FUTURE
English for Results
2

Sarah Lynn
Wendy Pratt Long

Series Consultants
Beatriz B. Díaz
Ronna Magy
Federico Salas-Isnardi

PEARSON
Longman

Future 2
English for Results

Pearson Education, 10 Bank Street, White Plains, NY 10606

Staff credits: The people who made up the **Future 2** team, representing editorial, production, design, and manufacturing, are Rhea Banker, Peter Benson, Elizabeth Carlson, Aerin Csigay, Dave Dickey, Nancy Flaggman, Irene Frankel, Mike Kemper, Katie Keyes, Melissa Leyva, Linda Moser, Liza Pleva, and Sherry Preiss.

Cover design: Rhea Banker
Cover photo: Kathy Lamm/Getty Images
Text design: Elizabeth Carlson
Text composition: Word & Image Design Studio Inc.
Text font: Minion Pro

Library of Congress Cataloging-in-Publication Data

Nishio, Yvonne Wong.
    Future: english for results / Yvonne Wong Nishio ... [et al.].
        p. cm.
    ISBN 978-0-13-240876-9 (student bk. intro)—ISBN 978-0-13-199144-6 (student bk.1)—ISBN 978-0-13-199148-4 (student bk. 2)—ISBN 978-0-13-199152-1 (student bk. 3)—ISBN 978-0-13-199156-9 (student bk. 4)—ISBN 978-0-13-240875-2 (student bk. 5)
    1. English language—Textbooks for foreign speakers. I. Title.
    PE1128.N56 2009
    428.0076--dc22

                                                                    2008021069

ISBN-13: 978-0-13199148-4
ISBN 10: 0-13-199148-5

1 2 3 4 5 6 7 8 9 10 —WC— 14 13 12 11 10 09

The authors would like to thank **Irene Frankel** for her inspiration, insight, and guidance throughout this project and **Peter Benson** for his patient answers, his unwavering support, and his great sense of humor.

Wendy Pratt Long, Sarah Lynn
authors of Student Book 2

Contents

Acknowledgments

The authors and publisher would like to extend special thanks to our Series Consultants whose insights, experience, and expertise shaped the course and guided us throughout its development.

Beatriz B. Díaz Miami-Dade County Public Schools, Miami, FL
Ronna Magy Los Angeles Unified School District, Los Angles, CA
Federico Salas-Isnardi Texas LEARNS, Houston, TX

We would also like to express our gratitude to the following individuals. Their kind assistance was indispensable to the creation of this program.

Consultants

Wendy J. Allison Seminole Community College, Sanford, FL
Claudia Carco Westchester Community College, Valhalla, NY
Maria J. Cesnik Ysleta Community Learning Center, El Paso, TX
Edwidge Crevecoeur-Bryant University of Florida, Gainesville, FL
Ann Marie Holzknecht Damrau San Diego Community College, San Diego, CA
Peggy Datz Berkeley Adult School, Berkeley, CA
MaryAnn Florez D.C. Learns, Washington, D.C.
Portia LaFerla Torrance Adult School, Torrance, CA
Eileen McKee Westchester Community College, Valhalla, NY
Julie Meuret Downey Adult School, Downey, CA
Sue Pace Santa Ana College School of Continuing Education, Santa Ana, CA
Howard Pomann Union County College, Elizabeth, NY
Mary Ray Fairfax County Public Schools, Falls Church, VA
Gema Santos Miami-Dade County Public Schools, Miami, FL
Edith Uber Santa Clara Adult Education, Santa Clara, CA
Theresa Warren East Side Adult Education, San Jose, CA

Piloters

MariCarmen Acosta American High School, Adult ESOL, Hialeah, FL
Resurrección Ángeles Metropolitan Skills Center, Los Angeles, CA
Linda Bolognesi Fairfax County Public Schools, Adult and Community Education, Falls Church, VA
Patricia Boquiren Metropolitan Skills Center, Los Angeles, CA
Paul Buczko Pacoima Skills Center, Pacoima, CA
Matthew Horowitz Metropolitan Skills Center, Los Angeles, CA
Gabriel de la Hoz The English Center, Miami, FL
Cam-Tu Huynh Los Angeles Unified School District, Los Angeles, CA
Jorge Islas Whitewater Unified School District, Adult Education, Whitewater, WI
Lisa Johnson City College of San Francisco, San Francisco, CA
Loreto Kaplan Collier County Public Schools Adult ESOL Program, Naples, FL
Teressa Kitchen Collier County Public Schools Adult ESOL Program, Naples, FL
Anjie Martin Whitewater Unified School District, Adult Education, Whitewater, WI
Elida Matthews College of the Mainland, Texas City, TX
Penny Negron College of the Mainland, Texas City, TX
Manuel Pando Coral Park High School, Miami, FL
Susan Ritter Evans Community Adult School, Los Angeles, CA
Susan Ross Torrance Adult School, Torrance, CA
Beatrice Shields Fairfax County Public Schools, Adult and Community Education, Falls Church, VA
Oscar Solís Coral Park High School, Miami, FL
Wanda W. Weaver Literacy Council of Prince George's County, Hyattsville, MD

Reviewers

Lisa Agao Fresno Adult School, Fresno, CA
Carol Antuñano The English Center, Miami, FL
Euphronia Awakuni Evans Community Adult School, Los Angeles, CA
Jack Bailey Santa Barbara Adult Education, Santa Barbara, CA
Robert Breitbard District School Board of Collier County, Naples, FL
Diane Burke Evans Community Adult School, Los Angeles, CA
José A. Carmona Embry-Riddle Aeronautical University, Daytona Beach, FL
Veronique Colas Los Angeles Technology Center, Los Angles, CA
Carolyn Corrie Metropolitan Skills Center, Los Angeles, CA
Marti Estrin Santa Rosa Junior College, Sebastopol, CA
Sheila Friedman Metropolitan Skills Center, Los Angeles, CA
José Gonzalez Spanish Education Development Center, Washington, D.C.
Allene G. Grognet Vice President (Emeritus), Center for Applied Linguistics
J. Quinn Harmon-Kelley Venice Community Adult School, Los Angeles, CA
Edwina Hoffman Miami-Dade County Public Schools, Coral Gables, FL
Eduardo Honold Far West Project GREAT, El Paso, TX
Leigh Jacoby Los Angeles Community Adult School, Los Angeles, CA
Fayne Johnson Broward County Public Schools, Ft. Lauderdale, FL
Loreto Kaplan, Collier County Public Schools Adult ESOL Program, Naples, FL
Synthia LaFontaine Collier County Public Schools, Naples, FL
Gretchen Lammers-Ghereben Martinez Adult Education, Martinez, CA
Susan Lanzano Editorial Consultant, Briarcliff Manor, NY
Karen Mauer ESL Express, Euless, TX
Rita McSorley North East Independent School District, San Antonio, TX
Alice-Ann Menjivar Carlos Rosario International Public Charter School, Washington, D.C.
Sue Pace Santa Ana College School of Continuing Education, Santa Ana, CA
Isabel Perez American High School, Hialeah, FL
Howard Pomann Union County College, Elizabeth, NJ
Lesly Prudent Miami-Dade County Public Schools, Miami, FL
Valentina Purtell North Orange County Community College District, Anaheim, CA
Mary Ray Fairfax County Adult ESOL, Falls Church, VA
Laurie Shapero Miami-Dade Community College, Miami, FL
Felissa Taylor Nause Austin, TX
Meintje Westerbeek Baltimore City Community College, Baltimore, MD

Thanks also to the following teachers, who contributed their ideas for the Persistence Activities:

Dave Coleman Los Angeles Unified School District, Los Angeles, CA
Renee Collins Elk Grove Adult and Community Education, Elk Grove, CA
Elaine Klapman Venice Community Adult School, Venice, CA (retired)
Yvonne Wong Nishio Evans Community Adult School, Los Angeles, CA (retired)
Daniel S. Pittaway North Orange County Community College District, Anaheim, CA
Laurel Pollard Educational Consultant, Tucson, AZ
Eden Quimzon Santiago Canyon College, Division of Continuing Education, Orange, CA

About the Series Consultants and Authors

SERIES CONSULTANTS

Dr. Beatriz B. Díaz has taught ESL for more than three decades in Miami. She has a master's degree in TESOL and a doctorate in education from Nova Southeastern University. She has given trainings and numerous presentations at international, national, state, and local conferences throughout the United States, the Caribbean, and South America. Dr. Díaz is the district supervisor for the Miami-Dade County Public Schools Adult ESOL Program, one of the largest in the United States.

Ronna Magy has worked as an ESL classroom teacher and teacher-trainer for nearly three decades. Most recently, she has worked as the ESL Teacher Adviser in charge of site-based professional development for the Division of Adult and Career Education of the Los Angeles Unified School District. She has trained teachers of adult English language learners in many areas, including lesson planning, learner persistence and goal setting, and cooperative learning. A frequent presenter at local, state and national, and international conferences, Ms. Magy is the author of adult ESL publications on life skills and test preparation, U.S. citizenship, reading and writing, and workplace English. She holds a master's degree in social welfare from the University of California at Berkeley.

Federico Salas-Isnardi has worked for 20 years in the field of adult education as an ESL and GED instructor, professional development specialist, curriculum writer, and program administrator. He has trained teachers of adult English language learners for over 15 years on topics ranging from language acquisition and communicative competence to classroom management and individualized professional development planning. Mr. Salas-Isnardi has been a contributing writer or consultant for a number of ESL publications, and he has co-authored curriculum for site-based workforce ESL and Spanish classes. He holds a master's degree in applied linguistics from the University of Houston and has completed a number of certificates in educational leadership.

AUTHORS

Wendy Pratt Long has previously worked as an EFL teacher and administrator. She has taught English to children, adolescents, and adults at all language levels in Mexico and Canada. She earned a master's degree in applied linguistics from the Universidad de las Americas, in Puebla, Mexico. Now working in the field of educational publishing, she has authored and co-authored ancillary materials including *Center Stage 2 Teacher's Edition*, *Summit 2 Workbook*, *Top Notch 2 Workbook*, *Top Notch Copy & Go* (Fundamentals and Level 3), and *Top Notch Assessment Packages* (Fundamentals and Levels 2 and 3). She has collaborated with Pearson Longman on numerous other projects, including the assessment programs for *Center Stage 2* and *Summit 2* and CD-ROMs for multiple levels of the *WorldView* and *Trends* series.

Sarah Lynn has taught ESL and EFL for 20 years in the United States and abroad, and she currently teaches ESL at the Harvard Bridge to Learning and Literacy Program in Cambridge, Massachusetts. Ms. Lynn holds a master's degree in TESOL from Columbia University. She has trained volunteers and given workshops on the teaching of reading, kinesthetic techniques in the classroom, and cross-cultural communication. She has developed curricula for adult education programs in the areas of reading, life skills, and civics, and she is the co-author of *Business Across Cultures*. She has also contributed to numerous teacher resource materials, including those for *Side by Side*, *Foundations*, and *Word by Word*.

Scope and Sequence

UNIT	VOCABULARY	LISTENING	SPEAKING AND PRONUNCIATION	GRAMMAR	
Pre-Unit **Getting Started** *page 2*	• Reasons for studying English • Ways to ask for help	• Listen to an introduction • Listen to ways of asking for help	• Introduce yourself • Greet people and ask where they are from • Talk about your goals for learning English • Ask for help	• Simple present of *be*	
1 **Making Connections** *page 5*	• Physical descriptions • Personalities	Listen to conversations about: • the way people look • personalities • getting to know someone	• Describe the way people look • Describe people by their personality • Make an introduction • Get to know someone you just met • Recognize appropriate topics for conversation • Word stress • Vowel sounds in unstressed syllables • Sentence stress	• Simple present: *be* + adjective • Simple present: *have* + object • *Be*: Compound sentences with *and/but* • *Be*: Additions with *and…, too/and…, not, either* • Simple present tense of *be*: *Yes/No* and information questions	
2 **All in the Family** *page 25*	• Family members • Ways to keep in touch with family	Listen to conversations about: • family members • things people have in common • keeping in touch with family Listen to a game show quiz about family members	• Talk about your life and family • Compare families in the U.S. and your country • Talk about what people have in common • Ask about keeping in touch with family members • Word stress • Strong and weak pronunciations of *do*	• Simple present affirmative and negative: *have/live/work* • Simple present: Additions with *and…, too/and… not, either* • Simple present: *Yes/No* and information questions	
3 **Lots To Do** *page 45*	• Clothes and materials • Daily errands • Problems with purchases	Listen to conversations about: • clothing someone needs or wants • errands and shopping plans • problems with purchases Listen to a radio interview with shoppers	• Talk about the types of store sales • Describe clothing you need or want • Talk about errands and shopping plans • Describe problems with purchases • Pronunciation of *need to* and *want to* • Pronunciation of *going to*	• Simple present: *want/need* + infinitive • *Be going to* + verb • Adverbs of degree: *very/too*	
4 **Small Talk** *page 65*	• Free-time activities • Types of classes • Chores • Reasons to decline an invitation	Listen to conversations about: • weekend activities • likes and dislikes • accepting or declining an invitation Listen to a radio talk show offering tips for doing chores	• Talk about your weekend activities • Communicate your likes and dislikes • Invite someone to do something • Accept or decline an invitation politely • Words with one unpronounced syllable • Pronunciation of *have to* and *has to*	• Adverbs of frequency • Questions with *How often/* frequency time expressions • Simple present: *like/love/hate* + infinitive • Modal: *have to*	

LIFE SKILLS	READING	WRITING	NUMERACY	PERSISTENCE
• Ask for help when you don't understand	• Locate the U.S. map and world map in your book	• Write questions to complete a conversation	• Unit and page numbers	• Learn about your book • Meet your classmates • Identify your goals for studying English
• Understand abbreviations on an ID card • Complete an application for an ID card • Complete a driver's license application	• Read an article about ways people learn • Take a quiz about learning styles • Reading Skill: Find the main idea • Problem-solving: Read about responding to impolite questions	• Describe the way people look • Write about your personality • Write learning tips to match your learning style	• Heights and weights • Telephone numbers • Street addresses • Dates • Social Security and ID numbers	• Find classmates with the same learning style and give tips for learning English • Play a game to remember your classmates' names • Make a booklet about the members of your class
• Ask about sending mail • Identify types of mail • Understand post office mailing services • Complete a post office customs form	• Read about a family • Read an advice column about managing responsibilities • Reading Skill: Retell information in your own words • Problem-solving: Read about a conflict with a family member	• Write about your life and family • Write a list of your responsibilities • Describe how people are similar	• Weights of letters and packages • Shipping times for post office mailing services	• Find things you and your classmates have in common • Make a poster about class members' personalities
• Count your change • Read a store ad • Understand types of sales, sale prices, and discounts • Read a sales receipt • Ask about a mistake on a sales receipt • Write a personal check	• Read an article about ways to pay for purchases • Reading Skill: Identify the writer's purpose • Problem-solving: Read about a problem with a purchase	• Write about clothes you need or want • Write about some people's errands • Write about how you will pay for your next big purchase • Write reasons that people are returning clothes	• Count change • Prices in a product ad • Percentages of sale discounts • Amounts of discounts, tax, and total on a sales receipt • Calculations of the cost of different payment methods	• Visualize your goals for learning English • Make a neighborhood shopping guide
• Read a community calendar • Talk about the schedule of an event • Complete a library card application	• Read a bar graph about free-time activities in the U.S. • Read advice about rude and polite behavior on an online message board • Reading Skill: Identify the topic • Problem-solving: Read about declining an invitation politely	• List your weekend plans • Write about your likes and dislikes • Write about what is rude or polite in your country	• Dates on a calendar • Starting and ending times for scheduled events • Amounts and percentages in a bar graph	• Make plans to practice English outside of class • Make a neighborhood activity guide

Text in red = Civics and American culture

UNIT	VOCABULARY	LISTENING	SPEAKING AND PRONUNCIATION	GRAMMAR	
5 **At Home** *page 85*	• Home repair problems • Types of repair people • Driving directions	Listen to conversations about: • home repairs • renting an apartment • getting directions Listen to directions on a recorded telephone message	• Describe home repair problems • Ask for information about an apartment • Ask for and give directions to community locations • Stress in two-word nouns • Voiced and voiceless *th* sounds	• Present continuous: Affirmative and negative statements • *There is/There are*: Affirmative and negative statements, questions, and short answers	
6 **In the Past** *page 105*	• Events with family and friends • Family activities • Milestones in a person's life • Commuting problems	Listen to conversations about: • events with family and friends • life milestones • a bad day Listen to a radio interview with a famous person	• Talk about past activities • Talk about personal milestones • Talk about a bad day • Extra syllable for –*ed* endings • Intonation of statements repeated as questions	• Simple past: Regular verbs • Simple past: Irregular verbs • Simple past: *Yes/No* questions and short answers • Simple past: Information questions	
7 **Health Watch** *page 125*	• Health problems • Symptoms • Common injuries	Listen to conversations about: • making a doctor's appointment • an injury • calling in sick to work	• Describe a symptom • Make a doctor's appointment • Talk about an injury • Report an absence to a work supervisor • Linking a consonant to a vowel sound • Pronunciation of *t* between two vowel sounds • Using pauses to organize sentences into thought groups	• Prepositions of time: *at/by/in/on/ from… to* • Simple past: Irregular verbs • Ways to express reasons: *because* + a subject and a verb; *for* + a noun	
8 **Job Hunting** *page 145*	• Job duties • Job skills • Fields of employment	Listen to a job interview about: • job duties and skills • work history • availability	• Talk about your skills at a job interview • Talk about things you can and can't do • Talk about your work experience • Explain your reason for changing jobs • Answer questions about your availability • Pronunciation of *can* and *can't* • Intonation of questions with *or*	• Can to express ability: Affirmative and negative statements, *Yes/No* questions and short answers • Time expressions with *ago, last, in,* and *later* • Ways to express alternatives: *or, and*	

LIFE SKILLS	READING	WRITING	NUMERACY	PERSISTENCE
• Read apartment ads • Understand abbreviations in rental ads • Know where to find apartment ads • Complete an application for an apartment • Interpret a map	• Read a U.S. map • Read an article about a U.S. city • Reading Skill: Skim to get the main idea • Problem-solving: Read about a problem getting repairs in a rental apartment	• Write about your community • Write driving directions • Write a housing classified ad	• Costs of rent, utilities, fees, and security deposit • Number of rooms in an apartment	• Find a classmate who lives in your area. Discuss what you like and dislike about your community. • Write a daily planner for studying English
• Recognize U.S. holidays • Make a holiday calendar	• Read a biography of Oprah Winfrey • Read a time line of a person's life • Reading Skill: Scan for information • Problem-solving: Read about a mistake at work	• Write about your past activities • Write about milestones in your life • Make a time line of your life • Write a short autobiography • Write an absence note to a teacher	• Dates on a calendar • Lengths of time • Times of day	• Set goals to use vocabulary strategies
• Read a medical appointment card • Read OTC medical labels • Read a prescription • Read prescription medicine labels and instructions • Ask questions about taking medicine	• Read an article about ways to manage stress • Take a stress quiz • Reading Skill: Use formatting clues to find main points • Problem-solving: Read about a problem with a coworker	• Complete a medical history form • Write about an injury • Write about stress in your life	• Dates and times of appointments • Medicine dosages • Expiration dates • Score a quiz and interpret the results	• Find classmates who share the same sources of stress. Talk about ways to manage stress. • Identify obstacles to class attendance and make plans to overcome them • Make a booklet of home remedies
• Read help-wanted ads • Understand abbreviations in help-wanted ads • Complete a job application	• Read a time line • Read an article about jobs in the U.S. • Read information about job interviews • Reading Skill: Predict the topic • Problem-solving: Read about what to say in a job interview when you've been fired	• Write about your dream job • Write about your job skills and work history • Write a time line • Write about a job you want in five years • Write about a person's availability	• Hourly wages • Telephone numbers • Periods of time • Percentages of workers in fields of employment • Starting and ending time of a work shift	• Find classmates who want the same job in five years. Talk about what you need to do to get the job. • Assign jobs to students to assist the teacher in class • Make a job skills booklet

Text in red = Civics and American culture

UNIT	VOCABULARY	LISTENING	SPEAKING AND PRONUNCIATION	GRAMMAR
9 **Parents and Children** *page 165*	• Types of schools • School subjects • Ways children misbehave in school	Listen to conversations about: • a parent-teacher conference and school events • a child's progress in school • a child's behavior in school	• Make plans for school events • Communicate with your child's teacher • Discuss your child's progress in school • Discuss your child's behavior in school • Pronunciation of *will* • The *'s* or *s'* possessive ending	• Future with *will* • Adverbs of manner • Object pronouns • Possessive nouns
10 **Let's Eat!** *page 185*	• Food containers and quantities • Types of food stores • Food on a restaurant menu	Listen to conversations about: • quantities of food • reasons for buying specific brands of food • ordering food at a restaurant Listen to a food commercial	• Talk about the food you need to buy • Compare different brands of food products • Order food at a restaurant • Weak pronunciation of *to, the, a,* and *of*	• Count nouns/Non-count nouns • *How much/How many* • Comparative adjectives with *than* • Quantifiers with plural and non-count nouns
11 **Call 911!** *page 205*	• Medical emergencies • Dangerous situations • Traffic violations	Listen to conversations about: • a medical emergency call to 911 • an emergency situation • a traffic stop Listen to a police officer talk about what to do if you are pulled over for a traffic violation	• Call 911 to report a medical emergency • Describe an emergency situation • Respond to a police officer's instructions during a traffic stop • Stressed syllables • The sound /h/ at the beginning of words	• Present continuous: Statements and questions • *There was/There were* • Compound imperatives
12 **The World of Work** *page 225*	• Job responsibilities • Reasons people change their work schedules	Listen to conversations about: • policies at work • covering a work shift • changing your work schedule Listen to a talk about company policies at a new employee orientation	• Ask questions about company policies • Ask a co-worker to cover your shift • Give reasons for missing work • Request a schedule change • Rising intonation in *Yes/No* questions • Falling intonation in statements and information questions	• Expressions of necessity: *must/have to* • Expressions of prohibition: *must not/can't* • Information questions with *Who* • Information questions with *What/ Which/When/Where* • *Can/Could* to ask permission

Text in red = Civics and American culture

LIFE SKILLS	READING	WRITING	NUMERACY	PERSISTENCE
• Leave and take a telephone message • Complete a telephone message form • Complete a school enrollment form	• Read about parent-teacher conferences and PTOs • Read about ways students can get help with schoolwork • Read an article about the cost of going to college • Interpret a bar graph • Reading Skill: Use information in charts and tables • Read a school newsletter • Problem-solving: Read about a problem with a child's behavior in school	• Write about the progress of students you know • Write about your educational goals	• Dates and times of school events • Telephone numbers • Percentages of students going to college • Costs of tuition and college expenses	• Create a portfolio of your English work • Make a poster about ways to improve your English skills
• Understand the importance of a healthy diet • Read ingredient and nutrition labels • Read food ads • Compare the healthfulness of two food products • Read and order food from a menu	• Read an article about the nutrients in food • Read an article about the effects of caffeine • Reading Skill: Get meaning from context • Problem-solving: Read about a parent's problem providing healthy meals for her family	• Write a food shopping list • Complete a healthy eating log • Compare food in a supermarket ad • Write a radio commercial for a food product • Keep a caffeine journal	• Quantities of food • Amounts on food labels • Prices of food products	• Plan a class picnic • Get to know a classmate over tea and cookies • Make a food shopping guide
• Call 911 to report a medical emergency • Identify fire hazards in the home • Understand fire safety devices and procedures • Create a fire escape plan • Identify ways to avoid accidents at home • Respond to a police officer's instructions • Complete an employee accident report	• Read about 911 calls • Read fire safety tips • Read about a woman's actions during a fire • Read an article about common causes of home injuries • Reading Skill: Identify supporting details • Problem-solving: Read about reporting an accident at work	• Write about what people are doing • Describe emergency situations • Write about the safety of your home	• Street addresses • Numbers of home injuries per year • Percentages of common household injuries	• Identify ways to improve your study skills and habits • Make a fire escape plan poster for your school
• Read a pay stub • Understand payroll deductions and overtime hours • Understand the Social Security program • Complete a vacation request form	• Read an employee manual • Read about overtime hours • Read about a problem at work • Read a FAQ about the Social Security program • Reading Skill: Think about what you know • Problem-solving: Read about a worker's problem with a schedule	• Write about your responsibilities • Write about your life after you retire	• Dates • Amounts of money on a pay stub • Calculations of earnings and deductions on a pay stub • Times on a schedule	• Form into one of three groups: employees, students, and parents. Discuss your responsibilities. • Review the unit goals you have achieved • Make an employee manual

Text in red = Civics and American culture

Correlations

UNIT	CASAS Reading Basic Skill Content Standards	CASAS Listening Basic Skill Content Standards	
1	**U1:** 1.1, 1.2, 1.3, 1.4, 2.2, 3.1, 3.2, 3.8; **L1:** 3.12, 6.1; **L2:** 2.5, 2.8, 3.10; **L3:** 2.5, 6.1; **L4:** 2.7, 4.1, 4.6; **L5:** 2.11, 2.12; **L6:** 3.10, 3.14; **L7:** 3.3, 3.6, 7.1; **L8:** 3.12, 6.1; **L9:** 4.1; **SWYK Expand:** 3.3, 3.6	**U1:** 1.4; **L1:** 1.1, 2.3; **L2:** 3.3, 3.4; **L3:** 3.2, 3.3, 3.4; **L4:** 3.4, 3.5; **L5:** 4.2, 4.3, 4.4; **L6:** 3.2; **L7:** 3.4; **L8:** 2.1, 3.3, 3.4; **L9:** 3.1; **SWYK Expand:** 2.1, 3.1, 3.2	
2	**U2:** 1.1, 1.2, 1.3, 1.4, 2.2, 3.1, 3.2, 3.8; **L1:** 2.5, 2.9, 3.12; **L2:** 3.12 ; **L3:** 3.12, 4.9; **L4:** 7.1, 7.2, 7.6; **L5:** 3.12; **L6:** 3.12; **L7:** 4.8. 4.10; **L8:** 3.12; **SWYK Review:** 3.11, 4.8; **SWYK Expand:** 3.10, 7.1, 7.8	**U2:** 1.4; **L1:** 1.1, 1.3; **L2:** 1.3, 2.1, 3.1, 3.3; **L3:** 1.3, 2.1, 3.1; **L4:** 1.3, 2.1, 3.1, 3.4; **L5:** 1.3, 2.1, 3.1; **L6:** 3.3; **L7:** 3.3, 3.5; **L8:** 3.3; **L9:** 3.3, 3.4, 3.5; **SWYK Review:** 3.4; **SWYK Expand:** 3.3, 3.4, 3.5	
3	**U3:** 1.1, 1.2, 1.3, 1.4, 2.2, 3.1, 3.2, 3.8; **L1:** 3.12; **L2:** 3.12, 4.8; **L3:** 3.12; **L4:** 4.1, 4.4, 4.6, 4.10, 6.2, 7.13; **L5:** 3.14; **L6:** 2.5; **L7:** 4.9, 7.1, 7.2, 7.3, 7.11; **L8:** 2.8, 3.12; **SWYK Review:** 2.11; **SWYK Expand:** 7.1, 7.8	**U3:** 1.4; **L2:** 1.5, 3.3, 3.4; **L3:** 1.5; **L4:** 2.1, 3.3, 3.4, 3.5; **L5:** 1.5, 3.7, 4.1; **L6:** 1.5, 3.4; **L7:** 3.4; **L8:** 3.4, 4.11; **SWYK Expand:** 3.4	
4	**U4:** 1.1, 1.2, 1.3, 1.4, 2.2, 3.1, 3.2, 3.8; **L1:** 3.12, 6.1; **L2:** 3.12, 6.1; **L3:** 4.6, 4.8, 4.9; **L4:** 4.6, 6.2; **L5:** 3.12, 6.1, 7.4; **L6:** 4.9, 7.8; **L7:** 3.11, 7.2; **L8:** 3.12; **L9:** 2.8; **SWYK Expand:** 7.8	**U4:** 1.4; **L1:** 1.1; **L2:** 1.3, 3.4; **L3:** 3.5; **L4:** 3.4, 5.1, 6.2; **L5:** 3.4, 6.1; **L6:** 3.4; **L7:** 3.3; **L8:** 1.5, 3.3, 3.4; **L9:** 3.2; **SWYK Review:** 1.5; **SWYK Expand:** 3.1, 3.2, 3.3, 3.4	
5	**U5:** 1.1, 1.2, 1.3, 1.4, 2.2, 3.1, 3.2, 3.8; **L1:** 3.12, 6.1; **L2:** 3.12, 6.1; **L3:** 2.8, 3.12; **L4:** 2.3, 2.7, 2.12, 4.6; **L5:** 2.8, **L6:** 2.3, 4.6; **L7:** 4.9, 6.2; **L8:** 4.9; **SWYK Review:** 2.3, 4.9; **SWYK Expand:** 3.12, 7.1	**U5:** 1.4; **L1:** 1.1; **L2:** 5.1, 7.7; **L3:** 4.4; **L4:** 3.4; **L5:** 5.1; **L6:** 1.3, 3.4; **L7:** 3.4; **L8:** 2.6; **SWYK Review:** 2.6; **SWYK Expand:** 4.8, 5.1	
6	**U6:** 1.1, 1.2, 1.3, 1.4, 2.2, 3.1, 3.2, 3.8; **L1:** 3.12, 6.1; **L2:** 3.12, 6.1; **L3:** 3.3; **L4:** 3.16, 4.3, 4.6; **L5:** 2.8; **L6:** 2.8; **L7:** 3.10, 7.2, 7.4; **L8:** 3.12, 6.1; **L9:** 3.11; **SWYK Review:** 3.11; **SWYK Expand:** 7.4	**U6:** 1.1, 1.4, 3.4; **L1:** 1.3, 3.4, 3.9; **L2:** 1.3, 3.4, 3.9; **L3:** 1.3, 3.2; **L4:** 5.1; **L5:** 3.6, 4.10, 5.1; **L6:** 3.9, **L7:** 3.4; **L8:** 3.4, 3.8; **L9:** 3.4, 3.8; **SWYK Review:** 3.4, 3.8; **SWYK Expand:** 3.3, 3.4, 3.5	
7	**U7:** 1.1, 1.2, 1.3, 1.4, 2.2, 3.1, 3.2, 3.8; **L1:** 3.12, 6.1; **L2:** 3.12, 4.6, 6.1; **L3:** 3.10, 4.6; **L4:** 3.11, 4.6, 7.13; **L5:** 3.11, 3.12, 6.1; **L6:** 3.11, 6.1; **L7:** 4.6, 4.9, 4.10, 6.2, 6.6; **L8:** 3.11; **L9:** 3.9; **SWYK Review:** 3.9; **SWYK Expand:** 3.10, 7.1, 7,8	**U7:** 1.4; **L1:** 1.1; **L2:** 3.4, 4.11; **L3:** 3.4; **L4:** 3.4, 3.5; **L5:** 1.5, 2.1, 4.11; **L6:** 1.3, 3.3; **L7:** 5.1; **L8:** 1.5, 2.1, 5.1; **SWYK Expand:** 3.3, 3.4	
8	**U8:** 1.1, 1.2, 1.3, 1.4, 2.2, 3.1, 3.2, 3.8; **L1:** 2.9, 2.11, 3.11, 3.12, 6.1; **L2:** 3.12, 6.1; **L3:** 3.11, 3.12, 6.1; **L4:** 2.6, 2.7, 3.11, 4.6; **L5:** 7.4; **L6:** 7.4; **L7:** 6.1, 7.2; **L8:** 3.11; **L9:** 3.11, 4.6; **SWYK Review:** 3.11, 7.4; **SWYK Expand:** 3.11, 7.8	**U8:** 1.4; **L1:** 3.4, **L2:** 1.5, 4.10; **L3:** 1.5, 3.2, **L4:** 3.4, 4.10; **L5:** 4.10, 5.2, 6.1; **L6:** 3.4; **L7:** 3.4, 4.10; **L8:** 3.3, 3.4, 3.6, 4.7; **SWYK Expand:** 3.3, 3.4, 3.5	
9	**U9:** 1.1, 1.2, 1.3, 1.4, 2.2, 3.1, 3.2, 3.8; **L1:** 2.3, 3.12, 6.1; **L2:** 2.6, 4.2, 4.3; **L3:** 3.3, 4.9; **L4:** 4.2, 4.3, 4.6; **L5:** 2.8, 2.9, 6.1; **L6:** 2.8, 2.9, 3.10; **L7:** 4.8, 4.9, 7.1, 7.8; **L8:** 2.8, 3.11; **L9:** 2.8, 3.10; **SWYK Review:** 2.8, 3.10, 4.6 **SWYK Expand:** 4.2, 4.3, 4.8, 7.8	**U9:** 1.4; **L1:** 4.10; **L2:** 4.3, 4.4; **L3:** 3.4; **L4:** 2.5, 3.1, 4.6, 4.10, 6.1; **L5:** 3.1, 4.6, 4.10, 6.1; **L6:** 1.3; **L7:** 4.3, 4.4; **L8:** 3.4; 4.3, 4.4; **SWYK Expand:** 3.4	
10	**U10:** 1.1, 1.2, 1.3, 1.4, 2.2, 3.1, 3.2, 3.8; **L1:** 2.3, 3.12, 6.1; **L2:** 3.12, 6.1; **L3:** 2.8; **L4:** 2.7, 4.1, 6.2, 6.6; **L5:** 3.3; **L6:** 2.9, 4.10; **L7:** 3.13, 6.6; **L8:** 2.3; **L9:** 2.8; **SWYK Review:** 2.8; **SWYK Expand:** 2.6, 4.1, 6.6, 7.3	**U10:** 1.4; **L1:** 1.1; **L2:** 4.10; **L3:** 3.4; **L5:** 1.3, 3.3, 4.10; **L7:** 3.4; 4.10; **L8:** 2.1	
11	**U11:** 1.1, 1.2, 1.3, 1.4, 2.2, 3.1, 3.2, 3.8; **L1:** 3.12, 6.1; **L2:** 3.12, 6.1; **L3:** 2.5; **L4:** 3.12, 4.9, 6.1, 6.6, 7.8; **L5:** 3.11, 3.12, 4.10, 6.1; **L6:** 2.8, 3.12, 6.1; **L7:** 3.12, 6.1, 7.3; **L8:** 3.11, 3.12, 6.1; **L9:** 3.3; **SWYK Review:** 3.3; **SWYK Expand:** 3.11, 7.8	**U11:** 1.4; **L1:** 1.1; **L2:** 3.4, 5.1, 6.4; **L3:** 3.4; **L4:** 4.10; **L5:** 1.3, 4.4, 4.10, 6.2; **L6:** 3.3, 3.4, 4.4, 4.10; **L7:** 3.3, 3.4 **L8:** 3.3, 4.10; **SWYK Expand:** 4.10, 6.4	
12	**U12:** 1.1, 1.2, 1.3, 1.4, 2.2, 3.1, 3.2, 3.8; **L1:** 2.12, 3.12, 6.1; **L2:** 2.12; **L3:** 2.12, 3.11; **L4:** 3.11, 4.1, 4.4, 4.7; **L5:** 7.8; **L6:** 4.8; **L7:** 6.2, 6.5, 6.6; **L8:** 3.11, 4.6; **L9:** 3.3; **SWYK Review:** 3.3; **SWYK Expand:** 7.9	**U12:** 1.4; **L1:** 4.10; **L2:** 3.6, 4.11, 5.4; **L3:** 3.3; **L4:** 3.4; **L5:** 5.2, 6.2; **L6:** 3.4; **L7:** 3.4, 5.1; **L8:** 6.3, 7.1; **L9:** 6.4; **SWYK Expand:** 4.10, 6.4	

CASAS Competencies	LAUSD ESL Beginning High Competencies	Florida Adult ESOL Course Standards
U1: 0.1.2, 0.1.4, 0.1.5, 0.1.7, 0.2.1, 0.2.4; **L1:** 7.4.1; **L4:** 0.2.2, 4.1.1; **L6:** 0.2.3; **L7:** 0.2.3, 7.4.1, 7.4.9; **SWYK Review:** 0.1.6; **SWYK Expand:** 4.4.1, 7.1.1, 7.1.2, 7.3.1, 7.3.2, 7.3.3, 7.3.4	3; 4; 5; 6; 7a, 63	3.01.01, 3.01.02, 3.01.03, 3.06.04
U2: 0.1.2, 0.1.4, 0.1.5, 0.1.7, 0.2.1, 0.2.4; **L1:** 6.6.5, 7.4.1; **L4:** 0.2.3, 7.1.1, 7.2.1, 7.5.5; **L5:** 7.5.5; **L6:** 0.2.3; **L7:** 2.4.2, 2.4.3, 2.4.4, 2.4.5; **SWYK Review:** 7.2.3; **SWYK Expand:** 7.1.1, 7.1.2, 7.1.4, 7.3.1, 7.3.2, 7.3.3, 7.4.8, 7.5.3, 7.3.4	4; 5; 7a; 24a	3.01.02, 3.01.03, 3.02.01, 3.02.07
U3: 0.1.2, 0.1.4, 0.1.5, 0.1.7, 0.2.1, 0.2.4; **L1:** 1.2.9, 7.4.3; **L2:** 1.2.9, 1.3.1; **L3:** 1.2.9, 1.31, 1.3.3, 1.6.4, 1.6.5; **L4:** 1.1.6, 1.2.1, 1.2.2, 1.2.4, 1.2.9, 1.3.3, 1.6.3, 1.6.4, 1.8.1; **L5:** 0.2.3, 1.2.6, 1.2.7; **L6:** 1.2.6, 1.2.7; **L7:** 1.3.1, 1.5.2, 1.8.1, 1.8.6; **L8:** 0.1.8, 1.3.3; **L9:** 1.3.3; **SWYK Review:** 1.3.3, 7.1.1; **SWYK Expand:** 1.2.6, 1.2.9, 1.3.3, 7.1.1, 7.1.2, 7.3.1, 7.3.2, 7.3.3, 7.3.4	3; 5; 7a; 7b; 8a; 24a; 27; 32; 33; 62a	3.01.03, 3.02.05, 3.04.01, 3.04.02, 3.04.06, 3.04.08,
U4: 0.1.2, 0.1.4, 0.1.5, 0.1.7, 0.2.1, 0.2.4; **L1:** 0.2.3, 2.6.1, 6.6.5, 7.4.3; **L2:** 2.6.1, 2.6.3, 2.8.2; **L3:** 0.2.3, 2.3.2, 2.6.1, 2.8.2; **L4:** 0.2.2, 2.3.2, 2.6.1, 2.5.6, 2.6.3; **L6:** 0.2.3, 2.6.1, 6.7.3; **L7:** 0.2.3, 7.7.1, 7.7.3, 7.7.4; **SWYK Review:** 2.6.1, 2.6.3, 7.1.1; **SWYK Expand:** 2.6.1, 2.6.3, 7.1.1, 7.1.2, 7.3.1, 7.3.2, 7.3.3, 7.3.4, 7.5.5	5; 7; 7a; 9a; 9b; 9c; 21; 22; 62a	3.01.02, 3.01.03, 3.02.02
U5: 0.1.2, 0.1.4, 0.1.5, 0.1.7, 0.2.1, 0.2.4; **L1:** 1.4.1, 1.4.7, 7.4.1; **L2:** 1.4.1, 1.4.7; **L3:** 1.4.1, 1.4.7; **L4:** 1.4.1, 1.4.2; **L5:** 1.4.1, 1.4.2; **L6:** 1.4.1, 2.2.1; **L7:** 1.4.2, 2.2.1; **L8:** 1.2.7, 2.2.1; **SWYK Review:** 2.2.1; **SWYK Expand:** 1.4.2, 1.4.5, 1.4.7, 5.31, 5.32, 7.3.1, 7.1.1, 7.1.2, 7.1.4, 7.3.2, 7.3.3, 7.3.4	17; 17a; 23a; 23b; 37; 38a; 38b; 38c; 38d; 39; 62b	3.01.03, 3.03.01, 3.04.04, 3.04.05, 3.04.06, 3.06.03
U6: 0.1.2, 0.1.4, 0.1.5, 0.1.7, 0.2.1, 0.2.4; **L1:** 7.1.4, 7.4.1; **L3:** 0.2.3, 7.4.3; **L4:** 2.3.2, 2.7.1; **L7:** 0.2.3, 6.7.1; **SWYK Review:** 0.1.6, 0.1.8; **SWYK Expand:** 0.1.6, 0.1.8, 2.7.1, 4.3.4, 4.4.1, 4.5.1, 4.6.4, 7.1.1, 7.1.2, 7.1.3, 7.3.1, 7.3.2, 7.3.3, 7.3.4, 7.4.1, 7.4.3	4; 5; 7; 7a; 11e; 16b; 25	3.01.02, 3.01.03, 3.02.03, 3.03.09, 3.03.11
U7: 0.1.2, 0.1.4, 0.1.5, 0.1.7, 0.2.1, 0.2.4; **L1:** 3.6.3, 7.4.1; **L2:** 3.1.2, 3.6.3; **L3:** 0.1.6, 3.1.2; **L4:** 0.1.8, 3.2.1, 3.3.1, 3.3.2, 7.3.4; **L5:** 0.1.6, 3.0.2, 3.0.3; **L6:** 0.2.3, 3.6.25, 5.6.3; **L7:** 0.2.3, 3.5.8, 3.5.9, 6.6.5, 7.5.4; **L8:** 0.1.8, 2.1.7, 3.5.4, 4.4.1; **L9:** 0.2.3, 1.2.7, 3.5.4, 3.6.3; **SWYK Review:** 0.1.6, 0.1.8, 3.1.2, 3.1.3, 3.6.3, 3.6.4; **SWYK Expand:** 3.1.2, 3.1.3, 3.3.1, 3.6.3, 3.6.4; 7.1.1, 7.1.2, 7.3.1, 7.3.2, 7.3.3, 7.3.4	10b; 17a; 17b; 42; 43; 44; 46; 47; 55a; 62	3.01.01, 3.01.06, 3.03.10, 3.03.11, 3.04.01, 3.05.01, 3.05.02, 3.05.03
U8: 0.1.2, 0.1.4, 0.1.5, 0.1.7, 0.2.1, 0.2.4; **L1:** 4.1.8, 7.1.1; **L2:** 0.1.6, 4.1.5, 4.1.8; **L3:** 0.1.6, 4.1.5, 4.1.8; **L4:** 4.1.2, 4.1.3, 4.1.6, 4.1.8, 4.2.5; **L5:** 4.1.2, 4.1.6, 4.1.8; **L6:** 4.1.6, 4.1.8, 6.7.3; **L7:** 0.2.3, 4.1.6, 4.1.8; **L8:** 4.1.6, 4.1.8; **L9:** 0.2.3; **SWYK Review:** 0.1.6, 4.1.5, 4.1.6, 4.1.7, 4.1.8; **SWYK Expand:** 0.1.6, 4.1.5, 4.1.6, 4.1.7, 4.1.8; 7.1.1, 7.1.2, 7.3.1, 7.3.2, 7.3.3, 7.3.4	7a; 51; 52a; 52b; 54a; 54b; 54c; 55b; 59a	3.03.01, 3.03.02, 3.03.03, 3.03.10, 3.03.11, 3.03.15
U9: 0.1.2, 0.1.4, 0.1.5, 0.1.7, 0.2.1, 0.2.4; **L1:** 2.8.1, 2.8.3, 7.4.1; **L2:** 0.1.6, 2.8.6; **L3:** 2.8.9, 7.7.4; **L4:** 2.1.7, 2.8.5; **L5:** 0.1.6, 0.1.8, 2.8.7, 7.5.1; **L6:** 0.1.6, 0.1.8, 7.5.1; **L7:** 0.2.3, 2.8.1, 6.6.5, 6.7.2, 7.1.1; **L8:** 0.1.6, 0.1.8, 2.8.6, 2.8.8; **L9:** 2.8.7; **SWYK Review:** 2.5.8, 2.8.3, 2.8.6, 2.8.8, 2.8.9, 5.6.5; **SWYK Expand:** 2.5.8, 2.8.3, 2.8.6, 2.8.8, 2.8.9, 5.6.5; 7.1.1, 7.1.2, 7.1.3, 7.1.4, 7.3.1, 7.3.2, 7.3.3, 7.3.4	13; 14; 17a; 17b; 21; 25	3.01.02, 3.01.04, 3.01.07, 3.02.09
U10: 0.1.2, 0.1.4, 0.1.5, 0.1.7, 0.2.1, 0.2.4; **L1:** 1.1.7, 1.2.8, 7.4.1; **L2:** 0.1.6 1.1.7, 1.2.8; **L3:** 0.2.3, 1.1.7, 1.2.8; **L4:** 1.2.8, 1.6.1, 3.5.1, 3.5.2, 3.5.9; **L5:** 0.1.6, 1.2.1, 1.2.2, 1.2.8, 3.5.2; **L6:** 1.2.1, 1.2.8, 3.5.2; **L7:** 0.2.3, 1.2.1, 1.2.2, 1.2.8, 3.5.2; **L8:** 0.1.6, 1.2.8, 2.6.4; **SWYK Review:** 1.1.4, 1.1.7, 1.2.2, 1.2.8; **SWYK Expand:** 0.1.6, 1.1.4, 1.1.7, 1.2.1, 1.2.2, 1.2.6, 1.2.8, 7.1.1, 7.1.2, 7.3.1, 7.3.2, 7.3.3, 7.3.4	32; 34; 35; 36	3.04.01, 3.04.02, 3.05.05, 3.05.06
U11: 0.1.2, 0.1.4, 0.1.5, 0.1.7, 0.2.1, 0.2.4; **L1:** 0.1.6, 0.1.8, 2.1.2, 2.5.1, 3.6.2, 3.6.4, 7.4.1; **L2:** 0.1.6, 0.1.8, 2.1.2, 2.2.1, 2.5.1, 3.6.2, 3.6.4; **L3:** 0.1.6, 0.1.8, .02.3, 2.1.2, 3.6.2, 3.6.4; **L4:** 1.4.8, 2.5.1, 3.4.2; **L5:** 0.1.8, 1.4.8, 7.3.1; **L6:** 1.4.8, 1.9.7; **L7:** 0.2.3, 1.4.8, 3.4.2; **L8:** 1.9.1, 1.9.7; **L9:** 1.9.1, 1.9.7; **SWYK Review:** 2.1.2, 2.5.1, 4.3.4; **SWYK Expand:** 2.1.2, 2.5.1, 3.4.8, 4.3.4, 4.4.1, 7.1.1, 7.1.2, 7.3.1, 7.3.2, 7.3.3, 7.3.4, 7.4.1	7a; 20; 23b; 42; 45b; 48; 49; 57	3.02.01, 3.03.08, 3.05.01, 3.05.02, 3.06.02, 3.06.04, 3.06.05, 3.07.03
U12: 0.1.2, 0.1.4, 0.1.5, 0.1.7, 0.2.1, 0.2.4; **L1:** 4.1.7, 4.1.8, 4.3.3, 4.4.1, 7.4.1; **L2:** 0.1.6, 4.1.7, 4.1.8, 4.4.1; **L3:** 4.1.7, 4.1.8, 4.4.1; **L4:** 1.1.6, 4.1.6, 4.2.1, 4.2.5, 4.4.3, 6.0.2, 6.6.5; **L5:** 1.1.6, 4.1.6, 4.4.1, 4.8.3; **L6:** 4.1.6, 4.4.3; **L7:** 0.2.3, 4.2.5, 5.5.9; **L8:** 4.1.6, 4.1.8, 4.25, 4.4.1, 4.4.2, 4.6.2; **SWYK Review:** 0.1.6, 4.2.4, 4.2.5, 4.3.2, 4.4.1, 4.4.2, 4.4.3, 4.4.4, 4.5.1, 4.6.1, 4.6.3; **SWYK Expand:** 0.1.6, 4.2.4, 4.2.5, 4.3.2, 4.4.1, 4.4.2, 4.4.3, 4.4.4, 4.5.1, 4.6.1, 4.6.3, 4.2.4, 7.1.1, 7.1.2, 7.1.4, 7.3.1, 7.3.2, 7.3.3, 7.3.4	7a; 8a; 8b; 11d; 11e; 46; 55; 55b; 55c	3.01.03, 3.02.01, 3.03.01, 3.03.02, 3.03.06, 3.03.07, 3.03.09, 3.03.10, 3.03.11

All units of *Future* meet most of the **EFF Content Standards**. For details, as well as for correlations to other state standards, go to www.pearsonlongman.com/future.

To the Teacher

Welcome to *Future*
English for Results

Future is a six-level, four-skills course for adults and young adults correlated to state and national standards. It incorporates research-based teaching strategies, corpus-informed language, and the best of modern technology.

KEY FEATURES

Future provides everything your students need in one integrated program.

In developing the course, we listened to what teachers asked for and we responded, providing six levels, more meaningful content, a thorough treatment of grammar, explicit skills development, abundant practice, multiple options for state-of-the-art assessment, and innovative components.

Future serves students' real-life needs.

We began constructing the instructional syllabus for *Future* by identifying what is most critical to students' success in their personal and family lives, in the workplace, as members of a community, and in their academic pursuits. *Future* provides outstanding coverage of life skills competencies, basing language teaching on actual situations that students are likely to encounter and equipping them with the skills they need to achieve their goals. The grammar and other language elements taught in each lesson grow out of these situations and are thus practiced in realistic contexts, enabling students to use language meaningfully, from the beginning.

Future grows with your students.

Future takes students from absolute beginner level through low-advanced proficiency in English, addressing students' abilities and learning priorities at each level. As the levels progress, the curricular content and unit structure change accordingly, with the upper levels incorporating more academic skills, more advanced content standards, and more content-rich texts.

Level	Description	CASAS Scale Scores
Intro	True Beginning	Below 180
1	Low Beginning	181–190
2	High Beginning	191–200
3	Low Intermediate	201–210
4	High Intermediate	211–220
5	Low Advanced	221–235

Future is fun!

Humor is built into each unit of *Future*. Many of the conversations, and especially the listenings, are designed to have an amusing twist at the end, giving students an extra reason to listen—something to anticipate with pleasure and to then take great satisfaction in once it is understood. In addition, many activities have students interacting in pairs and groups. Not only does this make classroom time more enjoyable, it also creates an atmosphere conducive to learning in which learners are relaxed, highly motivated, and at their most receptive.

Future puts the best of 21st-century technology in the hands of students and teachers.

In addition to its expertly developed print materials and audio components, *Future* goes a step further.

- Every **Student Book comes with a Practice Plus CD-ROM** for use at home, in the lab, or wherever students have access to a computer. The Practice Plus CD-ROM can be used both by students who wish to extend their practice beyond the classroom and by those who need to "make up" what they missed in class. The CD-ROM also includes the entire class audio program as MP3 files so students can get extra listening practice at their convenience.
- The **Workbook with Audio CD** gives students access to more listening practice than ever before possible.
- The **Tests and Test Prep** book comes with the *Future* Exam*View*® Assessment Suite, enabling teachers to print ready-made tests, customize these tests, or create their own tests for life skills, grammar, vocabulary, listening, and reading for students at three levels—on-level, pre-level, or above-level.
- The **Teacher Training DVD** provides demo lessons of real teachers using *Future* with their classes. Teachers can select from the menu and watch a specific type of lesson, such as a grammar presentation, or a specific type of activity, such as an information gap, at their own convenience.
- The **Companion Website** provides a variety of teaching support, including a pdf of the Teacher's Edition and Lesson Planner notes for each unit in the Student Book.

Future provides all the assessment tools you need.

- The **Placement Test** evaluates students' proficiency in all skill areas, allowing teachers and program administrators to easily assign students to the right classes.
- The **Tests and Test Prep** book for each level provides:
  - **Printed unit tests** with accompanying audio CD. These unit tests use standardized testing formats, giving students practice "bubbling-in" responses as required

for CASAS and other standardized tests. In addition, reproducible test prep worksheets and practice tests provide invaluable help to students unfamiliar with such test formats.

o The *Future* **Exam** *View® Assessment Suite* is a powerful program that allows teachers to create their own unique tests or to print or customize already prepared tests at three levels; pre-level, on-level, and above-level.

- **Performance-based assessment:** Lessons in the Student Book end with a "practical assessment" activity such as Role Play, Make it Personal, or Show What You Know. Each unit culminates with both a role-play activity and a problem-solving activity, which require students to demonstrate their oral competence in a holistic way. The **Teacher's Edition and Lesson Planner** provides speaking rubrics to make it easy for teachers to evaluate students' oral proficiency.

- **Self-assessment:** For optimal learning to take place, students need to be involved in setting goals and in monitoring their own progress. *Future* has addressed this in numerous ways. In the Student Book, checkboxes at the end of lessons invite students to evaluate their mastery of the material. End-of-unit reviews allow students to see their progress in grammar and writing. And after completing each unit, students go back to the goals for the unit and reflect on their achievement. In addition, the CD-ROM provides students with continuous feedback (and opportunities for self-correction) as they work through each lesson, and the Workbook contains the answer keys, so that students can check their own work outside of class.

Future addresses multilevel classes and diverse learning styles.

Using research-based teaching strategies, *Future* provides teachers with creative solutions for all stages of lesson planning and implementation, allowing them to meet the needs of all their students.

- The **Multilevel Communicative Activities Book** provides an array of reproducible activities and games that engage students through different modalities. Teachers' notes provide multilevel options for pre-level and above-level students, as well as extension activities for additional speaking and writing practice.

- The **Teacher's Edition and Lesson Planner** offers pre-level and above-level variations for every lesson plan as well as numerous optional and extension activities designed to reach students at all levels.

- The **Transparencies and Reproducible Vocabulary Cards** include picture and word cards that will help kinesthetic and visual learners acquire and learn new vocabulary. Teachers' notes include ideas for multilevel classes.

- The **Practice Plus CD-ROM** included with the Student Book is an extraordinary tool for individualizing instruction. It allows students to direct their own learning, working on precisely what they need and practicing what they choose to work on as many times as they like. In addition, the CD-ROM provides all the audio files for the book, enabling students to listen as they wish to any of the material that accompanies the text.

- The **Workbook with Audio CD**, similarly, allows students to devote their time to the lessons and specific skill areas that they need to work on most. In addition, students can replay the audio portions they want to listen to as many times as necessary, choosing to focus on the connections between the written and spoken word, listening for grammar pronunciation, and/or listening for general comprehension.

- The **Tests and Test Prep** book, as noted on page xiv, includes the *Future* **Exam** *View® Assessment Suite*, which allows teachers to print out prepared tests at three levels (pre-level, on-level, and above-level) and to customize existing tests or create their own tests using the databank.

Future's persistence curriculum motivates students to continue their education.

Recent research about persistence has given us insights into how to keep students coming to class and how to keep them learning when they can't attend. Recognizing that there are many forces operating in students' lives—family, jobs, childcare, health—that may make it difficult for them to come to class, programs need to help students:

- Identify their educational goals
- Believe that they can successfully achieve them
- Develop a commitment to their own education
- Identify forces that can interfere with school attendance
- Develop strategies that will help them try to stay in school in spite of obstacles
- Find ways to continue learning even during "stopping out" periods

Future addresses all of these areas with its persistence curriculum. Activities found throughout the book and specific persistence activities in the back of the book help students build community, set goals, develop better study skills, and feel a sense of achievement. In addition, the Practice Plus CD-ROM is unique in its ability to ensure that even those students unable to attend class are able to make up what they missed and thus persist in their studies.

Future supports busy teachers by providing all the materials teachers need, plus the teacher support.

The **Student Book**, **Workbook with Audio CD**, **Multilevel Communicative Activities Book**, and **Transparencies and Reproducible Vocabulary Cards** were designed to provide teachers with everything they need in the way of ready-to-use classroom materials so they can concentrate on responding to their students' needs. The **Future Teacher Training DVD** gives teachers tips and models for conducting various activity types in their classroom.

Future provides ample practice, with flexible options to best fit the needs of each class.

The Student Book provides 60–100 hours of instruction. It can be supplemented in class by using:
- Teacher's Edition and Lesson Planner expansion ideas
- Transparencies and Reproducible Vocabulary Cards
- Workbook exercises
- Multilevel Communicative Activities
- Tests
- CD-ROM activities
- Activities on the Companion Website (longmanusa.com/Future)

TEACHING MULTILEVEL CLASSES

Teaching tips for pair and group work

Using pair and group work in an ESL classroom has many proven benefits. It creates an atmosphere of liveliness, builds community, and allows students to practice speaking in a low-risk environment. Many of the activities in *Future* are pair and small-group activities. Here are some tips for managing these activities:
- Limit small groups to three or four students per group (unless an activity specifically calls for larger groups). This maximizes student participation.
- Change partners for different activities. This gives students a chance to work with many others in the class and keeps them from feeling "stuck."
- If possible, give students a place to put their coats when they enter the classroom. This allows them to move around freely without worrying about returning to their own seats.

- Move around the classroom as students are working to make sure they are on task and to monitor their work.
- As you walk around, try to remain unobtrusive, so students continue to participate actively, without feeling they are being evaluated.
- Keep track of language points students are having difficulty with. After the activity, teach a mini-lesson to the entire class addressing those issues. This helps students who are having trouble without singling them out.

Pairs and groups in the multilevel classroom

Adult education ESL classrooms are by nature multilevel. This is true even if students have been given a placement test. Many factors—including a student's age, educational background, and literacy level—contribute to his or her ability level. Also, the same student may be at level in one skill, but pre-level or above-level in another.

When grouping students for a task, keep the following points in mind:
- *Like-ability* groups (in which students have the same ability level) help ensure that all students participate equally, without one student dominating the activity.
- *Cross-ability* groups (in which students have different ability levels) are beneficial to pre-level students who need the support of their at- or above-level classmates. The higher-level students benefit from "teaching" their lower-level classmates.

For example, when students are practicing a straightforward conversation substitution exercise, like-ability pairings are helpful. The activity can be tailored to different ability levels, and both students can participate equally. When students are completing the more complex task of creating their own conversations, cross-ability pairings are helpful. The higher-level student can support and give ideas to the lower-level student.

The *Future* Teacher's Edition and Lesson Planner, the Teacher's Notes in the Multilevel Communicative Activities Book, and the Teacher's Notes in the Transparencies and Reproducible Vocabulary Cards all provide specific suggestions for when to put students in like-ability versus cross-ability groups, and how to tailor activities to different ability levels.

Unit Tour

Unit Opener

Each unit starts with a full-page photo that introduces the theme and vocabulary of the unit.

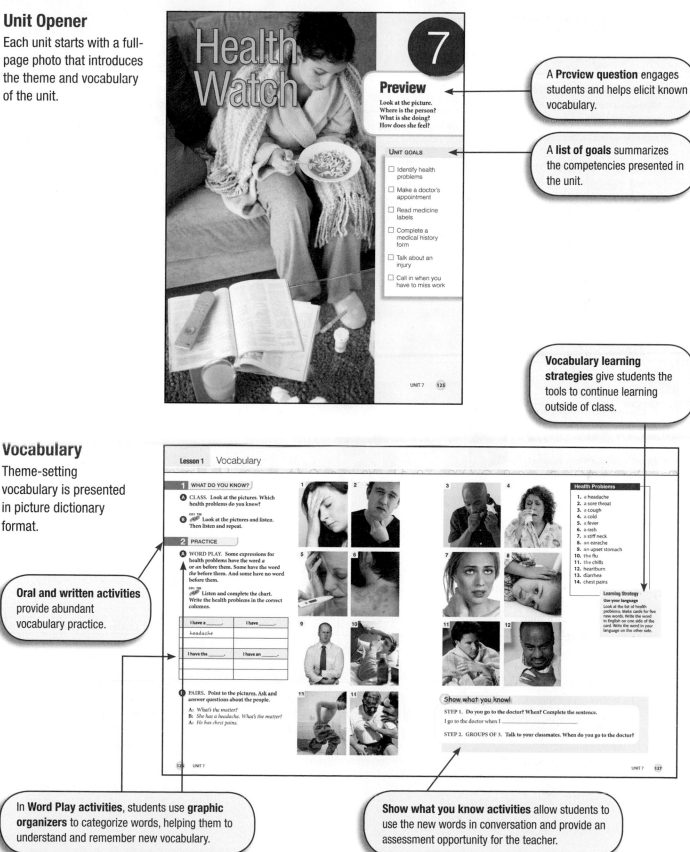

A **Preview question** engages students and helps elicit known vocabulary.

A **list of goals** summarizes the competencies presented in the unit.

Vocabulary learning strategies give students the tools to continue learning outside of class.

Vocabulary

Theme-setting vocabulary is presented in picture dictionary format.

Oral and written activities provide abundant vocabulary practice.

In **Word Play activities**, students use **graphic organizers** to categorize words, helping them to understand and remember new vocabulary.

Show what you know activities allow students to use the new words in conversation and provide an assessment opportunity for the teacher.

Listening and Speaking

Three listening lessons present the core competencies and language of the unit.

Before You Listen activities introduce new language and cultural concepts.

Prediction questions focus attention on the context-setting photo and encourage critical thinking.

The **Pronunciation Watch** and exercises focus on the sound patterns, stress, and intonation of English.

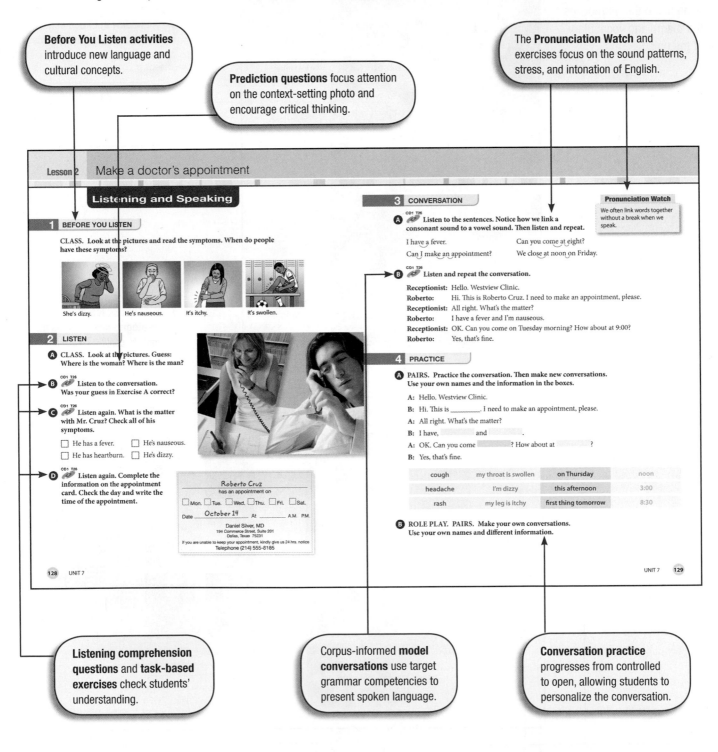

Lesson 2 Make a doctor's appointment

Listening and Speaking

1 BEFORE YOU LISTEN

CLASS. Look at the pictures and read the symptoms. When do people have these symptoms?

She's dizzy. He's nauseous. It's itchy. It's swollen.

2 LISTEN

A CLASS. Look at the pictures. Guess: Where is the woman? Where is the man?

B CD1 T26 Listen to the conversation. Was your guess in Exercise A correct?

C CD1 T26 Listen again. What is the matter with Mr. Cruz? Check all of his symptoms.

☐ He has a fever. ☐ He's nauseous.
☐ He has heartburn. ☐ He's dizzy.

D CD1 T26 Listen again. Complete the information on the appointment card. Check the day and write the time of the appointment.

Roberto Cruz
has an appointment on
☐ Mon. ☐ Tue. ☐ Wed. ☐ Thu. ☐ Fri. ☐ Sat.
Date _October 14_ At _____ A.M. P.M.
Daniel Silver, MD
194 Commerce Street, Suite 201
Dallas, Texas 75231
If you are unable to keep your appointment, kindly give us 24 hrs. notice
Telephone (214) 555-8185

128 UNIT 7

3 CONVERSATION

A CD1 T26 Listen to the sentences. Notice how we link a consonant sound to a vowel sound. Then listen and repeat.

I have a fever.   Can you come at eight?
Can I make an appointment?   We close at noon on Friday.

B CD1 T26 Listen and repeat the conversation.

Receptionist: Hello. Westview Clinic.
Roberto: Hi. This is Roberto Cruz. I need to make an appointment, please.
Receptionist: All right. What's the matter?
Roberto: I have a fever and I'm nauseous.
Receptionist: OK. Can you come on Tuesday morning? How about at 9:00?
Roberto: Yes, that's fine.

4 PRACTICE

A PAIRS. Practice the conversation. Then make new conversations. Use your own names and the information in the boxes.

A: Hello. Westview Clinic.
B: Hi. This is _____. I need to make an appointment, please.
A: All right. What's the matter?
B: I have, _____ and _____.
A: OK. Can you come _____? How about at _____?
B: Yes, that's fine.

cough	my throat is swollen	on Thursday	noon
headache	I'm dizzy	this afternoon	3:00
rash	my leg is itchy	first thing tomorrow	8:30

B ROLE PLAY. PAIRS. Make your own conversations. Use your own names and different information.

UNIT 7 129

Pronunciation Watch
We often link words together without a break when we speak.

Listening comprehension questions and **task-based exercises** check students' understanding.

Corpus-informed **model conversations** use target grammar competencies to present spoken language.

Conversation practice progresses from controlled to open, allowing students to personalize the conversation.

Grammar

Each unit presents three grammar points in a logical, systematic grammar syllabus.

Grammar charts present the target grammar point with minimal metalanguage.

Grammar Watch notes call attention to specific aspects of the grammar point.

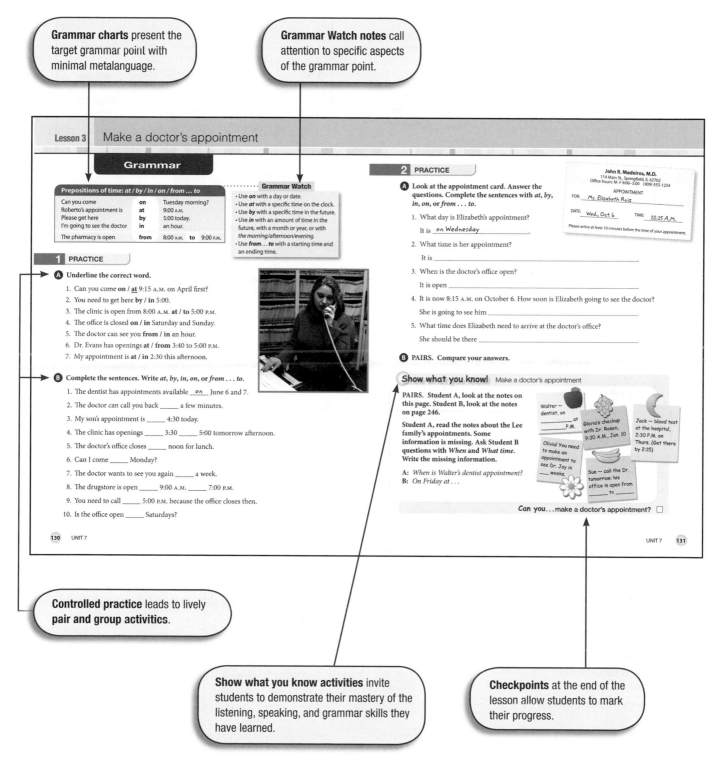

Controlled practice leads to lively **pair and group activities**.

Show what you know activities invite students to demonstrate their mastery of the listening, speaking, and grammar skills they have learned.

Checkpoints at the end of the lesson allow students to mark their progress.

Life Skills

The Life Skills lesson in each unit focuses on functional language, practical skills and authentic printed materials such as schedules, labels, and receipts.

Functional language related to the Life Skills topics is modeled and practiced.

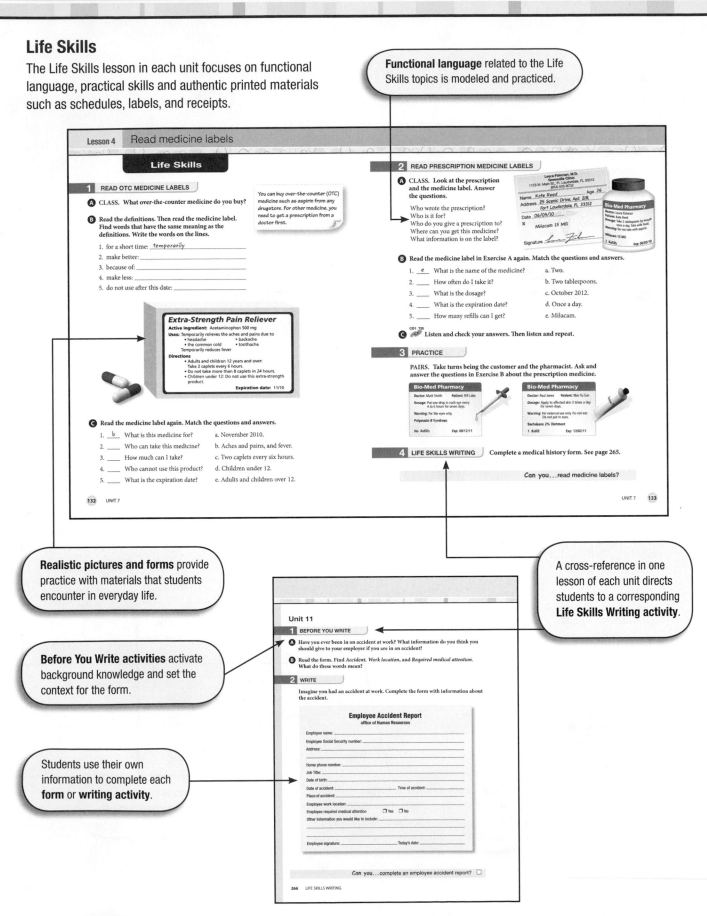

Realistic pictures and forms provide practice with materials that students encounter in everyday life.

Before You Write activities activate background knowledge and set the context for the form.

Students use their own information to complete each **form** or **writing activity**.

A cross-reference in one lesson of each unit directs students to a corresponding **Life Skills Writing activity**.

Reading

High-interest articles introduce students to cultural concepts and useful, topical information. Students read to learn while learning to read in English.

Pre-reading questions accompanied by pictures pre-teach vocabulary and activate students' background knowledge.

Essential **reading skills** such as finding the main idea, scanning for information, and getting meaning from context are introduced and practiced.

Comprehension questions check understanding of the article and build reading skills.

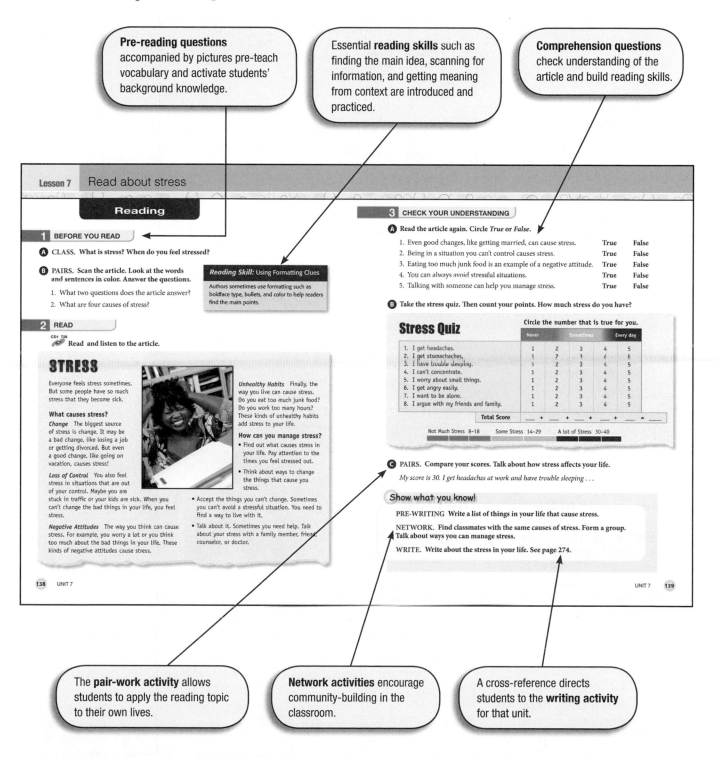

The **pair-work activity** allows students to apply the reading topic to their own lives.

Network activities encourage community-building in the classroom.

A cross-reference directs students to the **writing activity** for that unit.

Review

The Review page synthesizes the unit grammar through contextualized cloze or sentence writing activities.

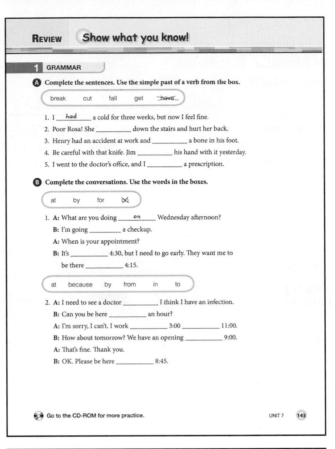

REVIEW — Show what you know!

1 GRAMMAR

A Complete the sentences. Use the simple past of a verb from the box.

break   cut   fall   get   ~~have~~

1. I ___had___ a cold for three weeks, but now I feel fine.
2. Poor Rosa! She _____ down the stairs and hurt her back.
3. Henry had an accident at work and _____ a bone in his foot.
4. Be careful with that knife. Jim _____ his hand with it yesterday.
5. I went to the doctor's office, and I _____ a prescription.

B Complete the conversations. Use the words in the boxes.

at   by   for   ~~on~~

1. **A:** What are you doing ___on___ Wednesday afternoon?
   B: I'm going _____ a checkup.
   A: When is your appointment?
   B: It's _____ 4:30, but I need to go early. They want me to be there _____ 4:15.

at   because   by   from   in   to

2. **A:** I need to see a doctor _____ I think I have an infection.
   B: Can you be here _____ an hour?
   A: I'm sorry, I can't. I work _____ 3:00 _____ 11:00.
   B: How about tomorrow? We have an opening _____ 9:00.
   A: That's fine. Thank you.
   B: OK. Please be here _____ 8:45.

Go to the CD-ROM for more practice.   UNIT 7   143

Expand

The final page of the unit allows students to review and expand on the language, themes, and competencies they have worked with throughout the unit.

> Lively **role-play activities** motivate students, allowing them to feel successful. Teachers can use these activities to assess students' mastery of the material.

> Cross-references direct students to the **Persistence Activity** and **Team Project** for that unit.

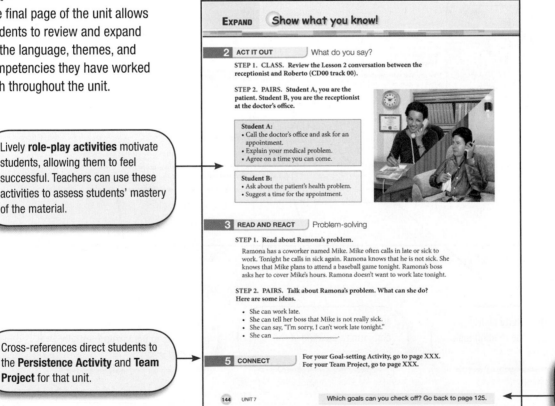

EXPAND — Show what you know!

2 ACT IT OUT — What do you say?

STEP 1. CLASS. Review the Lesson 2 conversation between the receptionist and Roberto (CD00 track 00).

STEP 2. PAIRS. Student A, you are the patient. Student B, you are the receptionist at the doctor's office.

Student A:
- Call the doctor's office and ask for an appointment.
- Explain your medical problem.
- Agree on a time you can come.

Student B:
- Ask about the patient's health problem.
- Suggest a time for the appointment.

3 READ AND REACT — Problem-solving

STEP 1. Read about Ramona's problem.

Ramona has a coworker named Mike. Mike often calls in late or sick to work. Tonight he calls in sick again. Ramona knows that he is not sick. She knows that Mike plans to attend a baseball game tonight. Ramona's boss asks her to cover Mike's hours. Ramona doesn't want to work late tonight.

STEP 2. PAIRS. Talk about Ramona's problem. What can she do? Here are some ideas.

- She can work late.
- She can tell her boss that Mike is not really sick.
- She can say, "I'm sorry, I can't work late tonight."
- She can _____.

5 CONNECT — For your Goal-setting Activity, go to page XXX.
For your Team Project, go to page XXX.

144   UNIT 7   Which goals can you check off? Go back to page 125.

> **Checkpoints** allow students to see the unit goals they have accomplished.

Persistence Activities

Persistence activities build community in the classroom, help students set personal and language goals, and encourage students to develop good study skills and habits.

Controlled activities provide scaffolding for the **real-life application activities** that follow.

Writing

After students have their Pre-Writing discussion in the Reading lesson, they are asked to write about the same subject. Topics are interesting and relevant to their lives.

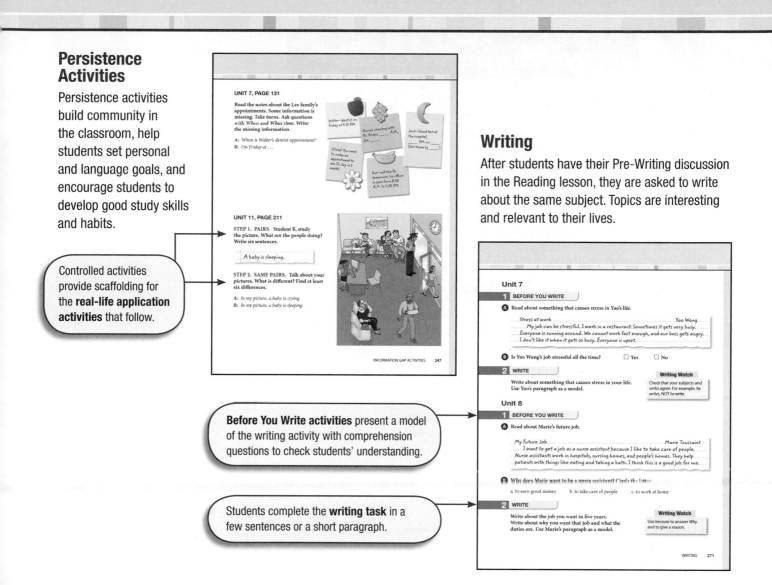

Before You Write activities present a model of the writing activity with comprehension questions to check students' understanding.

Students complete the **writing task** in a few sentences or a short paragraph.

Team Projects

Each unit includes a collaborative project that integrates all of the unit themes, language, and competencies in a community-building activity.

A **graphic organizer** helps students collect the information they need for the task.

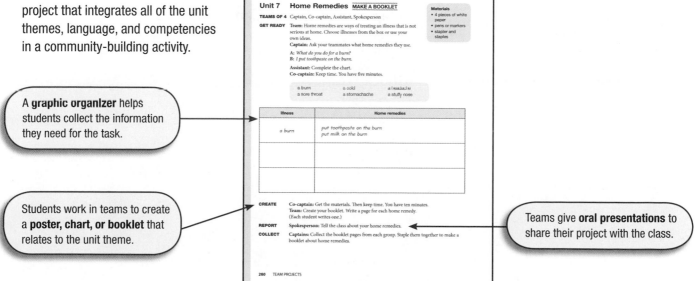

Students work in teams to create a **poster, chart, or booklet** that relates to the unit theme.

Teams give **oral presentations** to share their project with the class.

Pre-Unit

Getting Started

Welcome to Class

---

1 **LEARN ABOUT YOUR BOOK**

A CLASS. Turn to page iii. Answer the questions.

1. What information is on this page?

2. How many units are in this book?

3. Which unit is about food?

4. Which two units are about work?

B CLASS. Sometimes you will need to go to the back of the book to do activities. Look at the chart. Find the pages in the book and complete the chart.

Page	Activity
248	Persistence Activities
260	
272	
278	

C PAIRS. There is additional information for you in the back of the book. Find each section. Write the page number.

Grammar Reference _____   Map of the U.S. and Canada _____

Audio Script _____   Map of the World _____

Word List _____   Index _____

2 MEET YOUR CLASSMATES

A CD1 T2 Read and listen to the conversation.

Ayida: Hi. My name is Ayida .

Carmen: Hello, Ayida . I'm Carmen .

Ayida: Nice to meet you, Carmen .

Carmen: Nice to meet you, too.

Ayida: Where are you from?

Carmen: Peru . How about you?

Ayida: I'm from Haiti .

B PAIRS. Practice the conversation. Use your own names and information.

3 TALK ABOUT YOUR GOALS

A Why are you studying English? Check the boxes.

☐ to get a job or a better job

☐ to get United States citizenship

☐ to continue my education

☐ to help my children with schoolwork

☐ to get into a career program

☐ other goal: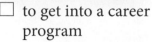

B NETWORK. GROUPS OF 3. Talk about your goals. Do you have any of the same goals?

A Complete the conversations. Use questions from the box.

> Can you speak more slowly?   Can you repeat that?
> How do you pronounce this?   How do you spell that?
> What does this word mean?   What's this called in English?

1. Where are you from?
   I'm sorry. Can you speak more slowly?
   Oh, sorry. Where are you from?
   I'm from Korea.

2. _____
   It's a pencil sharpener.
   Thank you.

3. Excuse me. _____
   Registration.
   New Student Registration
   Registration?
   Yes. That's right.

4. Can you help me?
   Sure.
   _____
   Occupation? It means a job or career.

5. Please turn to page 45.
   I'm sorry. _____
   Sure. Please turn to page 45.

6. My name is Chiao.
   Chiao? _____
   C-H-I-A-O.
   Thanks.

CD1 T3

B 🔘 Listen and check your answers.

C ROLE PLAY. PAIRS. Choose one conversation from Exercise A.
Make your own conversation. Use different information.

Making Connections

Preview

Look at the picture.
Where are the people?
What are they doing?

UNIT GOALS

☐ Describe
the way
people look

☐ Complete an
application

☐ Describe
personalities

☐ Get to know
someone

1 WHAT DO YOU KNOW?

A CLASS. Look at the pictures. What are some words that describe the people?

Bruno: short, thin

CD1 T4

B Look at the pictures and listen. Listen again and repeat.

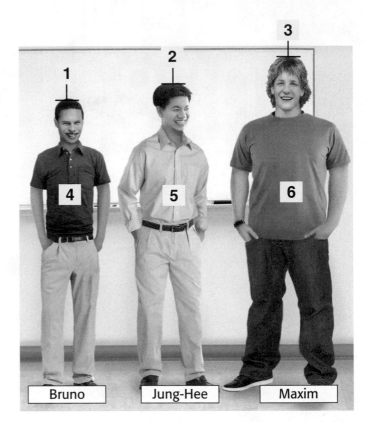

2 PRACTICE

A Choose one person in the pictures. Write a list of words to describe that person.

B PAIRS. Student A, read your list to your partner. Student B, listen and identify the person in the picture.

A: *Short. Curly hair. Slim.*
B: *Bruno?*
A: *Yes.*

C WORD PLAY. Look at the underlined words. Which word describes hair length? Which word describes hair type? Which word describes hair color?

He has <u>short</u>, <u>curly</u> <u>brown</u> hair.
     1   2   3

D Write four other phrases to describe hair. Add commas.

	1	2	3	
She has				hair.

Felix   Basia   Ana   Mai

Kwami   Yusef   David

Physical Descriptions

Height
1. short
2. average height
3. tall

Weight
4. thin/slim
5. average weight
6. heavy

Hair Type
7. bald
8. curly
9. wavy
10. straight

Hair Length
11. short
12. shoulder-length
13. long

Facial Hair
14. a beard
15. a mustache
16. a goatee

Learning Strategy

Personalize

Think of someone you know well. Look at the list of physical descriptions. Write four words to describe that person.

Show what you know!

STEP 1. Look at the list of physical descriptions. Which words describe you? Write the words on a piece of paper. Put your paper in a box.

STEP 2. CLASS. Take a piece of paper from the box. Read the description to the class. Who is it?

Listening and Speaking

1 BEFORE YOU LISTEN

PAIRS. Read the words in the box. Then complete the chart.

attractive   beautiful   good-looking   handsome   ~~pretty~~

Words for women only	Words for men only	Words for women and men
pretty		

Some words describe only women. Some words describe only men. Some words describe both women and men.

2 LISTEN

CD1 T5

A Look at the picture. Listen to the conversation between two friends, Tania and Eva. What does Tania want to know more about?

a. a party   b. Eva's friend   c. a teacher

CD1 T5

B Listen again. Answer the questions.

1. Where is Tania going tonight?
   a. to her class   b. to her job   c. to a party

2. What does Tania say about Eva's friend?
   a. "He's attractive."   b. "He's good-looking."   c. "He's handsome."

3. What does Eva's friend look like?
   a.    b.    c.

CD1 T6

C Listen to the whole conversation. Complete the sentence.

Victor is Eva's _____.
a. friend   b. boyfriend   c. brother

3 CONVERSATION

CD1 T7

A Listen to the words. Then listen and repeat.

par·ty   to·night   beau·ti·ful   at·trac·tive

CD1 T8

B Listen to the words. Mark (●) the stressed syllable.

1. hand·some   2. in·vit·ing   3. pret·ty   4. in·tro·duce

CD1 T9

C Listen and repeat the conversation.

Tania: Hi, Eva.

Eva: Hi, Tania. Are you coming to my party tonight?

Tania: Of course. Are you inviting your friend?

Eva: Which friend?

Tania: You know—he's handsome and he has short, black hair.

Pronunciation Watch

A syllable is a part of a word. For example, the word *party* has two syllables: par·ty. In words with more than one syllable, one syllable is stressed. The stressed syllable is long and loud.

---

4 PRACTICE

A PAIRS. Practice the conversation. Then make new conversations. Use the information in the boxes and your own names.

A: Hi, _____.

B: Hi, _____. Are you coming to my party tonight?

A: Of course. Are you inviting your friend?

B: Which friend?

A: You know—he's _____ and he has _____, _____ hair.

| thin |
| average height |
| average weight |

| wavy |
| long |
| curly |

| red |
| brown |
| black |

B ROLE PLAY. PAIRS. Make your own conversations. Use different words to describe the friend.

Describe the way people look

Grammar

Simple present: be + adjective

Affirmative			Negative			
I	**am**		I	**am**		
They	**are**	tall.	They	**are**	**not**	heavy.
He	**is**		He	**is**		

Simple present: have + object

Affirmative			Negative			
I	**have**		I	**do**		
They		black hair.	They		**not**	**have** black hair.
He	**has**		He	**does**		

> **Grammar Watch**
>
> Contractions are short forms.
> Here are some examples:
>
> • *he is not* = **he's not / he isn't**
> • *he does not* = **he doesn't**
>
> • *they are* = **they're**
> • *they are not* = **they're not /**
>   **they aren't**
>
> For more contractions, see
> page 286.

1 PRACTICE

A Complete the sentences.

My sister and brother ____are____ very good-looking, but they don't look alike.
                            (is / are)

My sister _____ brown eyes, but my brother _____ blue eyes. My sister
              (is / has)   (has / have)

_____ long hair. It _____ curly. My brother's hair _____
 (has / is)   (are / is)   (has / is)

short. And it _____ curly—it's straight. Also, my sister _____ tall, and
               (isn't / is)   (is / are)

my brother _____ average height. But my sister and brother _____ alike
            (have / is)   (is / are)

in one way: They _____ both thin.
                  (are / have)

B Complete the sentences. Write the correct forms of *be* or *have*. Use contractions
for the negative sentences.

1. Omar ___has___ brown hair.

2. Na-Young (not) ___isn't___ thin.

3. Jeff and Rob _____ blond hair.

4. Josh and his brother _____ tall.

5. Amy's hair (not) _____ curly.

6. Marko's eyes _____ green.

7. Ivana and Olga _____ very attractive.

8. Steve (not) _____ a beard.

A PAIRS. Look at the picture. Describe the people. Talk about their height, weight, and hair. There is more than one possible answer.

Shakira has long, wavy, blond hair. She's short and thin.

Yao Ming   Venus Williams   Jorge Garcia   Shakira   Cee-Lo Green   Zhang Ziyi

B WRITE. Write two sentences to describe each person. Use a separate piece of paper.

Show what you know! Describe the way people look

STEP 1. WRITE. Describe someone in the class. Write three sentences.

> This person is tall and heavy.

STEP 2. PAIRS. Student A, read your sentences. Student B, guess the person.

A: *This person is tall and heavy.*
B: *Is it Laura?*
A: *No, it isn't. This person has straight, blond hair.*
B: *Is it Sofia?*
A: *Yes!*

Can you...describe the way people look? ☐

Complete an application

Life Skills

1 COMPLETE AN APPLICATION

A **PAIRS.** Read the application for an identification card. Ask and answer the questions.

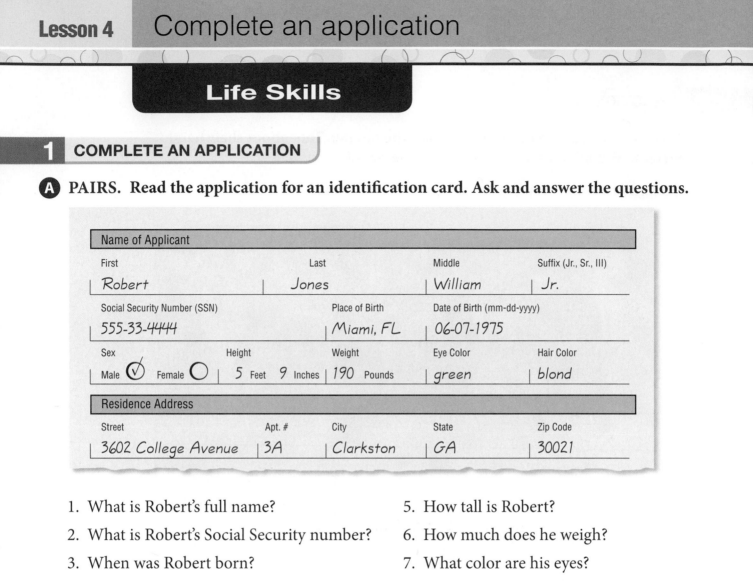

Name of Applicant			
First	Last	Middle	Suffix (Jr., Sr., III)
Robert	Jones	William	Jr.

Social Security Number (SSN)	Place of Birth	Date of Birth (mm-dd-yyyy)
555-33-4444	Miami, FL	06-07-1975

Sex	Height	Weight	Eye Color	Hair Color
Male ✓ Female ○	5 Feet 9 Inches	190 Pounds	green	blond

Residence Address				
Street	Apt. #	City	State	Zip Code
3602 College Avenue	3A	Clarkston	GA	30021

1. What is Robert's full name?

2. What is Robert's Social Security number?

3. When was Robert born?

4. Where was he born?

5. How tall is Robert?

6. How much does he weigh?

7. What color are his eyes?

8. What is Robert's residence address?

B Look at Teresa Santos's identification card. Match the abbreviations and the words.

1. __b__ F   a. height

2. _____ DOB   b. female

3. _____ BRN   c. black

4. _____ BLK   d. weight

5. _____ Ht.   e. brown

6. _____ Wt.   f. date of birth

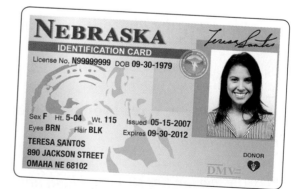

NEBRASKA
IDENTIFICATION CARD
License No. N99999999 DOB 09-30-1979

Sex F   Ht. 5-04   Wt. 115   Issued 05-15-2007
Eyes BRN   Hair BLK   Expires 09-30-2012
TERESA SANTOS
890 JACKSON STREET
OMAHA NE 68102
DONOR
DMV

A PAIRS. Student A, look at Joseph Smith's application.
Student B, look at Joseph Smith's identification card on page 245.

Student A, ask questions. Complete the missing information
on the application.

Title	Name (Last, First, Middle)		
Mr. Ms. Mrs. Miss	*Smith*	*Joseph*	*Charles*

SSN	Sex	Date of Birth (mm–dd–yyyy)
987-65-4321	M ☑ F ☐	

Height		Weight	Eye Color	Hair Color
Feet	Inches	*185* Pounds		

Residence Address

Street	Apt. #	City	State	Zip Code
	4E	*Chicago*	*IL*	*60604*

B SAME PAIRS. Student A, look at Ana Martinez's identification card.
Student B, look at Ana Martinez's application on page 245.

Student A, answer Student B's questions.

NEW YORK STATE
Governor of the State of New York
IDENTIFICATION CARD

ID: 123 456 789

Martinez, Ana M
101 Chestnut St.
Yonkers, NY 10701
DOB: 05-07-1987
SEX: F EYES: BRN HAIR: BRN HT: 5-04

ISSUED: 10-20-2006 EXPIRES: 05-07-2011

Complete a driver's license application. See page 256.

Can you...complete an application? ☐

Describe personalities

Listening and Speaking

1 BEFORE YOU LISTEN

A GROUPS OF 3. Look at the words to describe people. Read the definitions. Match the words and definitions.

~~bossy~~ cheerful laid-back moody outgoing shy sweet talkative

1. always tells other people what to do _____*bossy*_____
2. is nervous when speaking to other people _____
3. likes to talk a lot _____
4. changes feelings quickly and often _____
5. is relaxed and not worried about anything _____
6. is happy and positive _____
7. is kind, gentle, and friendly _____
8. enjoys meeting new people _____

CD1 T10
B Listen and check your answers.

2 LISTEN

CD1 T11
A Look at the picture. Listen to more of Tania and Eva's conversation. What are they talking about?

a. classmates   b. Victor   c. friends

CD1 T11
B Listen again. What is Victor like? Check the words.

☐ laid-back   ☐ outgoing   ☐ bossy
☐ sweet   ☐ quiet   ☐ moody

CD1 T12
C Listen to the whole conversation. Read the sentences. Circle *True* or *False*.

1. Tania is talkative.   **True**   **False**
2. Tania likes talkative guys.   **True**   **False**

3 CONVERSATION

CD1 T13

A Listen to the words. Notice the unstressed vowels. Then listen and repeat.

about   quiet   talkative   beautiful   attractive

CD1 T14

B Listen and repeat the conversation.

Tania: So tell me more about Victor. What's he like?

Eva: Well, he's outgoing and he has a lot of friends.

Tania: Yeah? What else?

Eva: He's sweet but he's a little quiet.

> **Pronunciation Watch**
>
> The vowel sound in a stressed syllable is long and clear. Vowels in unstressed syllables often have a very short, quiet sound. For example, a·bóut.

4 PRACTICE

A PAIRS. Practice the conversation. Then make new conversations. Use the information in the boxes.

A: So tell me more about Victor. What's he like?

B: Well, he's _____ and he _____.

A: Yeah? What else?

B: He's _____ but he's a little _____.

funny	tells great jokes
outgoing	loves adventure
interesting	tells great stories
talkative	moody
friendly	bossy
cheerful	shy

B MAKE IT PERSONAL. PAIRS. Talk about the personalities of your friends or family members.

A: *My best friend's name is Marie.*

B: *What's she like?*

A: *She's friendly. She's nice and she isn't bossy.*

Describe personalities

Grammar

Be: Compound sentences with *and* / *but*		
He's outgoing	**and**	he has a lot of friends.
He's sweet	**but**	he's a little quiet.

Grammar Watch

- Use *and* to join two sentences with similar ideas.
- Use *but* to join two sentences with opposite ideas.

1 PRACTICE

A Complete the sentences. Write *and* or *but*.

1. He's from Brazil _____but_____ now he lives in the U.S.

2. Sarah is my friend. She's funny _____ she's sweet.

3. My hair is straight _____ it's shoulder length.

4. I'm shy _____ my brother is outgoing.

5. I like long hair _____ my wife's hair is short.

B Write sentences. Use the words in parentheses, the correct form of *be*, and *and* or *but*.

1. (Tina / shy / her sister / talkative) _Tina is shy but her sister is talkative._

2. (Ken / outgoing / he / moody) _____

3. (The food / delicious / the waiter / friendly) _____

4. (The class / good / the teacher / funny) _____

5. (Emily / cheerful / she / laid-back) _____

C Complete the sentences. Write adjectives to make true sentences.

1. I'm _____shy_____ and I'm _____quiet_____.

2. I'm _____ and I'm _____.

3. I'm _____ but I'm _____.

4. My teacher is _____ and he's/she's _____.

D PAIRS. Compare your answers.

Be: Additions with *and ...*, *too* / *and ...not*, *either*

Affirmative statement	Addition		
Eva is a student	**and**	I	**am, too.**
		they	**are, too.**
		he	**is, too.**

Negative statement	Addition		
Victor isn't a teacher	**and**	I	**'m not, either.**
		you	**aren't, either.**
			're not, either.
		she	**isn't, either.**
			's not, either.

· · · · · · · · · · **Grammar Watch**

- Use an addition as a way to avoid repeating the same information in the second part of the sentence.
- Use *too* for affirmative sentences.
- Use *not, either* for negative sentences.
- Use a comma before *too* and *either*.

2 PRACTICE

Complete the sentences. Write the correct forms of *be* and *too* or *either*.

1. He isn't tall and his wife <u>isn't, either</u>.

2. Greg is funny and his dad _____.

3. Sun is in my English class and Oscar and Fernando _____.

4. My brothers are not outgoing and I _____.

5. My friend is beautiful and her daughter _____.

Show what you know!   Describe personalities

STEP 1. WRITE. Think about your own personality. Write four sentences with *be*. Write two affirmative sentences and two negative sentences.

> I am outgoing and I am quiet.

STEP 2. GROUPS OF 5. Tell your partners about your personality. Do you have the same personality as other members of your group? Make sentences with *too* or *either*.

Marta is outgoing and I am, too.

Can you...describe personalities? ☐

Reading

1 BEFORE YOU READ

PAIRS. What is your learning style? For example, do you like to study alone or with other people? Do you like to study in a quiet room or in a noisy place?

2 READ

CD1 T15
 Listen. Read the article.

What is a Learning Style?

Some people learn best when they study with classmates. Other people like to study alone. Some people learn how to do things by reading books. Other people learn things best by talking to people. There are many ways to learn new information. These ways of learning are called learning styles. Here are some learning styles.

 Visual Learners
Visual learners learn best by seeing. They remember new information best when it is in pictures, graphs, and maps. They are also good at spelling and remembering faces.

 Auditory Learners
Auditory learners learn best by talking and listening. They remember information best when they hear it. They have a "good ear" for language and remember names easily. They are good at discussions and interviewing. They find it difficult to study in noisy places.

 Kinesthetic Learners
Kinesthetic learners learn best by doing things. They like doing projects. They remember new information best if they act it out or role-play. They "speak" with their hands a lot. They find it difficult to sit down and study for long periods.

3 CHECK YOUR UNDERSTANDING

A Read the article again. What is the main idea of the article? How do you know?

a. People learn best by doing things.

b. People learn in different ways.

c. Some people use two learning styles.

Reading Skill: Finding the Main Idea

The main idea is the most important idea in the article. The first paragraph usually tells the main idea.

B How do you learn best? Take the quiz.

Learning Styles Quiz

How do you learn new information? What do you do in these situations?

1 You have a new cell phone. You don't know how to use it.

☐ I read the instructions in the user's manual.

☐ I ask a friend to explain it to me.

☐ I play with the phone until I understand how to use it.

2 You're going to a new restaurant in your neighborhood. You don't know exactly where it is.

☐ I look at a map.

☐ I call the restaurant and ask for directions.

☐ I start walking until I find it.

3 You can't remember how to spell a word.

☐ I write the word different ways. I choose the way that looks right.

☐ I say the word and write the letters as they sound.

☐ I use my finger to "write" the word and decide what feels right.

4 You need to memorize a new word.

☐ I draw a picture of the work in my notebook.

☐ I close my eyes and say the word over and over again.

☐ I say the word as I write it over and over again.

C Look at the quiz. How many responses do you have for each symbol? Write the numbers. The symbol with the most responses is your learning style.

____ 👁 responses = visual learner

____ 👂 responses = auditory learner

____ ✋ responses = kinesthetic learner

> Many people use more than one learning style. For example, a person may learn best by talking and doing.

D PAIRS. Compare your quiz results. What is your learning style? Do the results surprise you?

Show what you know!

PRE-WRITING. NETWORK. Find classmates with the same learning style. Talk about how you learn English best.

WRITING. Write a list of learning tips for your learning style. See page 268.

Get to know someone

Listening and Speaking

1 BEFORE YOU LISTEN

CLASS. Imagine that you are meeting someone for the first time. In this country, which questions are OK to ask? Check the questions.

☐ What do you do?   ☐ Where are you from?

☐ Are you married?   ☐ Where do you live?

☐ How old are you?   ☐ Do you have children?

2 LISTEN

A **CLASS.** Look at the picture. Who are the people? Where are they?

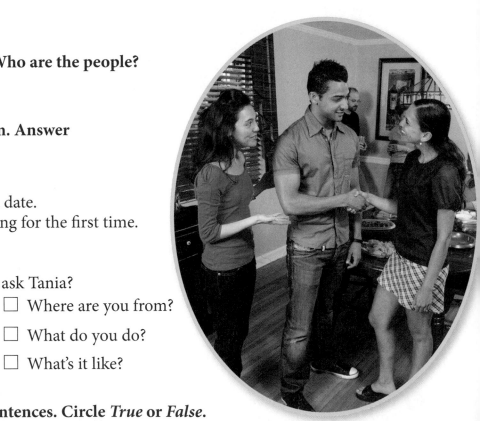

CD1 T16

B Listen to the conversation. Answer the questions.

1. What's happening?
   a. Victor is asking Tania for a date.
   b. Victor and Tania are meeting for the first time.
   c. Tania is saying good-bye.

2. Which questions does Victor ask Tania?
   ☐ Are you a student?   ☐ Where are you from?

   ☐ Is it nice?   ☐ What do you do?

   ☐ Are you from Ecuador?   ☐ What's it like?

CD1 T16

C Listen again. Read the sentences. Circle *True* or *False*.

1. Tania is a student.   True   False

2. Eva is a student.   True   False

3. Victor is from Ecuador.   True   False

CD1 T17

D Listen to the whole conversation. Answer the question.

What is Victor's job? _____

3 CONVERSATION

CD1 T18

A Listen to the sentences. Then listen and repeat.

Pronunciation Watch

In English, the important words in a sentence are stressed. They are long and loud. In words with more than one syllable, only one syllable is stressed.

Are you a student, too?   No, I'm not.

I work at a restaurant.   I'm a waiter.

CD1 T19

B Listen to the sentences. Mark (●) the stressed words.

1. Nice to meet you.   2. Where are you from?   3. How about you?

CD1 T20

C Listen and repeat the conversation.

Eva: I want to introduce you to my friend. Victor, this is Tania. Tania, this is Victor.

Victor: Nice to meet you.

Tania: Nice to meet you, too.

Victor: So, are you a student?

Tania: Yes, I am. Eva and I are in the same English class.

Victor: Oh, that's nice. Where are you from?

Tania: Ecuador.

Victor: Really? What's it like?

Tania: It's a very beautiful country.

4 PRACTICE

A GROUPS OF 3. Practice the conversation.

B ROLE PLAY. GROUPS OF 3. Student A, introduce Student B to Student C. Continue the conversation.

A: *I want to introduce you to my friend. _____, this is _____.*

   _____, this is _____.

B: *Nice to meet you.*

C: *Nice to meet you, too.*

B: *So, _____ . . .*

Grammar

Simple present tense of *be*: *Yes / No* and information questions

Yes / No questions with *be*			Short answers					
Are	you	a student?	**Yes,**	I	**am**.	**No,**	I	**am** **not**.

Information questions with *be*			Short answer	
Where	**are**	you from?	Ecuador.	

PRACTICE

A Match the questions and answers.

1. __d__ Where is your family from?
2. _____ Are they students?
3. _____ What is your country like?
4. _____ How old is your daughter?
5. _____ Are you from Russia?
6. _____ What's your name?

a. Yes, they are.
b. She's four.
c. No, I'm not.
d. Brazil.
e. I'm Jennifer.
f. It's beautiful.

B Read the answers. Write questions about the underlined information.

1. **A:** _What is your last name?_

   B: My last name is <u>Chow</u>.

2. **A:** _____

   B: Pei-Ling's address is <u>240 Colson Drive</u>.

3. **A:** _____

   B: They're from <u>Cuba</u>.

4. **A:** _____

   B: Peter is <u>twenty-four years old</u>.

5. **A:** _____

   B: <u>Yes</u>. His sisters are tall.

6. **A:** _____

   B: <u>No</u>. He's not outgoing. He's really shy!

7. **A:** _____

   B: Mike's phone number is <u>555-9874</u>.

8. **A:** _____

   B: <u>Yes</u>. Ted and Chris are students.

C PAIRS. Ask your partner three questions from Exercises A and B.

1 GRAMMAR

A Complete the conversations. Write the correct forms of the words in parentheses.

1. **A:** Excuse me. ___*Are you*___ Anthony Jenkins?
      (you / be)

   B: No, I _____. Anthony _____ the tall guy over there.
      (not / be)   _(be)_

   He _____ short, dark hair.
      (have)

   A: Oh, I see him. Thanks.

2. **A:** You look familiar. _____ a student at the English Language Center?
      (you / be)

   B: Yes, I _____. I _____ in level two.
      _(be)_   _(be)_

   A: Me, too. _____ your teacher?
      (who / be)

   B: Ted Graham. He _____ a really good teacher.
      _(be)_

B Complete the sentences. Underline the correct words.

My name **has / is** Ellen. **I'm / I have** eighteen years old. This is my sister, Isabel. We're twins. As you can see, we look alike. My hair **is / am** long and brown, **and / but** my sister's hair is, **either / too**. We both **have / are** brown eyes. **I'm / I have** not tall, **but / and** my sister isn't, **too / either**.

We are very similar, **and / but** we're not alike in every way. My sister **is / has** talkative, **but / and** I'm quiet. My sister **has / is** outgoing, **but / and** I'm shy. My sister is always cheerful, **and / but** I am sometimes moody. Oh, and one more difference: I **am / are** sweet, **but / and** my sister **is / are** bossy. Don't tell my sister I wrote that!

Go to the CD-ROM for more practice.

2 ACT IT OUT   What do you say?

STEP 1. CLASS. Review the Lesson 8 conversation between Eva, Victor, and Tania (CD 1 track 16).

STEP 2. ROLE PLAY. GROUPS OF 3. Imagine you are at a party.
Student A, introduce Students B and C.
Students B and C, continue the conversation. Make small talk.

3 READ AND REACT   Problem-solving

STEP 1. Read about Victor's problem.

Victor is at work. He meets a new co-worker, Jim, for the first time.
First they talk about where they are from. Then Jim asks Victor, "How
much money do you make?" Victor doesn't want to answer the question.

STEP 2. PAIRS. What is Victor's problem? What can he do?
Here are some ideas.

- He can say nothing and then talk about something different.
- He can answer the question and feel bad.
- He can say, "I'd rather not say."
- He can _____.

4 CONNECT

For your Community-building Activity, go to page 248.
For your Team Project, go to page 274.

Which goals can you check off? Go back to page 5.

All in the Family

Preview

Look at the picture.
What do you see?

UNIT GOALS

- ☐ Identify family members
- ☐ Talk about your life and family
- ☐ Talk about what people have in common
- ☐ Ask about sending mail
- ☐ Complete a customs form
- ☐ Ask about family members

Manny Tina Manuel Isabel   Marta   Maria Tony Carlos

1 WHAT DO YOU KNOW?

A CLASS. Look at the pictures of Marta's family. Find Marta in each picture. Guess: Who are the other family members in the pictures? Which family relationships do you know?

I think number 1 is Marta's brother.

CD1 T21

B   Look at the pictures and listen. Listen again and repeat.

2 PRACTICE

A PAIRS. Student A, ask a question about Marta's family. Student B, answer.

A: *Who is Marta's mother-in-law?*
B: *Sandra. Who are Marta's grandchildren?*

Ben   Marta   Tina   Eva   Felix

B PAIRS. Look at the pictures. Student A, say two names and point to the two people in the pictures. Student B, say the relationship.

A: *Ben and Ann.*
B: *Brother and sister.*

C WORD PLAY. PAIRS. Look at the list of family members. Which words are for females? Which are for males? Which are for both? Complete the diagram.

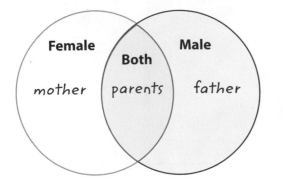

Female   Both   Male

mother   parents   father

12   13   14   15   16

Marta   Ben   Sandra   Tom   Ann

Tommy   Liz   Marta   Ben

Family Members

1. brother	14. mother-in-law
2. sister	15. father-in-law
3. father	16. sister-in-law
4. mother	17. son
5. aunt	18. daughter
6. cousin	19. children
7. uncle	20. parents
8. fiancé	21. grandmother
9. fiancée	22. grandfather
10. niece	23. granddaughter
11. nephew	24. grandson
12. wife	25. grandchildren
13. husband	

Liz   Marta   Ben   Mary   Tommy   Sue   Benny

Show what you know!

STEP 1. GROUPS OF 3. Talk about your own families.

A: *Do you have family in this country?*
B: *Yes, I have a sister and a . . .*

STEP 2. Tell the class about your partners' families.

Andrea's sister lives here. Her brother . . .

Listening and Speaking

1 BEFORE YOU LISTEN

A READ. Look at the picture. Read about the Garcia family. Which members of the Garcia family live together? Who did they live with in Mexico?

My name is Inez Garcia.
This is a picture of my family.
This is me, my husband,
and my two kids. We live in
an apartment in Los Angeles.
In Mexico, we lived with
my mother and father.

B CLASS. In your country, which family members usually live together? Do you think this is the same for people in the U.S.?

2 LISTEN

A CLASS. Look at the picture of two new coworkers, Amy and Babacar. What do people talk about when they are getting to know each other?

CD1 T22

B Listen to the conversation. Answer the questions.

1. What size family does Babacar have?
   a. big   b. small

2. How many brothers does Babacar have?
   a. one   b. two

3. Where do Babacar's sisters live?
   a. Somalia   b. Senegal

CD1 T23

C Listen to the whole conversation. Complete the sentence.

Babacar's brother lives **far from / with** Babacar.

3 CONVERSATION

CD1 T24

A **Listen. Then listen again and repeat the sentences.**

I have a brother and a sister.
We live in the same apartment.
He works in a hospital.

CD1 T25

B **Listen and repeat the conversation.**

Amy: Tell me about your family.

Babacar: Well, I don't have a very big family. I have a brother and two sisters.

Amy: Do they live here?

Babacar: My sisters live in Senegal, but my brother lives here.

4 PRACTICE

A PAIRS. Practice the conversation.

B MAKE IT PERSONAL. PAIRS. Talk about your own families.

A: *Tell me about your family.*
B: *I have a very big family. I have …*

Grammar

Simple present affirmative and negative: *have / live / work*

Affirmative			Negative			
I	**have**	two sisters.	I		**have**	a big family.
We	**live**	in New York.	We	**don't**	**live**	in Miami.
They	**work**	in a school.	They		**work**	in an office.
He	**has**	a brother.	He		**have**	a sister.
She	**lives**	in Senegal.	She	**doesn't**	**live**	here.
My brother	**works**	in a hospital.	My sister		**work**	in a hospital.

Grammar Watch

- With *he, she,* or *it,* the simple present verb ends in *-s.*
- Use *don't* or *doesn't* to make a sentence negative.
- Use the base form of the verb with *don't* and *doesn't.*

1 PRACTICE

A Complete the sentences. Underline the correct words.

1. My cousin **has** / **have** a wife and two children.
2. They **doesn't** / **don't** have children.
3. Her cousin **work** / **works** in a theater.
4. My mother-in-law **lives** / **live** on South Street.
5. Our grandparents **doesn't** / **don't** live here.
6. We **don't** / **doesn't** work on weekends.
7. Shelly and Kirk **have** / **has** twins.

B Complete the sentences. Write the correct forms of the words in parentheses.

1. Clara (work) _____ works _____ at a beauty salon.
2. His sister-in-law (not have) _____ doesn't have _____ a job.
3. Nina's fiancé (live) _____ near the city.
4. Her husband (work) _____ with her brother.
5. I (not live) _____ with my parents.
6. Our family (live) _____ in Colombia.
7. They (not work) _____ in a big office.
8. Emilio (not have) _____ any cousins.

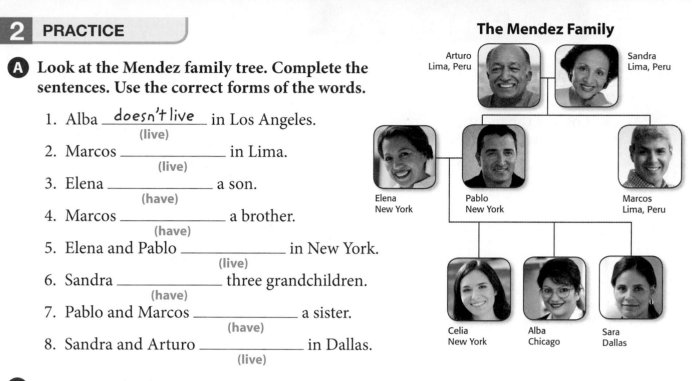

The Mendez Family

A Look at the Mendez family tree. Complete the sentences. Use the correct forms of the words.

1. Alba __doesn't live__ in Los Angeles.
   (live)
2. Marcos _____ in Lima.
   (live)
3. Elena _____ a son.
   (have)
4. Marcos _____ a brother.
   (have)
5. Elena and Pablo _____ in New York.
   (live)
6. Sandra _____ three grandchildren.
   (have)
7. Pablo and Marcos _____ a sister.
   (have)
8. Sandra and Arturo _____ in Dallas.
   (live)

B PAIRS. Make three new sentences about the Mendez family.

Elena and Pablo have three daughters. They live . . .

Show what you know! Talk about your life and family

STEP 1. Complete the sentences about your family and life. Write two true sentences and one false sentence.

I have _____.

I live in _____.

I work in _____.

STEP 2. GROUPS OF 3. Play a guessing game. Student A, read your sentences to your group. Students B and C, guess which sentence is false.

A: *I have four sisters. I live in Oak Park. I work in a hotel.*
B: *I think the first sentence is false. I don't think you have four sisters.*

STEP 3. Tell the class about one of your partners.

Manuel has two sisters. He lives in Oak Park. He works in a hotel.

Can you… talk about your life and family? ☐

Reading

1 BEFORE YOU READ

PAIRS. Look at the picture.
What is the man doing? How does
he feel? Do you ever feel like that?

2 READ

CD1 T26

Listen. Read the letters in a newspaper advice column.

Dear Kate
Advice for Your Life

Dear Kate,

My husband and I both work. I work days and he works two jobs, days and evenings. We have three kids (ages 8, 10, and 14). They need a lot of my time. They need me to help them with homework. I take them to school activities and sports events. And then there is all the housework! The cooking, the laundry, the cleaning, the shopping, the bills! I need to do a million things at the same time. Help! I can't do it all!
Tired Tania

Dear Tania,

You're right. You can't do it all. You're trying to do too much.

First, ask yourself, "What is most important?" You can't do everything. Only do the important things.

Second, get help. Ask your children to help with the housework. They can do the dishes, take out the garbage, do the laundry, and do other chores. Ask your husband to help on the weekends.

Third, say no. You already have many responsibilities. When people ask you to do something extra, say, "I'm sorry, but I don't have the time right now."

Finally, take some time for yourself. Make sure you get a little time every day to do something you like. Watch a TV program, take a bath, or read a magazine. Take care of yourself first. Then you will have the energy to take care of others.
Kate

A Read Tania's letter to Kate. Then read the sentences. Circle *True* or *False*.

1. Tania works two jobs.   True   False

2. Tania is a student.   True   False

3. Tania has three children.   True   False

4. Tania takes care of her kids in the afternoon.   True   False

5. Tania takes her children to school activities and sports events.   True   False

6. Tania does a lot of housework.   True   False

B Read Kate's letter to Tania. Check the advice she gives.

☐ Only do the things that are important.

☐ Ask other people for help.

☐ Go to bed earlier and get more sleep.

☐ Say, "no" when people try to give you more responsibilities.

☐ Make a schedule of your time.

☐ Take a little time each day for yourself.

C PAIRS. Student A, what is Tania's problem? Student B, what is Kate's advice? Explain in your own words.

D GROUPS OF 3. Do you agree with Kate's advice? Do you have any other advice for Tania?

Reading Skill:
Retelling Information

Retell means to say in your own words what you read or hear. The words are different, but the meaning is the same.

Show what you know!

PRE-WRITING. PAIRS. What are your family, school, and work responsibilities? Is Kate's advice helpful to you?

WRITE. Write a list of your responsibilities. See page 268.

Talk about what people have in common

Listening and Speaking

1 BEFORE YOU LISTEN

CLASS. Look at the picture of three brothers. What are some things that family members have in common?

2 LISTEN

A **CLASS.** Look at the picture of two neighbors, Ming and Tina. Guess: What are they talking about?

CD1 T27

B 💿 Listen to the conversation. Was your guess in Exercise A correct?

CD1 T27

C 💿 Listen again. Read the sentences. Circle *True* or *False*.

1. Tina looks like her sister.

    True   **False**

2. Tina has a friend named Lili.

    True   **False**

3. Tina has a lot in common with her sister.

    True   **False**

4. Tina's sister works in a bank.

    True   **False**

5. Tina's sister doesn't have any children.

    True   **False**

CD1 T28

D 💿 Listen to the whole conversation. Answer the questions.

1. Does Ming have any sisters?   _____

2. Does Ming have any brothers?   _____

3 CONVERSATION

CD1 T29

A **Listen. Then listen and repeat the sentences.**

Do you have any sisters?
Yes, I do.

Do you have a lot in common?
Actually, we do. She works in a bank, and I do, too.

CD1 T30

B **Listen and repeat the conversation.**

Ming: Tina, is this your sister? You two look alike.
Tina: Yeah, that's my sister, Lili.
Ming: Do you have a lot in common?
Tina: Actually, we do. She works in a bank, and I do, too.
And we both have new babies.

4 PRACTICE

A PAIRS. Practice the conversation. Then make new conversations. Use the information in the boxes.

A: Tina, is this your _____? You two look alike.

B: Yeah, that's my _____, Lili.

A: Do you have a lot in common?

B: Actually, we do. She works in a _____,

and I do, too. And we both have _____.

niece	restaurant	two kids
aunt	clothing store	a son
cousin	hospital	a boy and a girl

B MAKE IT PERSONAL. PAIRS. Talk about your own family members. Do you have a lot in common?

I have a lot in common with my sister Anna. She . . .

Talk about what people have in common

Grammar

Simple present: Additions with *and…, too / and…not, either*

Affirmative				Negative			
Lili works in a bank,	**and**	I you we they	**do, too.**	Trang doesn't live in Denver,	**and**	I you we they	**don't, either.**
		he she	**does, too.**			he she	**doesn't, either.**

---

1 PRACTICE

A **Complete the sentences. Match the sentence beginnings and endings.**

1. __b__ I speak Farsi, and my husband   a. doesn't, either.

2. ____ She lives with her parents, and her brothers   b. does, too.

3. ____ They don't live in an apartment, and we   c. do, too.

4. ____ Pablo doesn't work in an office, and Ursula   d. don't, either.

> **Grammar Watch**
> - Use *too* for affirmative sentences.
> - Use *not, either* for negative sentences.
> - Use a comma before *too* and *either*.

B **Complete the sentences. Use the words in the box.**

> do, too   does, too   doesn't, either   don't, either

1. Mark has two nephews, and Jason _____*does, too*_____.

2. They don't work on weekends, and we _____.

3. My son doesn't live with me, and my daughter _____.

4. My wife works for her father, and my brothers-in-law _____.

5. Todd and Mikah don't have any children, and we _____.

6. Her sisters-in-law live on Walnut Street, and her father-in-law _____.

7. I don't have any brothers, and Melanie _____.

8. My husband works long hours, and I _____.

9. Marilyn doesn't live in the city, and her sisters _____.

A PAIRS. Look at the Nash family. How are the people similar?

Tampa ——— Vancouver ——— Seattle

B WRITE. Write six sentences about the people. Use *too* and *either*. Use a separate piece of paper.

> Douglas has gray hair, and Emily does, too.
> Brian doesn't live in Vancouver, and Brad doesn't, either.

Show what you know!   Talk about what people have in common

STEP 1. Complete the questions. Use your own ideas.

Do you have any family in _____?

Do you live in _____? Do you work in _____?

STEP 2. GROUPS OF 5. Student A, read one question from Step 1. Other students, answer the question. Give true information.

Tia: *Do you have any family in Chicago?*
Jan: *Yes, my brother lives in Chicago.*

STEP 3. Tell the class about what the people in your group have in common. Use *too* and *either*.

Jan has family in Chicago, and I do, too. In-Ho lives . . .

Can you... talk about what people have in common? ☐

Life Skills

1 ASK ABOUT SENDING MAIL

A **PAIRS.** Match the pictures with words from the box.

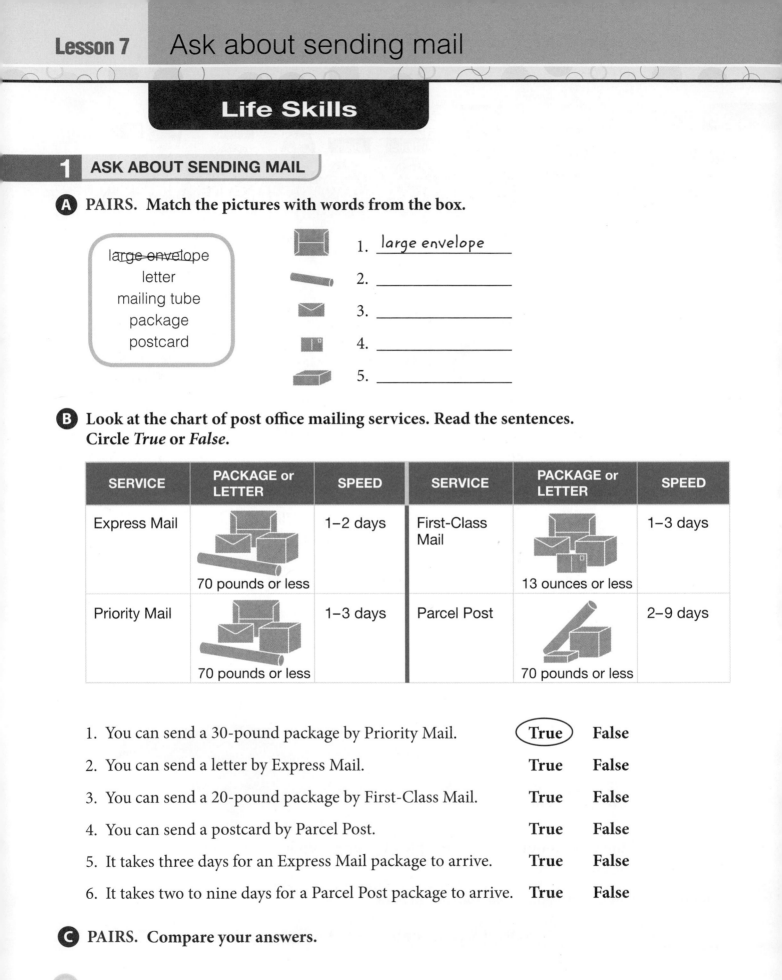

~~large envelope~~
letter
mailing tube
package
postcard

1. _large envelope_
2. _____
3. _____
4. _____
5. _____

B Look at the chart of post office mailing services. Read the sentences. Circle *True* or *False*.

SERVICE	PACKAGE or LETTER	SPEED	SERVICE	PACKAGE or LETTER	SPEED
Express Mail	70 pounds or less	1–2 days	First-Class Mail	13 ounces or less	1–3 days
Priority Mail	70 pounds or less	1–3 days	Parcel Post	70 pounds or less	2–9 days

1. You can send a 30-pound package by Priority Mail.   (True)   False

2. You can send a letter by Express Mail.   True   False

3. You can send a 20-pound package by First-Class Mail.   True   False

4. You can send a postcard by Parcel Post.   True   False

5. It takes three days for an Express Mail package to arrive. True   False

6. It takes two to nine days for a Parcel Post package to arrive. True   False

C **PAIRS.** Compare your answers.

D PAIRS. Look at the list of extra mailing services. Then read what each customer wants. Which mailing service is the best match for each customer?

Extra Mailing Services

Certificate of Mailing
You get a receipt to show you mailed the item on a certain date.

Delivery Confirmation
You can find out when your package is delivered.

Certified Mail
You get a receipt to show you mailed the item. You can find out when the item is delivered and who signs for it.

Insurance
If your package is lost or damaged, you get money back.

Registered Mail
You get a receipt to show you mailed the item. Your item is both certified and insured.

COD (Collect on Delivery)
The person who receives the item pays for the cost of mailing.

I want a receipt to show I mailed this letter today. And I want to know when the letter arrives. I don't need insurance.

I'm sending a gift to my brother. I want my money back if the package gets lost. I don't need the package certified.

2 PRACTICE

CD1 T31

Listen to a conversation between a customer and a post office clerk. Write the missing words.

Customer: Hello. I'd like to mail this _____.

Clerk: How do you want to send it?

Customer: How long does _____ take?

Clerk: Two to nine days.

Customer: OK. I'll send it _____.

Clerk: Do you want _____ or insurance?

Customer: Yes. _____, please.

3 LIFE SKILLS WRITING   Complete a post office customs form. See page 257.

Can you...ask about sending mail? ☐

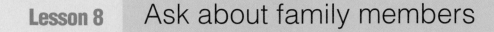

Listening and Speaking

1   BEFORE YOU LISTEN

CLASS. Do you watch game shows? Which game shows do you watch?

2   LISTEN

CD1 T32

A   Listen to the game show. What is Trevor answering questions about?

CD1 T32

B   Listen again. Match the name and the person's relationship to Trevor.

1. _____ Ann   a. brother-in-law

2. _____ Paul   b. sister-in-law

3. _____ Alex   c. mother-in-law's brother

4. _____ Danielle   d. wife

CD1 T32

C   Listen again. Answer the questions.

1. Where do Trevor's wife's grandparents live?
   a. with Trevor   b. in San Antonio   c. in a big house

2. How many sisters does Trevor's mother-in-law have?
   a. two   b. three   c. five

3. What does Trevor's brother-in-law do?
   a. He's an artist.   b. He's an engineer.   c. He's an accountant.

4. When does Danielle work?
   a. at night   b. during the day   c. on weekends

3 CONVERSATION

A CLASS. Look at the pictures. What are some ways that people keep in touch with their family and friends? Match the pictures and the words in the box.

> call   e-mail   visit   write

1. _____

2. _____

3. _____

4. _____

CD1 T33

B Listen and repeat the conversation.

Emil: Do you keep in touch with your family?

Adela: Yeah. I call my parents a lot.

Emil: Really? How often?

Adela: About once a week. How about you? Do you call your family a lot?

Emil: No, not really. I usually just e-mail.

4 PRACTICE

A PAIRS. Practice the conversation.

B MAKE IT PERSONAL. PAIRS. Do you keep in touch with your family? Who do you keep in touch with? How? How often?

I keep in touch with my brother Amir. I usually . . .

Grammar

Simple present: Yes / No questions and answers

Do	you they	**visit** **call**	your family? their parents?	Yes,	I they	**do.**	No,	I they	**don't.**
Does	he she	**live** **have**	near you? children?		he she	**does.**		he she	**doesn't.**

Simple present: Information questions and answers

When Where How	**do** **does** **does**	you he she	**visit** **live?** **keep**	them? in touch?	On holidays In Vancouver. By e-mail.

> ····· **Grammar Watch**
>
> Other question words
> **How often** do you call?
> **How many** kids do you have?
> **Which** family members live here?

PRACTICE

A Complete the questions. Underline the correct word.
Then match the questions and answers.

1. __c__ **Do** / **Does** you have any sisters?   a. Yes, they do.

2. ____ **Do** / **Does** he visit his family often?   b. Yes, we do.

3. ____ **Do** / **Does** your niece have children?   c. Yes, I do.

4. ____ **Do** / **Does** your parents work?   d. No, he doesn't.

5. ____ **Do** / **Does** you and your son live in Dallas, too?   e. Yes, she does.

CD1 T34
B 💿 Listen and check your answers.

C Complete the questions. Use the correct form of the words in parentheses.

1. What _____do_____ your brothers _____do_____? (do)

2. How often _____ your cousins _____ their parents? (visit)

3. When _____ your husband _____ to school? (go)

4. How _____ you _____ in touch with your family? (keep)

5. Where _____ your uncle _____? (work)

6. How many kids _____ Sharon _____? (have)

1 GRAMMAR

A Complete the questions. Use *do* or *does* and the words in parentheses.

	Nyoro	Ji-Na	Hector	Rahim	Nu
Place of work	at a hospital	at a hospital	at a hospital	in an office	in an office
Number of children	1	0	0	3	2
Place of residence	in-laws' house	rented apartment	brother's apartment	own house	in-laws' house

1. _____Do_____ Nyoro and Rahim _____have_____ children?
   (have)

2. Where ___does___ Nyoro ___work___?
   (work)

3. _____ Nyoro and Nu _____ with their in-laws?
   (live)

4. _____ Hector _____ children?
   (have)

5. Where _____ Ji-Na _____?
   (live)

6. How many children _____ Rahim _____?
   (have)

7. Where _____ Nu and Rahim _____?
   (work)

B PAIRS. Answer the questions in Exercise A. Use the information in the chart.

C Complete the sentences. Use the information in the chart and the words in the box.

> do, too   does, too   don't, either   doesn't, either

1. Nyoro works at a hospital, and Ji-Na and Hector __do, too._____.

2. Nyoro has children, and Rahim _____.

3. Ji-Na doesn't work in an office, and Hector _____.

4. Nu doesn't live in an apartment, and Nyoro and Rahim _____.

Go to the CD-ROM for more practice.

2 ACT IT OUT What do you say?

STEP 1. CLASS. Review the conversations in Lessons 2 and 5 (CD 1 tracks 22 and 27).

STEP 2. ROLE PLAY. PAIRS. You are co-workers talking at lunch.

Student A, ask questions about Student B's family or friends.	**Student B**, answer the questions. Talk about: • where they live and work • what they have in common with each other • who looks alike

3 READ AND REACT Problem-solving

STEP 1. Read about Jin-Hee's problem.

Jin-Hee is married and has two children. Every weekend Jin-Hee's mother-in-law comes to visit. Her mother-in-law tells Jin-Hee how to cook, how to take care of the children, and how to manage the house. Jin-Hee doesn't like her mother-in-law's advice.

STEP 2. PAIRS. What is Jin-Hee's problem?
What can she do? Here are some ideas.

- She can tell her mother-in-law not to visit anymore.
- She can ask her husband to talk to his mother.
- She can listen to her mother-in-law and then do things her own way.
- She can _____.

4 CONNECT For your Community-building Activity, go to page 248.
For your Team Project, go to page 275.

Which goals can you check off? Go back to page 25.

Lots to Do

Preview

Look at the picture.
Where are the people?
What are they doing?

UNIT GOALS

- ☐ Identify clothes and materials

- ☐ Describe your wants and needs

- ☐ Count your change

- ☐ Read a store ad

- ☐ Read a sales receipt

- ☐ Write a personal check

- ☐ Talk about shopping plans

- ☐ Describe problems with purchases

1 WHAT DO YOU KNOW?

A CLASS. Look at the pictures. Which clothes do you know? Which materials do you know?

CD1 T35

B Look at the pictures and listen. Listen again and repeat.

2 PRACTICE

A PAIRS. Talk about the clothes.

A: *I like this coat.*
B: *It's nice. What's it made of?*
A: *Wool.*
B: *I like these jeans.*

B WORD PLAY. PAIRS. What clothes are made of these materials? Write the words in the chart.

Wool	Leather	Fleece	Cotton
a coat			

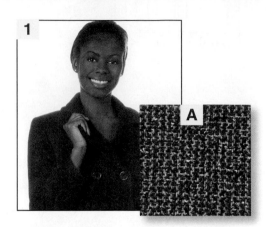

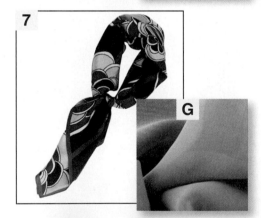

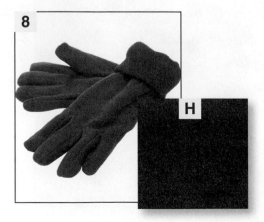

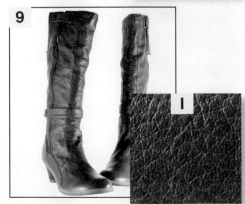

2

Clothes and Materials

Things You Wear	**Materials**
1. a coat	A. wool
2. a jacket	B. corduroy
3. a raincoat	C. vinyl
4. a windbreaker	D. nylon
5. jeans	E. denim
6. a sweatshirt	F. cotton
7. a scarf	G. silk
8. gloves	H. fleece
9. boots	I. leather

Learning Strategy

Use pictures.

Look at the list of clothes and materials. Make cards for five new words. Write the word in English on one side of the card. Paste a picture of the clothes or material to the other side.

4

5

6

Show what you know!

STEP 1. Think about your clothes.
Make a list of five items. Include the color and the material.

> *a black wool coat*
> *a blue denim jacket*

STEP 2. PAIRS. Describe your clothes to your partner.
Do you and your partner have any of the same clothes?

Clara: *I have a black wool coat.*
Charles: *Me, too. I have a . . .*

STEP 3. Report to the class.

Clara: *Charles and I have black wool coats.*

Describe your wants and needs

Listening and Speaking

1 BEFORE YOU LISTEN

CLASS. What is a summer clearance sale? What other kinds of sales are there? Do you look for sales when you shop?

2 LISTEN

CD1 T36

A Listen to an interviewer talking to three shoppers at Big Deals clothing store. Match the clothing to the shopper who talks about each item.

1. _____ Alicia Duran   2. _____ Gladys Flores   3. _____ John Nichols

a.    b.    c.

CD1 T36

B Listen again. Look at the chart. Check (✓) the reason each person shops at Big Deals.

	Alicia Duran	Gladys Flores	John Nichols
It's convenient.			
They have great prices.			
It's easy to return things.			

3 CONVERSATION

CD1 T37

A **Listen. Then listen and repeat.**

need to	I need to buy a raincoat.
like to	I don't like to shop.
want to	I want to buy some jeans.

CD1 T38

B **Listen and repeat the conversation.**

Anwar: Oh, it's so rainy this month!

Maryan: I know! It really feels like spring now. I need to buy a raincoat. Look. Those are nice.

Anwar: Yes, they are. Let's go in and look around.

Pronunciation Watch

The word *to* usually has a short, weak pronunciation when another word comes after it. In informal conversation, *want to* often sounds like "wanna."

4 PRACTICE

A PAIRS. Practice the conversation. Then make new conversations. Use the information in the boxes.

A: Oh, it's so _____ this month!

B: I know! It really feels like _____ now.

I need to buy _____ . Look. Those are nice.

A: Yes, they are. Let's go in and look around.

hot	summer	some shorts
cold	winter	some gloves
cool	fall	some jeans

B MAKE IT PERSONAL. PAIRS. Talk about the clothes that you need or want this season. Where do you shop? Why do you shop there?

A: *What clothes do you need this fall?*
B: *I need a new sweater.*

Describe your wants and needs

Grammar

Simple present: *want / need* + infinitive

Affirmative				Negative			
I They	**want** **need**	**to buy**	a raincoat.	I They	**don't**	**want** **need**	**to return**	these boots.
He She	**wants** **needs**	**to exchange**	this hat.	He She	**doesn't**	**want** **need**	**to get**	it now.

1 PRACTICE

Grammar Watch

- Use *want* and *need* + an infinitive.
- An infinitive = *to* + the base form of the verb.
- You can also use *want / need* + a noun.
  I want a denim jacket.
  He needs a sweatshirt.

A Complete the conversations. Write the correct forms of the verbs in the boxes.

buy   come   leave   return

1. **A:** Denise and I want ___to buy___ a few things at the

   store later today. Do you want _____ with us?

   B: Sure. I need _____ a blouse that I bought last week.

   A: OK. No problem. What time do you want _____?

be   buy   come   go   leave   spend

2. **A:** I want _____ downtown tomorrow morning.

   Do you want _____ with me?

   B: Well, I need _____ a birthday present for my mom.

   But I don't want _____ a lot of money right now.

   A: Then this is the perfect time to shop—they're having big sales!

   B: Really? That's great!

   A: Yeah. But we need _____ early. I want _____ home by 12:00.

CD1 T39

B 📀 Listen and check your answers.

A Look at the pictures. Write a sentence about what each customer wants or needs to do. Use *need* or *want* + an infinitive. There may be more than one right answer.

1. Mary ___needs to go to the shoe store___.
   (need / want + go)

2. Jim _____.
   (need / want + go)

3. Larry _____.
   (need / want + buy)

4. Ray _____.
   (need / want + get)

5. Hector _____.
   (need / want + return)

6. Mariko _____.
   (need / want + exchange)

B PAIRS. Compare your answers.

Show what you know! Describe your wants and needs

STEP 1. Complete the sentences about your clothing needs or wants. Use *buy, get, return,* or *exchange.*

I need to _____.   I want to _____.

STEP 2. GROUPS OF 5. Play the Memory Game. Talk about shopping for clothes.

Kwon-Su: *I want to buy new gloves.*
Julio: *Kwon-Su wants to buy new gloves. I need to return a wool sweater.*
Silvia: *Kwon-Su wants to buy new gloves. Julio needs to return a wool sweater. I need to get a new umbrella.*

Can you… describe your wants and needs? ☐

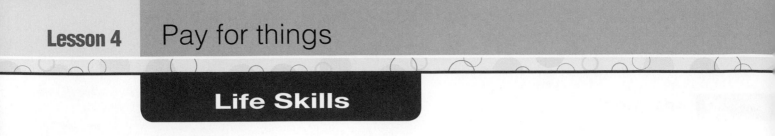

Life Skills

1 COUNT YOUR CHANGE

Calculate the change for each purchase. Write the amount on the line.

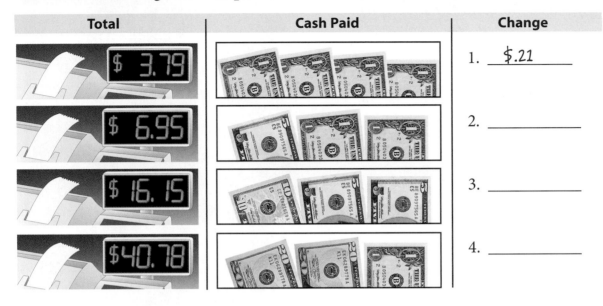

Total	Cash Paid	Change
$ 3.79		1. _$.21_
$ 6.95		2. _____
$ 16.15		3. _____
$40.78		4. _____

2 READ A STORE AD

PAIRS. Read the store ad. What's on sale? How much is the discount on each item?

MAYFIELD Department Store **Summer Sale!**

Wednesday, July 24 – Sunday, July 28

All men's and women's swimwear **30%off**
Regular price: $40
Sale price **$28**

All sunglasses **40%off**
Regular price: $30
Sale price **$18**

All flip-flops **50%off**
Regular price: $5
Sale price **$2.50**

Can you...count your change and read a store ad? ☐

3 READ A SALES RECEIPT

PAIRS. Read the store sales receipt. Answer the questions.

1. What is the date on the receipt?

2. What is the discount on the swimsuit?

3. How much does the swimsuit cost before tax?

4. How much is it after tax?

5. How much change does the customer get?

```
+ MAYFIELD +
  DEPARTMENT STORE
     07/28/10
Women's Swimwear
1 swimsuit          $30.00
Discount 30%         -9.00
Subtotal             21.00
FL Sales Tax 6%       1.26
Total                22.26
CASH                 30.00
Change                7.74
```

4 PRACTICE

A **PAIRS. Read the store ad on page 52 again. Then check the discounts and prices on the receipts. Circle the three mistakes, according to the information in the ad.**

1.
```
+ MAYFIELD +
  DEPARTMENT STORE
     07/25/10
Men's Swimwear
1 swimsuit      $25.00
Discount 20%     -5.00
Subtotal         20.00
FL Sales Tax 6%   1.20
Total           $21.20
CASH             21.20
Change            0.00
```

2.
```
+ MAYFIELD +
  DEPARTMENT STORE
     07/26/10
Men's Footwear
1 flip-flops    $85.00
Discount 50%    -42.50
Subtotal         42.50
FL Sales Tax 6%   2.55
Total           $45.05
CASH             50.00
Change            4.95
```

3.
```
+ MAYFIELD +
  DEPARTMENT STORE
     07/27/10
Women's Accessories
1 sunglasses    $30.00
Discount 30%     -9.00
Subtotal         21.00
FL Sales Tax 6%   1.26
Total           $22.26
CASH             23.00
Change            0.74
```

CD1 T40

B **Read and listen to the conversation. Then listen and repeat.**

A: Excuse me. I think there's a mistake. The ad says <u>all swimwear is 30 percent off</u>.

B: Yes, that's right.

A: But my receipt says <u>20 percent off</u>.

B: Oh, I'm sorry. I'll take care of that.

C **PAIRS. Make new conversations. Use the information in the incorrect sales receipts in Exercise A.**

5 LIFE SKILLS WRITING

Write a personal check. See page 258.

Can you...read a sales receipt? ☐

Talk about shopping plans

Listening and Speaking

1 BEFORE YOU LISTEN

CLASS. Look at the pictures of someone running errands. Where did the man go? What other errands do people run?

2 LISTEN

CD1 T41

A Listen to the conversation between Debbie and her son Antonio. Complete the sentences.

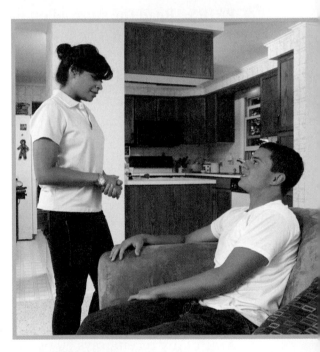

1. They are talking about plans for _____.
   a. today   b. tomorrow

2. _____ is going to relax tomorrow.
   a. Antonio   b. Debbie

3. _____ is going to be busy tomorrow.
   a. Antonio   b. Debbie

CD1 T41

B Listen again. Number Debbie's activities in the order you hear them.

_____ go to the supermarket

_____ go to the ATM

_____ go to the hardware store

CD1 T42

C Listen to the whole conversation. Complete the sentence.

After the conversation, Antonio _____.
a. takes a nap   b. goes to the deli   c. goes to work

3 CONVERSATION

CD1 T43

A **Listen. Then listen and repeat.**

going to	I'm going to relax. I'm going to stop at the bank.
going to	I'm going to the post office. You're going to the store with me.

Pronunciation Watch

In informal conversation, *going to* often has the pronunciation "gonna" when it comes before another verb. It does not have this pronunciation when it is the only verb.

CD1 T44

B **Listen and repeat the conversation.**

Debbie: So, what are your plans for tomorrow?

Antonio: Nothing. I'm going to relax. Why?

Debbie: Well, I have a lot to do. First, I need to go to the ATM. Then I need to go to the hardware store. Then I'm going to stop at the supermarket.

Antonio: Wow. You're going to be busy.

4 PRACTICE

A **PAIRS. Practice the conversation. Then make new conversations. Use the information in the boxes.**

A: So, what are your plans for tomorrow?

B: Nothing. I'm going to relax. Why?

A: Well, I have a lot to do. First, I need to go to the __________.
Then I need to go to the __________. Then I'm going
to stop at the __________.

B: Wow. You're going to be busy.

library drugstore bank
grocery store deli post office
bakery gas station laundromat

B **MAKE IT PERSONAL. PAIRS. Talk about the errands you need to run this week.**

A: *What errands do you need to run?*
B: *Tomorrow I need to go to my son's school. Then I need to . . .*

Grammar

Be going to

Affirmative						Negative					
I	'm					I	'm not				
We They	're	**going to**	relax	tomorrow. on Thursday. next week.		We They	're not aren't	**going to**	run errands	tomorrow. on Thursday. next week.	
He She	's					He She	's not isn't				

Grammar Watch

we are = **we aren't** = **we're not**

he is = **he isn't** = **he's not**

1 PRACTICE

A Complete the sentences. Use the correct forms of *be going to*. Use contractions if possible.

1. She _'s going to_ stop at the post office later.

2. I _____ cash my check after work.

3. They _____ return the movies to the video store tomorrow.

4. Dan _____ buy some bread at the bakery tonight.

5. My mom _____ take the car to the car wash this weekend.

6. You _____ pick up the kids after school tomorrow.

B Complete the sentences. Use the correct forms of *be going to* and the words in parentheses.

1. The clothes are dirty. My brother ___*is going to take*___ them to the laundromat.

(take)

2. There's a big sale at Griffon's on Saturday. The parking lot _____ crowded.

(be)

3. We need to run a lot of errands. We _____ time to relax.

(not have)

4. Sally _____ late. She _____ dinner.

(work)   (not cook)

5. Hector and Maria _____ a movie tonight. Their kids

(see)

_____ home with their grandmother.

(stay)

6. I _____ a ride to work tomorrow. I _____ the bus.

(get)   (not take)

A PAIRS. Look at the pictures. Talk about what the people are going to do. There is more than one correct answer.

In picture 1, the man is going to send a package.

B WRITE. On a separate piece of paper, write a sentence for each picture in Exercise A.

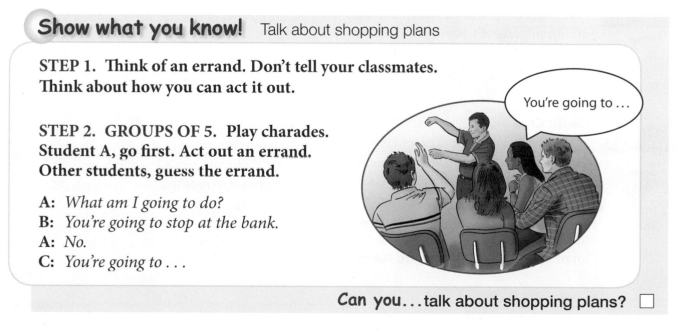

Show what you know! Talk about shopping plans

STEP 1. Think of an errand. Don't tell your classmates. Think about how you can act it out.

STEP 2. GROUPS OF 5. Play charades. Student A, go first. Act out an errand. Other students, guess the errand.

A: *What am I going to do?*
B: *You're going to stop at the bank.*
A: *No.*
C: *You're going to . . .*

You're going to . . .

Can you... talk about shopping plans? ☐

Reading

1   BEFORE YOU READ

PAIRS. What are the different ways to pay for large purchases, such as a TV or furniture?

2   READ

CD1 T45

 Listen. Read the article.

How would you like to pay for that?

Are you thinking of making a big purchase soon, like a big-screen TV or a new computer? What is the best way to pay for it? We interviewed three shoppers who just bought a new $475 Sonpanic TV.

Each shopper paid for the TV in a different way. Read how each shopper paid for the TV. Then compare how much it really cost them. You may be surprised by the differences!

Brian

Credit Card

"I paid with my credit card. I like to use my credit card because it gives me time to pay the bill. I can buy something in October, but I don't get the bill until November. I get a month to make my payment. I make sure to pay the total amount on the bill. That way I don't have to pay the credit card company any interest."

Cost of Sonpanic TV	$475.00
5% sales tax	+ $23.75
Total cost of the TV	$498.75

Cindy

Credit Card

"I paid with my credit card. I like to pay with credit because I never have enough money to pay for big purchases. The credit card lets me pay just a small amount every month. The problem is that it takes a long time to pay off the whole bill. And I pay a lot of interest to the credit card company."

Minimum monthly payment	$10.00
Number of months	× 98
Total cost of the TV	$980.00

Rent-to-Own

Craig

"I bought my TV at the rent-to-own store because I don't have a lot of money right now, and I don't have a credit card. At a rent-to-own store, I can get a new TV and bring it home the same day. If I move, or I don't have enough money, I can return the TV to the store. Every week, I pay $24. At the end of the year, the TV belongs to me."

Weekly payment	$24.00
Number of weeks	× 52
Real cost of the TV	$1,248.00

3 CHECK YOUR UNDERSTANDING

A Read the article again. What's the purpose of the article? How do you know?

1. To compare the real cost of different ways to pay.
2. To recommend the Sonpanic TV.
3. To tell shoppers to pay for TVs with a credit card.

> **Reading Skill:**
> Identifying Purpose
>
> Authors write articles for different reasons. This is the author's purpose. Knowing the author's purpose helps you understand the main idea.

B Underline the advantages and disadvantages of each way to pay in the article. Then complete the chart.

Ways to pay	Advantages	Disadvantages
Credit card (pay the whole amount)		
Credit card (pay the minimum amount)		
Rent-to-own		

C PAIRS. Which is the best way to pay for the Sonpanic TV? Why?

Show what you know!

PRE-WRITING. PAIRS. Think about an expensive product you want to buy. How are you going to pay for it? Explain your answer.

WRITE. Write about how you are going to pay for your next expensive purchase. See page 269.

Describe problems with purchases

Listening and Speaking

1 BEFORE YOU LISTEN

PAIRS. Look at the pictures. What's the problem with each piece of clothing? Match the pictures to the reasons for returning clothes.

> There's a hole in it.   It's too tight.   A button is missing.
> They're too loose.   ~~The zipper is broken~~.   A seam is ripped.

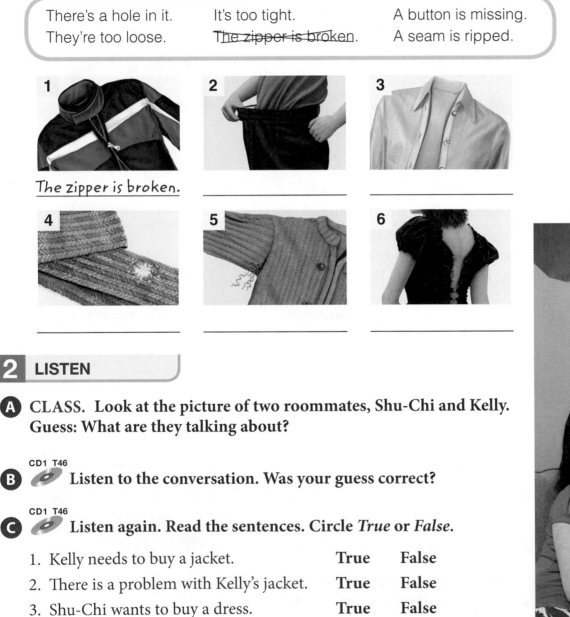

1. _The zipper is broken._

2. _____

3. _____

4. _____

5. _____

6. _____

2 LISTEN

A **CLASS.** Look at the picture of two roommates, Shu-Chi and Kelly. Guess: What are they talking about?

CD1 T46

B Listen to the conversation. Was your guess correct?

CD1 T46

C Listen again. Read the sentences. Circle *True* or *False*.

1. Kelly needs to buy a jacket.	**True**	**False**
2. There is a problem with Kelly's jacket.	**True**	**False**
3. Shu-Chi wants to buy a dress.	**True**	**False**

CD1 T47

D Listen to the whole conversation. Complete the sentence.

Shu-Chi's dress is really a _____.

3 CONVERSATION

CD1 T48

Listen and repeat the conversation.

Shu-Chi: Hi Kelly. Where are you going?

Kelly: I'm going to Kohn's. I need to return this jacket.

Shu-Chi: How come?

Kelly: The zipper is broken.

Shu-Chi: That's annoying . . . Um, could you do me a favor?

Kelly: What is it?

Shu-Chi: Could you return a dress for me?

Kelly: Sure. What's wrong with it?

Shu-Chi: It's too short.

4 PRACTICE

A **PAIRS. Practice the conversation. Then make new conversations. Use the information in the boxes.**

> **A:** Hi, _____ . Where are you going?
>
> **B:** I'm going to Kohn's. I need to return this _____ .
>
> **A:** How come?
>
> **B:** _____
>
> **A:** That's annoying . . . Um, could you do me a favor?
>
> **B:** What is it?
>
> **A:** Could you return a _____ for me?
>
> **B:** Sure. What's wrong with it?
>
> **A:** It's too _____ .

| blouse |
| windbreaker |
| sweater |

| A button is missing. |
| A seam is ripped. |
| There's a hole in it. |

| sweatshirt |
| coat |
| T-shirt |

| tight |
| long |
| big |

B **ROLE PLAY. PAIRS. Make your own conversations. Use different items of clothing and reasons. Remember, some clothing words are plural. Make any changes necessary. For example: *I need to return these pants.***

Describe problems with purchases

Grammar

Adverbs of degree: *very / too*		
It's	**very**	expensive. (It costs a lot of money.)
It's	**too**	expensive. (It's $100, but I only have $90.)

PRACTICE

A Complete the sentences. Underline *very* or *too*.

1. This raincoat doesn't cost a lot. It's <u>**very**</u> / **too** cheap.
2. She wears size 8. That dress is size 6. It's **very** / **too** small for her.
3. The prices at the clearance sale are **very** / **too** good. A lot of people are going to be there.
4. This sweater is **very** / **too** pretty. I want to buy it.
5. I can't wear these shoes. They're **very** / **too** tight.
6. This scarf is **very** / **too** colorful. It looks great with my coat.

B Complete the conversations. Write *very* or *too*.

1. **A:** We can't go to the store now because it's ___too___ late. The store closes in ten minutes.

   B: Well, we can go tomorrow morning. It opens at 8:00.

   A: That's _____ early for me. I get up at 9:00 on Saturdays.

2. **A:** The coffee shop on Oak Street is _____ good. I get coffee and egg sandwiches for breakfast there sometimes.

   B: I think the service there is _____ slow. I'm always late for school when I stop there.

3. **A:** Let me see your new blouse . . . . Oh, it's _____ beautiful.

   B: Thanks. But it's _____ big. I need to exchange it for a smaller size.

4. **A:** This coat is _____ warm. It's perfect for cold winter days.

   B: Are you going to buy it?

   A: No, it's _____ expensive. It's $90, and I only have $60.

1 GRAMMAR

A Complete the conversation. Use the correct forms of the verbs.
Use contractions if possible.

A: I think I _'m going to run_____ some errands this afternoon.
  (be going to / run)

B: Oh. What do you need to do?

A: First I _____ at the bank. Then I _____.
  (need / stop)   (be going to / get groceries)
  Why? What are your plans for today?

B: Well, I _____ at the swimming pool. I think it's open until 6:00.
  (be going to / relax)

A: That sounds great. Can I come with you? Maybe I really _____
    (not need / run)
  any errands today after all!

B WRITE. Look at the picture of customers returning clothes at an exchange counter.
Why are the people returning the clothes? Write a reason for each customer.

1. _It's too tight._____ 4. _____

2. _____ 5. _____

3. _____ 6. _____

C PAIRS. Compare your answers.

Go to the CD-ROM for more practice.

2 ACT IT OUT — What do you say?

STEP 1. CLASS. Review the Lesson 2 conversation between Anwar and Maryan (CD 1 track 38).

STEP 2. ROLE PLAY. PAIRS. Talk about the clothes you want and need to buy. Make a list. Look at the pictures or use your own ideas.

3 READ AND REACT — Problem-solving

STEP 1. Read about Lan's problem.

Lan's son lives in a city far away. He can't be with her on Mother's Day. He sends Lan flowers. Lan knows that the flowers are expensive. But the flowers are old and not very nice.

STEP 2. PAIRS. What is Lan's problem? What can she do? Here are some ideas.

- She can tell her son about the problem with the flowers.
- She can tell her son, "The flowers are beautiful."
- She can call the flower shop and ask for a refund.
- She can _____.

4 CONNECT

For your Goal-setting Activity, go to page 249.
For your Team Project, go to page 276.

Which goals can you check off? Go back to page 45.

Small Talk

Preview

**Look at the picture.
Where are the people?
What are they doing?**

UNIT GOALS

- [ ] Talk about your weekend activities

- [ ] Plan activities using a calendar

- [ ] Complete a library card application

- [ ] Communicate likes and dislikes

- [ ] Invite someone to do something

- [ ] Accept or decline an invitation

1 WHAT DO YOU KNOW?

A CLASS. Look at the pictures. Which free-time activities do you know?

CD1 T49

B Look at the pictures and listen. Listen again and repeat.

2 PRACTICE

A GROUPS OF 5. Play charades. Student A, go first. Act out a free-time activity. Other students, guess the activity.

B WORD PLAY. GROUPS OF 3. Look at the list of free-time activities. Which are outdoor activities? Which are indoor activities? Which can be both? Complete the chart.

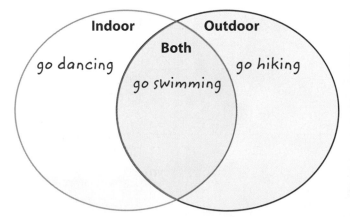

Indoor / Outdoor / Both

go dancing

go swimming

go hiking

 1 2

 5 6

 9 10

 11 12

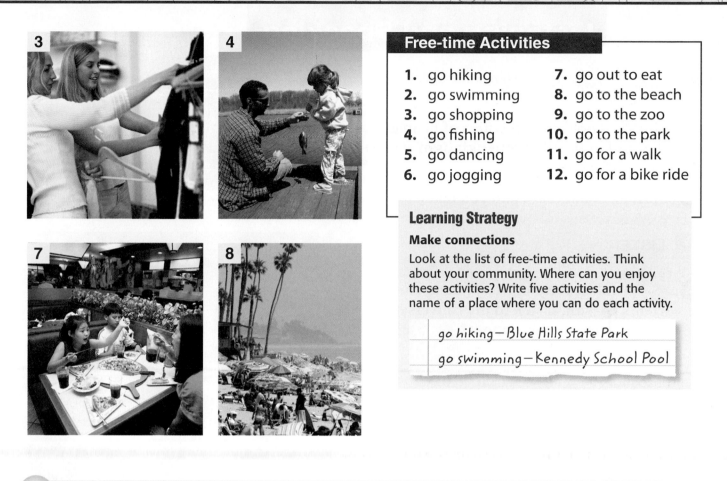

3

4

7

8

Free-time Activities

1. go hiking
2. go swimming
3. go shopping
4. go fishing
5. go dancing
6. go jogging
7. go out to eat
8. go to the beach
9. go to the zoo
10. go to the park
11. go for a walk
12. go for a bike ride

Learning Strategy

Make connections

Look at the list of free-time activities. Think about your community. Where can you enjoy these activities? Write five activities and the name of a place where you can do each activity.

go hiking—Blue Hills State Park

go swimming—Kennedy School Pool

Show what you know!

STEP 1. Look at the list of free-time activities. Write two activities that you do in your free time.

_____   _____

STEP 2. GROUPS OF 4. Ask your group members, *What do you do in your free time?* Write their names and activities on the lines.

Student 1: _____   _____

Student 2: _____   _____

Student 3: _____   _____

STEP 3. Report to the class. What are the three most popular activities in your group?

Listening and Speaking

1 BEFORE YOU LISTEN

A CLASS. Look at the pictures of people taking classes. What other kinds of classes do people take?

B CLASS. What classes do you take?

a guitar class

a computer class

2 LISTEN

CD1 T50

A Look at the picture of Mario and his friend, Bi-Yun. Listen to the conversation. What are they talking about?

a. weekend plans
b. school
c. swimming lessons

CD1 T50

B Listen again. Answer the questions.

1. Who does Bi-Yun usually see on Sunday?

   a. her family   b. her friends

2. What does Mario usually do on Saturday mornings?

   a.    b.

CD1 T51

C Listen to the whole conversation. Answer the question.

Which level class do you think Mario is in?

a. beginning   b. intermediate   c. advanced

3 CONVERSATION

A CD1 T52

💿 Listen. Notice that one syllable is not pronounced. Then listen and repeat the words.

| every | usually | interesting |
| (2 syllables) | (3 syllables) | (3 syllables) |

Pronunciation Watch

Some words have a syllable that is not pronounced. For example, the word *family* looks like it has three syllables (fam·i·ly) but we pronounce it as two syllables (fam·ily).

B CD1 T53

💿 Listen to the words. How many syllables do you hear?

1. ____ evening   2. ____ favorite   3. ____ different

C CD1 T54

💿 Listen and repeat the conversation.

Mario: What are you doing this weekend?

Bi-Yun: I'm going to go to the beach with my family.

Mario: Really? Sounds like fun.

Bi-Yun: Yeah. We usually go to the beach on Sunday. What about you?

Mario: Well, I have a guitar class. I have a guitar class every Saturday morning.

4 PRACTICE

A PAIRS. Practice the conversation. Then make new conversations. Use the information in the boxes.

A: What are you doing this weekend?

B: I'm going to _____ with my family.

A: Really? Sounds like fun.

B: Yeah. We usually _____ on Sunday. What about you?

A: Well, I have a _____ class. I have a _____ class every _____ .

go out to eat
go for a bike ride
go hiking

karate
painting
computer

Friday evening
Saturday afternoon
Sunday morning

B Think about your plans for this weekend. Write three things you plan to do.

1. _____   2. _____   3. _____

C MAKE IT PERSONAL. PAIRS. Talk about your weekend plans with your partner.

Grammar

Adverbs of frequency

With action verbs					With *be*			
I We They	**always** **usually** **often**	**go**		to the beach.	I	**am**	**always** **usually** **often**	at the beach.
He She	**sometimes** **hardly ever** **never**	**goes**			We They	**are**	**sometimes** **hardly ever** **never**	
					He She	**is**		

0%   100%

| never | hardly ever | sometimes | often | usually | always |

Grammar Watch

- Adverbs of frequency go *before* action verbs.
- Adverbs of frequency go *after* forms of *be*.

1 PRACTICE

A **Complete the sentences. Underline the correct words.**

1. She works on Saturday mornings. She **never** / **often** sleeps late on Saturdays.

2. I can't go to the movies with you Thursday night. I **always** / **hardly ever** take a computer class after work on Thursdays.

3. There are very few good restaurants in my area. I **hardly ever** / **often** go out to eat.

4. Ty is an excellent student. He **always** / **sometimes** does his homework.

5. My friend Tanya is afraid of the water. She **often** / **never** goes swimming.

6. Their son likes video games. He **sometimes** / **never** spends hours on the computer.

B **Rewrite the sentences. Use the adverbs in parentheses.**

1. (always) The kids are busy. (usually) They get homework help after school.
   The kids are always busy. They usually get homework help after school.

2. (never) Marcus is on time. (sometimes) He gets to class thirty minutes late.
   _____

3. (usually) They go dancing on weekends. (hardly ever) They stay home.
   _____

4. (never) They are home on Sundays. (always) They are at their cousin's house.
   _____

Questions with *How often* / frequency time expressions

| How often | do | you
they | exercise? |
| | does | he
she | |

| Every day. |
| Every Monday. |
| Once a week. |
| Twice a month. |

2 PRACTICE

PAIRS. Look at Felipe's calendar. Ask and answer five questions with *how often*.

A: *How often does Felipe have dinner at his grandma's?*
B: *Once a week.*

Felipe's Calendar

Sun.	Mon.	Tues.	Wed.	Thurs.	Fri.	Sat.
1 play soccer	2 have a computer class	3 have dinner at grandma's	4 go jogging with Hong	5	6 go jogging with Hong	7 rent a DVD
8	9 have a computer class	10 go jogging with Hong	11	12 have dinner at grandma's	13 go jogging with Hong	14 rent a DVD
15 play soccer	16 have a computer class	17 go jogging with Hong	18 have dinner at grandma's	19 go jogging with Hong	20	21 rent a DVD
22	23 have a computer class	24	25 go jogging with Hong	26 go jogging with Hong	27 have dinner at grandma's	28 rent a DVD

Show what you know! Talk about your weekend activities

STEP 1. Write three questions with *how often* to ask your classmates about their activities.

How often do you go to the movies?

STEP 2. GROUP OF 3. Ask your classmates your questions from Step 1. Write each person's name and answers on a separate piece of paper.

STEP 3. Tell the class about one of your classmates' activities.

Gigi goes to the movies once a month.

Can you...talk about your weekend activities? ☐

Life Skills

1 PLAN ACTIVITIES

CD1 T55

A 🔘 **Look at the calendar for the Greenville Community Center. Read and listen to how we talk about events. Then listen and repeat.**

- The swim team meets every Saturday from 1:00 to 4:00 P.M.

- The dance class meets on the second Friday of the month at 8:00 P.M.

- The ESL class meets on Mondays and Wednesdays from 7:00 to 9:00 P.M.

East Windsor **June**
Community Center Calendar

Sunday	Monday	Tuesday	Wednesday	Thursday	Friday	Saturday
	1 7:00 – 9:00 P.M. ESL class	2 9:00 – 10:00 A.M. exercise class	3 7:00 – 9:00 P.M. ESL class	4 9:00 – 10:00 A.M. exercise class	5 8:00 P.M. movie club	6 1:00 – 4:00 P.M. swim team
7 8:00 a.m.– 4:00 P.M. hiking club	8 7:00 – 9:00 P.M. ESL class	9 9:00 – 10:00 A.M. exercise class	10 7:00 – 9:00 P.M. ESL class	11 9:00 – 10:00 A.M. exercise class	12 8:00 – 10:00 P.M. dance class	13 1:00 – 4:00 P.M. swim team
14	15 7:00 – 9:00 P.M. ESL class	16 9:00 – 10:00 A.M. exercise class	17 7:00 – 9:00 P.M. ESL class	18 9:00 – 10:00 A.M. exercise class	19 8:00 P.M. movie club	20 1:00 – 4:00 P.M. swim team
21 9:00 A.M.– 12:00 P.M. jogging club	22 7:00 – 9:00 P.M. ESL class	23 9:00 – 10:00 A.M. exercise class	24 7:00 – 9:00 P.M. ESL class	25 9:00 – 10:00 A.M. exercise class	26	27 1:00 – 4:00 P.M. swim team
28	29 7:00 – 9:00 P.M. ESL class	30 9:00 – 10:00 A.M. exercise class				

B **PAIRS. Look at the community calendar again. Circle *True* or *False*. Correct the false information.**

1. The hiking club meets on the first ~~Saturday~~ *Sunday* of the month. True **False**

2. The jogging club meets on the fourth Sunday of the month. True False

3. The dance class meets from 8:00 to 10:00 P.M. True False

4. The exercise class meets every Monday and Wednesday. True False

5. The movie club meets at 8:00 P.M. True False

6. The swim team meets every Thursday. True False

7. The ESL class meets on Tuesdays and Thursdays. True False

C **PAIRS. Ask and answer questions about the calendar.**

A: *When does the swim team meet?*
B: *It meets every Saturday from 1:00 to 4:00 P.M. When does the . . . ?*

CD1 T56

A Listen to the schedule of events. Write the events on the calendar. Then listen again. Write the times of each event on the calendar.

Greenville September
Community Center Calendar

Sunday	Monday	Tuesday	Wednesday	Thursday	Friday	Saturday
		1	2	3	4	5
6	7 Labor Day	8	9	10	11 Lunch Club: Hilda's Café 12:00 P.M.	12
13	14	15	16	17	18	19
20	21	22	23	24	25	26
27	28	29	30			

B PAIRS. Compare your answers.

3 LIFE SKILLS WRITING
Complete a library card application. See page 259.

Can you...plan activities using a calendar? ☐

Listening and Speaking

1 BEFORE YOU LISTEN

A CLASS. Look at the pictures. What are some other activities that people have to do?

B CLASS. Which activities do you have to do?

cook

vacuum

exercise

iron

2 LISTEN

CD1 T57

A Listen to an interview on a radio show. What problem do the people discuss?

a. People often don't have a lot of free time.
b. People have to do things they don't enjoy.

CD1 T57

B Read the ideas from the interview. Listen again. Number the ideas in the order you hear them.

a. _____ After you do something you hate, do something you like.

b. _____ Put a time limit on the activities you hate to do.

c. _____ When you need to do something you hate, do something you like at the same time.

C Read the examples from the interview. Match each example to one of the ideas in Exercise B. Write the letter of the correct idea.

1. _____ If you hate to wash dishes, then do something you love while you wash the dishes. Wash the dishes and watch TV.

2. _____ Say it's 1:00 and you need to clean the house. Decide what time you're going to finish cleaning, say, 3:00. When it's 3:00, you stop.

3. _____ If you hate to do laundry, but you love to read, then say to yourself: "I'm going to do the laundry. Then I'm going to read for half an hour."

D GROUPS OF 3. Look at the picture. What is the man's problem? What are some solutions? Use the ideas from the radio show or your own ideas.

I need to exercise, but I really hate to do it!

3 CONVERSATION

CD1 T58

Listen and repeat the conversation.

Jane: You know, I really hate to do the laundry.

Karen: Me, too. And do you know what else I hate?

Jane: No. What?

Karen: I hate to iron.

Jane: Not me. I actually like it.

Karen: You're kidding.

Jane: No, really. I find it relaxing.

4 PRACTICE

A PAIRS. Practice the conversation. Then make new conversations. Use the information in the boxes.

A: You know, I really hate to   .

B: Me, too. And do you know what else I hate?

A: No. What?

B: I hate to   .

A: Not me. I actually like it.

B: You're kidding.

A: No, really. I find it relaxing.

clean the house
do the dishes
get up early

cook
vacuum
exercise

B MAKE IT PERSONAL. PAIRS. Make your own conversations. Use your own information.

Grammar

Simple present: *like / love / hate + infinitive*					
I You We They	**like don't like love hate**	**to do the laundry**.	He She	**likes doesn't like loves hates**	**to iron**.

hate = ☹
not like = ☹
like = ☺
love = 😊

---

1   PRACTICE

A   **Write sentences. Use the correct form of the verbs *like, love,* or *hate* and an infinitive.**

1. My brother / not like / eat vegetables _My brother doesn't like to eat vegetables._

2. Mrs. Lynn / love / go to the beach _____

3. Her daughters / hate / clean their rooms _____

4. Some children / not like / go swimming _____

5. Our neighbors / like / have loud parties _____

6. She / love / go hiking in the mountains _____

B   **WRITE. Look at the pictures. Write a sentence for each picture. Use *like, love,*
or *hate* and an infinitive. There can be more than one correct answer.**

the kids

Kyung-Ah

Niraj   Niraj's Dad

Sally   James

1. _The kids love to play soccer._   3. _____

2. _____   4. _____

C   **PAIRS. Compare your answers.**

A READ AND WRITE. Read the information. Look at the bar graph. On a separate piece of paper, write three sentences about the survey.

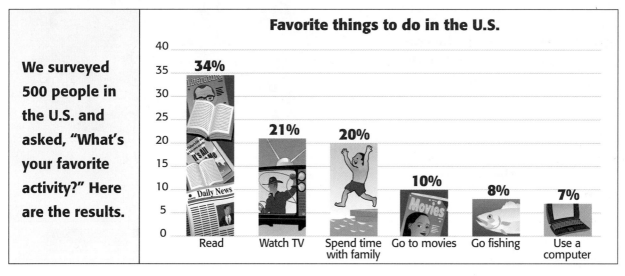

We surveyed 500 people in the U.S. and asked, "What's your favorite activity?" Here are the results.

Favorite things to do in the U.S.

Read — 34%
Watch TV — 21%
Spend time with family — 20%
Go to movies — 10%
Go fishing — 8%
Use a computer — 7%

Thirty-four percent of the people like to read.

B PAIRS. What do people in your country like to do in their free time?

In my country, a lot of people like to go out to eat.

Show what you know! Communicate likes and dislikes

STEP 1. What activities do you like? Love? Hate? Write four sentences.

1. _____

2. _____

3. _____

4. _____

STEP 2. PAIRS. Compare your answers. Talk about your likes and dislikes.

A: *I love to go fishing.*
B: *Not me. I love to read.*
A: *Well, I like to read, too.*

Can you...communicate likes and dislikes? ☐

Reading

1 BEFORE YOU READ

PAIRS. Look at the picture of people at a movie theater. How is the young man being rude? Do you think this behavior is rude in all countries?

2 READ

CD1 T59

Listen. Read the online message board posts.

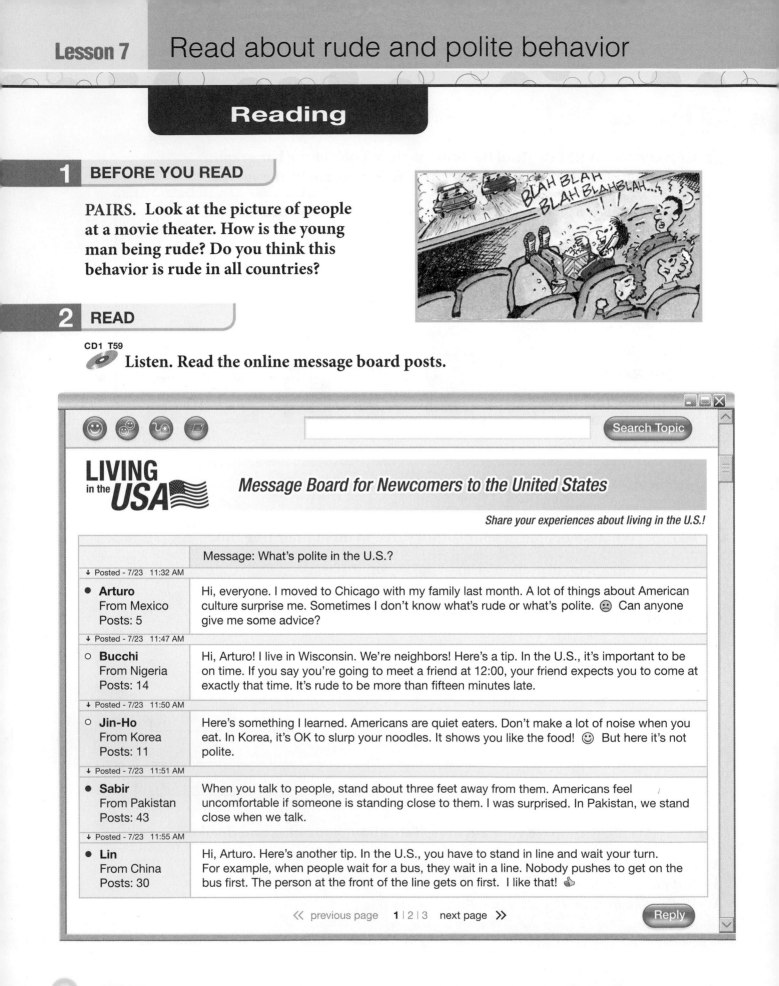

LIVING in the USA

Message Board for Newcomers to the United States

Share your experiences about living in the U.S.!

	Message: What's polite in the U.S.?
↓ Posted - 7/23 11:32 AM	
● **Arturo** From Mexico Posts: 5	Hi, everyone. I moved to Chicago with my family last month. A lot of things about American culture surprise me. Sometimes I don't know what's rude or what's polite. ☹ Can anyone give me some advice?
↓ Posted - 7/23 11:47 AM	
○ **Bucchi** From Nigeria Posts: 14	Hi, Arturo! I live in Wisconsin. We're neighbors! Here's a tip. In the U.S., it's important to be on time. If you say you're going to meet a friend at 12:00, your friend expects you to come at exactly that time. It's rude to be more than fifteen minutes late.
↓ Posted - 7/23 11:50 AM	
○ **Jin-Ho** From Korea Posts: 11	Here's something I learned. Americans are quiet eaters. Don't make a lot of noise when you eat. In Korea, it's OK to slurp your noodles. It shows you like the food! ☺ But here it's not polite.
↓ Posted - 7/23 11:51 AM	
● **Sabir** From Pakistan Posts: 43	When you talk to people, stand about three feet away from them. Americans feel uncomfortable if someone is standing close to them. I was surprised. In Pakistan, we stand close when we talk.
↓ Posted - 7/23 11:55 AM	
● **Lin** From China Posts: 30	Hi, Arturo. Here's another tip. In the U.S., you have to stand in line and wait your turn. For example, when people wait for a bus, they wait in a line. Nobody pushes to get on the bus first. The person at the front of the line gets on first. I like that! 👍

《 previous page   1 | 2 | 3   next page 》   Reply

A Read the message board posts again. What is the topic of the posts?

a. advice about eating quietly
b. rude and polite behavior in the U.S.
c. surprising things about U.S. culture

Reading Skill:
Identifying Topics

The topic of an article is the subject the author is writing about. Identifying the topic of an article will prepare you to understand it.

B What is the main idea of the message board posts?

a. Americans are quiet eaters.
b. Rude and polite behavior is not the same in all countries.
c. Life in the U.S. is difficult.

C Complete the advice that Arturo received.

1. Don't be more than _____ minutes late for an appointment with friends.

2. Don't make a lot of _____ when you eat.

3. When you talk to people, stand about _____ feet away from them.

4. When you are at a bus stop or in a store, you have to _____ your turn.

D PAIRS. Imagine you are writing a post on the message board. What advice will you give Arturo about living in the U.S.?

Show what you know!

PRE-WRITING. PAIRS. Look at the advice in Exercise C. Is this advice correct for your country?

WRITE. Write about what is rude or polite in your country. See page 269.

Accept or decline an invitation

Listening and Speaking

1 BEFORE YOU LISTEN

A CLASS. Look at the pictures. What are some other reasons that people say no to invitations?

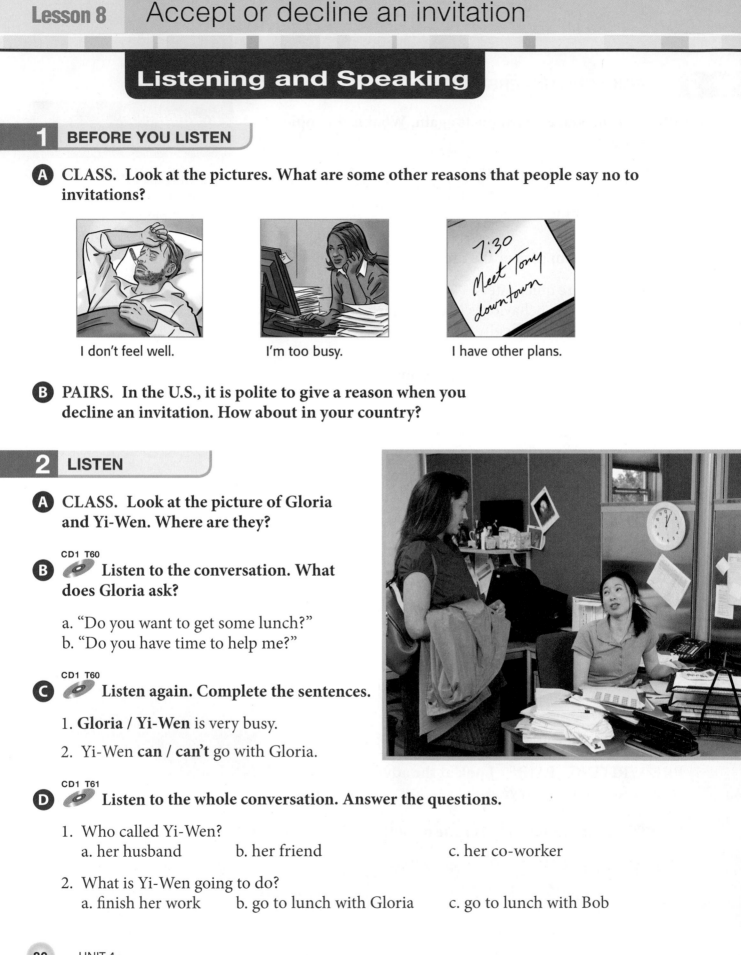

I don't feel well.

I'm too busy.

I have other plans.

B PAIRS. In the U.S., it is polite to give a reason when you decline an invitation. How about in your country?

2 LISTEN

A CLASS. Look at the picture of Gloria and Yi-Wen. Where are they?

CD1 T60

B Listen to the conversation. What does Gloria ask?

a. "Do you want to get some lunch?"
b. "Do you have time to help me?"

CD1 T60

C Listen again. Complete the sentences.

1. **Gloria / Yi-Wen** is very busy.

2. Yi-Wen **can / can't** go with Gloria.

CD1 T61

D Listen to the whole conversation. Answer the questions.

1. Who called Yi-Wen?
   a. her husband   b. her friend   c. her co-worker

2. What is Yi-Wen going to do?
   a. finish her work   b. go to lunch with Gloria   c. go to lunch with Bob

3 CONVERSATION

A 💿 **Listen. Notice the pronunciation of *have to* and *has to*. Then listen and repeat.**

have to   I have to finish some work.
has to   She has to make some calls.

CD1 T63

B 💿 **Listen. Circle the words you hear.**

1. a. have to
   b. have a

2. a. have to
   b. have a

3. a. has to
   b. has a

4. a. has to
   b. has a

CD1 T64

C 💿 **Listen and repeat the conversation.**

Gloria: Do you want to get some lunch?

Yi-Wen: Sorry, I can't. I have to finish some work.

Gloria: Oh. Are you sure?

Yi-Wen: Yes, I'm sorry. I really can't.

Gloria: Well, how about a little later?

Yi-Wen: Thanks, but I don't think so. Not today.

4 PRACTICE

A **PAIRS. Practice the conversation. Then make new conversations. Use the information in the boxes.**

A: Do you want to _____ ?

B: Sorry, I can't. I have to _____ .

A: Oh. Are you sure?

B: Yes, I'm sorry. I really can't.

A: Well, how about a little later?

B: Thanks, but I don't think so. Not today.

B **ROLE PLAY. PAIRS. Make your own conversations. Student A, invite your partner to do something. Student B, accept or decline the invitation.**

walk over to the deli
take a walk
get some coffee

go to a meeting
run some errands
make some calls

To accept an invitation, you can say:
• Sure. I'd love to.
• That sounds like fun.
• Sounds great.

Accept or decline an invitation

Grammar

Modal: *have to*

	Affirmative				Negative		
I You We They	**have to**	**finish**	some work.	I You We They	**don't have to**	**stay**	at work late.
He She	**has to**	**work**	a lot.	He She	**doesn't have to**	**work**	on weekends.

PRACTICE

drive	get up	~~go~~	study	take	visit

A **Complete the sentences. Use the infinitive forms of the verbs in the box.**

1. We don't have _____to go_____ to the grocery store. We have a lot of food.

2. He has _____ tonight. There's a big test tomorrow.

3. Kara doesn't have _____ to work. She takes the bus every day.

4. Their flight leaves at 6:00 in the morning. They have _____ early.

5. Claude has _____ his daughter to the doctor. She's sick.

6. I have _____ my mother. She's in the hospital.

B **Complete the sentences. Use the correct forms of *have to* and the words in parentheses.**

1. I'm coming home on time tonight. I _*don't have to work late*_ .
   (not work late)

2. Alice _____ home with her son. He's sick.
   (stay)

3. I can watch your kids on Saturday night. You _____ a babysitter.
   (not get)

4. Monica _____ this weekend. She can go to the zoo with us.
   (not work)

5. Babu _____ the bus to work. He doesn't have a car.
   (take)

6. The movie theatre is always crowded. We _____ tickets early.
   (buy)

C **PAIRS. Compare your answers.**

1 GRAMMAR

A Complete the conversation. Underline the correct words.

A: Hi, David. Do you want to come over to watch the game?

B: Sorry, I can't. I **have** / <u>**have to**</u> go to the supermarket.

A: The supermarket is open late. You can **always** / **never** go later.

B: Actually, I can't. My sister is coming over tonight and I **have** / **have to** get food for dinner.

A: OK. Too bad.

B: What about next Saturday? You know I love **watch** / **to watch** the games on your new TV.

A: Great. Make sure you **don't have** / **don't have to** run any errands next Saturday!

CD1 T65

B 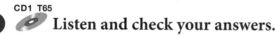 Listen and check your answers.

C Rewrite the statements. Use the adverbs in parentheses.

1. I go to the mall on weekends.

   (sometimes) _I sometimes go to the mall on weekends._

2. Dave works on Tuesday and Thursday mornings.

   (usually) _____

3. Ted is absent from English class.

   (always) _____

4. My brother cooks breakfast on Sundays.

   (often) _____

5. Ralph eats meat or fish.

   (never) _____

6. We are at home during the week.

   (hardly ever) _____

Go to the CD-ROM for more practice.

2 ACT IT OUT | What do you say?

STEP 1. CLASS. Review the Lesson 5 conversation between Jane and Karen (CD 1 Track 58).

STEP 2. PAIRS. Talk about the errands and chores you need to do every week. Talk about which things you like and dislike. Find something you both like to do.

3 READ AND REACT | Problem-solving

STEP 1. Read about Max's problem.

Max has a friend at work named Fran. Fran invites him to go dancing tomorrow night. Max doesn't have any plans tomorrow night but he doesn't want to go dancing.

STEP 2. PAIRS. What is Max's problem? What can he do? Here are some ideas.

- He can say, "Thanks, but I don't want to go dancing."
- He can say, "Thanks, but I have plans tomorrow night."
- He can say yes to the invitation but then not go.
- He can _____.

4 CONNECT

For your Study Skills Activity, go to page 250.
For your Team Project, go to page 277.

Which goals can you check off? Go back to page 65.

At Home

Preview

**Look at the picture.
What do you see?
What is the problem?**

UNIT GOALS

- ☐ Describe problems in your home
- ☐ Read apartment ads
- ☐ Complete an application for an apartment
- ☐ Ask about an apartment
- ☐ Get directions

1 WHAT DO YOU KNOW?

A CLASS. Look at the pictures. Which household problems do you know?

CD2 T2

B 💿 Look at the pictures and listen. Listen again and repeat.

2 PRACTICE

A PAIRS. Student A, point to a picture. Ask, "What's the problem?" Student B, identify the problem.

A: *(points to a picture) What's the problem?*
B: *The ceiling is leaking.*
A: *Right!*

B WORD PLAY. PAIRS. Complete the chart. Use the words in the box. Words can be written more than once.

| ceiling | door | faucet | lock | sink |
| toilet | washing machine | | window | |

Things that leak	Things that get stuck	Things that get clogged
faucet	window	sink

2

3

Household Problems

1. The ceiling is leaking.
2. The faucet is leaking.
3. The toilet is clogged.
4. The sink is clogged.
5. The lock is broken.
6. The mailbox is broken.
7. The window is stuck.
8. The door is stuck.
9. The washing machine isn't working.
10. The stove isn't working.
11. There's no heat.
12. There's no hot water.

5

6

Learning Strategy

Make labels

Look at the list of household problems. Think of the things in your home. Make cards for five things. Write the word on a card. Put the cards on the things in your home.

a faucet

8

9

OUT OF ORDER

Show what you know!

STEP 1. Look at the list of household problems. Circle the problem you think is the worst.

STEP 2. GROUPS OF 3. What is the worst household problem? Explain your answer.

I think number 5 is the worst problem because . . .

Listening and Speaking

1   BEFORE YOU LISTEN

CLASS. Look at the pictures. When there is a problem in your home, who fixes it?

an electrician

a plumber

a locksmith

a building manager

2   LISTEN

A   CLASS. Look at the picture of Harry fixing the radiator in his apartment. Guess: Who is he talking to?

a. a plumber
b. the building manager
c. his friend

B   CD2 T3   Listen to the conversation. Was your guess in Exercise A correct?

C   CD2 T3   Listen again. What does Joe say?

a. Call the building manager.
b. Buy a new radiator.
c. Fix the radiator.

D   CD2 T4   Listen to the whole conversation. Why can't Harry follow Joe's advice?

_____

_____

3 CONVERSATION

CD2 T5

Listen and repeat the conversation.

Harry: Hello?

Joe: Hi, Harry. It's Joe.

Harry: Oh, hi, Joe. Can I call you back?

Joe: Sure. No problem.

Harry: Thanks. My radiator is broken and I'm trying to fix it.

Joe: You should call the building manager.

4 PRACTICE

A PAIRS. Practice the conversation. Then make new conversations. Use your own names and the information in the boxes.

A: Hello?

B: Hi, _____. It's _____.

A: Oh, hi, _____. Can I call you back?

B: Sure. No problem.

A: Thanks. _____ and I'm trying to fix it.

B: You should call _____.

My lock is broken	a locksmith
My bathroom light isn't working	an electrician
My faucet is leaking	a plumber

B ROLE PLAY. PAIRS. Make your own conversations. Use your own names and different information.

Grammar

Present continuous

Affirmative			
I	**am**		
We	**are**	**fixing**	the radiator now.
He	**is**		

Negative			
I	**am**		
We	**are**	**not calling**	the building manager.
He	**is**		

Grammar Watch

Use the present continuous for events taking place at the present time.

1 PRACTICE

A Complete the sentences. Use the present continuous and the verbs in parentheses.

1. The building manager (help) _____*is helping*_____ the tenant.

2. Thanks for fixing the oven. I (use) _____ it now.

3. The dishwasher (make) _____ a loud noise. Can you look at it?

4. That lock is broken. I (try) _____ to fix it.

5. That washing machine (not work) _____. It's out of order.

6. We (not wait for) _____ the building manager to fix the broken light.

   My husband (fix) _____ it right now.

B Read the sentences. Correct the mistake in each sentence.

1. The sink is ~~leak~~ leaking, and it's making a big mess.

2. We're are looking for a good plumber.

3. I not calling the building manager.

4. The stove in my apartment not working.

5. The building manager are fixing the problem.

6. They're not use the broken sink.

Complete the e-mail. Use the present continuous and the words in the box.

leak   buy   ~~work~~   not work   fix   paint   wait

Hi Linda,

How are you? It's pretty busy around here. Everyone in the family __is working__ on our
<u>1.</u>

house today. The house is old and there are a lot of problems. The bathroom sink

_____ and there is water all over the floor. The light in the kitchen _____.
2.   3.

The lock on the front door is broken. Right now my uncle Charlie _____ the sink.
4.

The kids _____ the living room walls. We _____ for Tom to
5.   6.

get back from the hardware store. He _____ a new lock for the front door. There is
7.

so much work to do—I have to go! Talk to you soon!

Elaine

Show what you know!   Describe problems in your home

STEP 1. PAIRS. Student A, look at the picture on this page. Student B, look at the picture on page 246. Don't show your picture to your partner.

STEP 2. SAME PAIRS. Talk about the pictures. What are the people doing? What problems do you see? What are the differences in your pictures?

A: *In my picture, a man is fixing a sink in a kitchen.*
B: *In my picture, a man is cooking . . .*

Can you . . . describe problems in your home? ☐

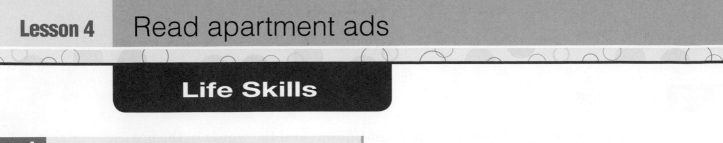
1   READ APARTMENT ADS

Ⓐ **Look at the ad for a rental apartment. Read the sentences. Circle *True* or *False*.**

> Furnished 2-bedroom, 1-bathroom apartment on the third floor of an elevator building.
> Large living room. Sunny eat-in kitchen with separate dining room. Washer/dryer in
> basement. Convenient location. Near shopping and public transportation. No pets allowed.
>
> **Rent:** $1,200/month   **Fee:** One month's rent
> **Security Deposit:** One month's rent   **Utilities Included:** heat, hot
> **Contact:** Joshua 510-555-5432   water, air-conditioning, and
>   electricity

1. The apartment has two bathrooms.   **True**   (**False**)

2. The building has an elevator.   **True**   **False**

3. The apartment is close to stores and transportation.   **True**   **False**

4. The rent includes electricity.   **True**   **False**

5. It's OK to have a pet.   **True**   **False**

6. The security deposit for this apartment is $1,200.   **True**   **False**

Ⓑ **PAIRS. Check your answers.**

Ⓒ **Look at the abbreviations below. Then look at the ad in Exercise A.
Circle the words for each abbreviation. Then write the words on the lines.**

1. A/C *air-conditioning*   7. EIK _____   13. mo. _____

2. apt. _____   8. fl. _____   14. nr. _____

3. BA _____   9. furn. _____   15. sec. dep. _____

4. BR _____   10. ht. _____   16. trans. _____

5. bsmt. _____   11. hw. _____   17. util. incl. _____

6. DR _____   12. LR _____   18. W/D _____

Ⓓ   CD2 T6   **Listen and check your answers. Then listen and repeat.**

2 PRACTICE

A Look at the newspaper apartment ads. Read the sentences.
Write the correct letter of the apartment ad next to each sentence.

a.
South End. Large 2 BR, LR, EIK, 2 BA. W/D. Ht. + hw. not incl. Pets allowed. No fee. $1,200/mo. 1 mo. sec. dep. Available immediately. Call Rick 207-555-1212.

b.
Downtown. Sunny furn. 1 BR apt. A/C. Pkg. garage. Nr. trans. Pets OK. $950/mo. Util. incl. No fee. City Properties 207-555-8765.

c.
North Square. Nice 2 BR, LR, DR. No pets. $1,200/mo. Ht. hw. incl. Nr. schools. Fee + 2 mo. sec. dep. Maven Realty 207-555-9989.

1. __b__ It has one bedroom.
2. ____ It has air-conditioning.
3. ____ It has a washer and dryer.
4. ____ No pets are allowed.
5. ____ It has an eat-in kitchen.

6. ____ It has two bathrooms.
7. ____ It is close to transportation.
8. ____ Utilities are not included in the rent.
9. ____ It is furnished.
10. ____ There is a fee.

B GROUPS OF 3. Read about the two families. Which apartment in Exercise A is best for each family? Explain your answer.

The Marshalls

The Marshalls are a family of four (a mother and three children). Mrs. Marshall works in the South End. She can spend $1,250 a month on rent and utilities. She can pay $3,000 for a security deposit. She doesn't have a car.

The Wilsons

The Wilsons are a family of three (a mother, a father, and a six-month-old baby). The parents both work downtown. They have a dog. They have a car. They can spend up to $1,000 a month on rent and utilities.

C GROUPS OF 3. Look at the list of ways to find an apartment. Which do you think is the best way? Explain your answer.

- ☐ reading newspaper ads
- ☐ reading Internet postings
- ☐ going to a real estate agent
- ☐ talking with friends and neighbors
- ☐ looking for rental signs in the neighborhood
- ☐ bulletin boards in supermarkets
- ☐ other: _____

3 LIFE SKILLS WRITING

Complete an application for an apartment. See page 260.

Can you...read apartment ads? ☐

Listening and Speaking

1 BEFORE YOU LISTEN

CLASS. Imagine you are calling about an apartment for rent. Read the questions. What other questions can you ask?

How much is the rent?
Is a security deposit required?
Are utilities included?
How many bedrooms are there?
Is it furnished?
Is there a laundry room in the building?
Are pets allowed?

2 LISTEN

CD2 T7

A 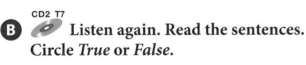 **Look at the picture of Paula calling a landlady. Listen to the conversation. Why is Paula calling?**

a. She wants information about an apartment.
b. She has a question about her rent.
c. She has a problem with her apartment.

CD2 T7

B  **Listen again. Read the sentences. Circle *True* or *False*.**

1. There are two bedrooms.

   True   **False**

2. There's a large living room.

   True   **False**

3. There's a laundry room in the building.

   True   **False**

4. There's a park around the corner.

   True   **False**

CD2 T8

C **Listen to the whole conversation. Why isn't Paula interested in the apartment anymore?**

a. She needs three bedrooms.   b. She wants to live near a park.   c. It is too expensive.

3 CONVERSATION

CD2 T9

A 📀 Listen. Then listen and repeat.

• bus stop   • laundry room   • dishwasher   • living room

CD2 T10

B 📀 Listen and repeat the conversation.

Landlady: Hello?

Paula: Hi, I'm calling about the apartment for rent. Can you tell me about it?

Landlady: Sure. There are two bedrooms and a large living room.

Paula: Is there a laundry room?

Landlady: No, there isn't. But there's a laundromat down the street.

Paula: I see. Is there a park nearby?

Landlady: Yes, there is—just around the corner.

Pronunciation Watch

Sometimes we put two words together to make a noun. The first word is usually stressed.

4 PRACTICE

A PAIRS. Practice the conversation. Then make new conversations. Use the information in the boxes.

A: Hello?

B: Hi, I'm calling about the apartment for rent. Can you tell me about it?

A: Sure. There are two bedrooms and a ⬚⬚⬚⬚⬚⬚⬚.

B: Is there a ⬚⬚⬚⬚⬚⬚?

A: No, there isn't. But there's ⬚⬚⬚⬚⬚⬚.

B: I see. Is there a ⬚⬚⬚⬚⬚⬚ nearby?

A: Yes, there is—just around the corner.

sunny kitchen	dishwasher	a microwave	bus stop
new bathroom	parking lot	free parking on the street	shopping center
big closet	balcony	a big window in the living room	supermarket

B ROLE PLAY. PAIRS. Make your own conversations. Student A, imagine you are going to rent your house or apartment. Answer Student B's questions with true information. Student B, you want to rent a house or apartment. Ask questions.

Ask about an apartment

Grammar

There is / There are

Affirmative		Negative	
There is	a park nearby.	**There isn't a** **There's no**	bus stop near here.
There are	two bedrooms.	**There aren't any** **There are no**	restaurants in the neighborhood.

Questions			Short answers			
	Is there **Are there**	a laundry room? a lot of windows?	Yes,	there is. there are.	No,	there isn't. there aren't.
How many bedrooms	**are there?**		Two.	**(There are** two.)		

1 PRACTICE

Grammar Watch

Use *there is / there are* to talk about a thing or things in a certain place.

A Complete the sentences. Underline the correct words.

1. <u>There is</u> / There are a bus stop near the apartment.
2. **Is there** / **Are there** a bathtub?
3. **Are there** / **Is there** a lot of children in the neighborhood?
4. **There is** / **There are** two windows in the kitchen.
5. **There's** / **There isn't** no elevator in the building.
6. **There aren't** / **There isn't** a lot of traffic on this street.

B Complete the conversation. Use the correct form of *there is / there are.* **Some sentences are negative.**

A: So, tell me about your new apartment. How many bedrooms ___are there___?

B: _____ two. And they're nice and big.

A: That's good. How are the neighbors?

B: Well, _____ an older woman next door. She seems very friendly.

A: And how's the neighborhood?

B: I like it a lot. _____ a lot of stores around the corner.

A: That's convenient. _____ any supermarkets?

B: No, _____, but _____ a convenience store down the street.

Read the answers. Write the questions. Use *Is there* and *Are there*.

1. **A:** Is there a bus stop nearby?

   B: Yes, there is. The #2 bus stop is across the street.

2. **A:** _____

   B: No. There are no families with children in the building.

3. **A:** _____

   B: Yes, there is. There's a supermarket 10 minutes from here.

4. **A:** _____

   B: Sorry. There aren't any furnished apartments available.

5. **A:** _____

   B: Yes, there is. There's a laundry room in the basement.

6. **A:** _____

   B: Four. There are four closets in the apartment.

Show what you know! Ask about an apartment

STEP 1. PAIRS. Student A, you are looking for an apartment. Look at the questions on this page. Student B, you have an apartment for rent. Look at your apartment information in the ad on page 246.

STEP 2. SAME PAIRS. Student A, ask about Student B's apartment. Take notes.

STEP 3. SAME PAIRS. Change roles. Student A, use the apartment ad on this page. Answer Student B's questions.

Ask about:	Notes
number of bedrooms	
number of bathrooms	
laundry room	
parking	
rent, fees, security deposit	

APARTMENT FOR RENT. 3 BR, 2 BA, LR, DR. W/D in basement, nr. transportation, $1,200/mo. 1 mo. fee + 1 mo. sec. dep.

Can you... ask about an apartment? ☐

Reading

1 BEFORE YOU READ

A Look at the map of the continental U.S. Write the region names on the map. Use the words in the box.

~~Midwest~~   Northeast   South   Southwest   West Coast   West

Midwest

B PAIRS. Compare your answers.

C Skim the article on page 99. What is one of the important ideas discussed in the article?

D PAIRS. Compare your answers.

Reading Skill:
Skimming

Skimming means you do not read every word. Instead, you read quickly to get the general idea of the article.

2 READ

CD2 T11

Listen. Read the article.

Record Growth in Springville

Springville is growing fast. It is like many other cities in the South and Southwest. These are the fastest growing regions in the U.S. "Every day I meet another newcomer," says Amy Mark, a Springville real-estate agent.

New residents say they moved to Springville because of the warm weather, jobs, low cost of living, and natural beauty. The area is popular with people from the large, expensive cities of the Northeast and the West Coast. "We moved to Springville last year.

One of Springville's new housing developments

We exchanged a tiny apartment in Boston for this big, beautiful house," says Jim Walker. "We love it here."

But not everyone loves the growth. "We moved here from Philadelphia to get closer to nature, but instead we are stuck in traffic all the time," says Joanna Fields. Pam Foster, a longtime resident, agrees. "We're replacing the area's natural beauty with shopping malls and new houses. People come here to get away from the big city, but they're just bringing the big city with them."

3 CHECK YOUR UNDERSTANDING

A Read the article again. Then answer the questions on a separate piece of paper.

1. What are four reasons people move to Springville?

2. What are two problems caused by Springville growth?

B PAIRS. Compare your community to Springville. How is it the same? How is it different?

Show what you know!

PRE-WRITING. NETWORK. PAIRS. Find a partner who lives in your community. Talk about what you like and dislike about your community.

WRITE. Write about your community. See page 270.

Get directions

Listening and Speaking

1 BEFORE YOU LISTEN

A Look at the pictures. Write the directions on the lines.

> Turn right.   Turn left.   ~~Go straight~~.   Go through one traffic light.

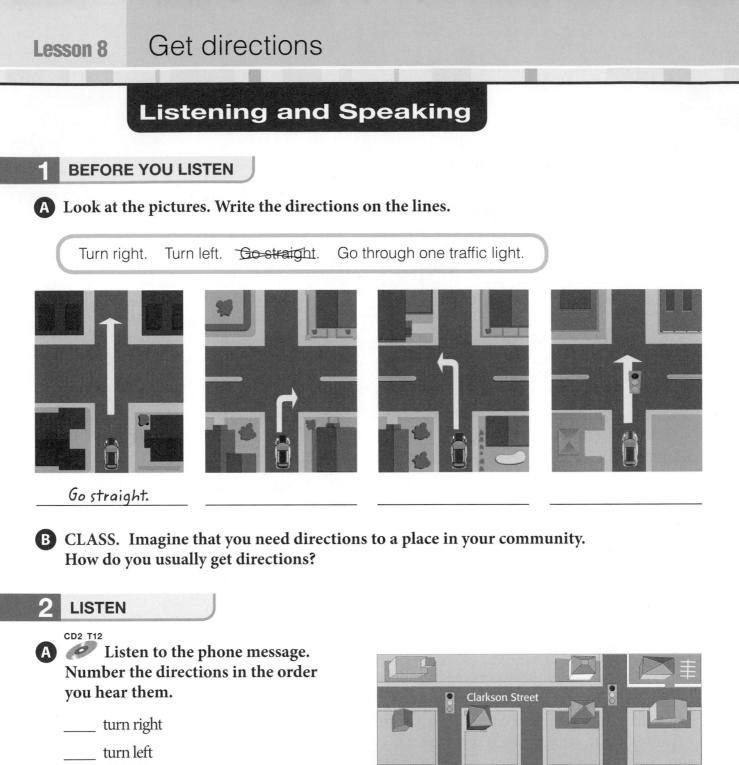

Go straight. _____   _____   _____   _____

B CLASS. Imagine that you need directions to a place in your community. How do you usually get directions?

2 LISTEN

CD2 T12

A Listen to the phone message. Number the directions in the order you hear them.

____ turn right

____ turn left

____ go straight

____ go through one traffic light

CD2 T12

B Listen again. Find the "start here" box. Follow the directions on the map. Draw the route on the map. Then circle the library.

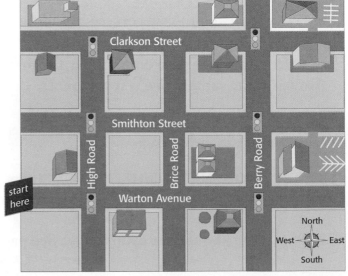

3 CONVERSATION

A 🔘 **Listen. Then listen and repeat.**

CD2 T13

Then turn right.   It's on the left.
It's on Third Street.   Thanks.

B 🔘 **Carrie has a new neighbor, Lan. Lan doesn't know her way around the neighborhood yet. Listen and repeat the conversation.**

CD2 T14

Lan: Can you give me directions to Save-Rite Pharmacy?
Carrie: Sure. Go straight on Third Street.
Lan: OK. Go straight on Third Street.
Carrie: All right. At the stop sign, turn right onto Davis Road.
Lan: At the stop sign, turn right onto Davis Road.
Carrie: Exactly. Save-Rite Pharmacy is on the left.

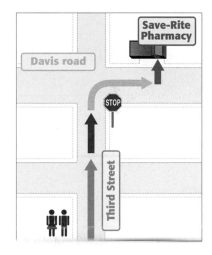

4 PRACTICE

A **PAIRS. Practice the conversation. Then make new conversations. Use the directions on the maps.**

A: Can you give me directions to ⬚⬚⬚⬚ ?

B: Sure. Go straight on ⬚⬚⬚⬚ .

A: OK. Go straight on ⬚⬚⬚⬚ .

B: All right. At the ⬚⬚⬚⬚ , turn ⬚⬚⬚⬚ onto ⬚⬚⬚⬚ .

A: At the ⬚⬚⬚⬚ , turn ⬚⬚⬚⬚ onto ⬚⬚⬚⬚ .

B: Exactly. ⬚⬚⬚⬚ is on the left .

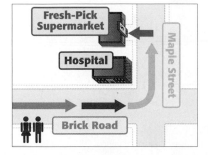

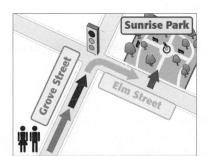

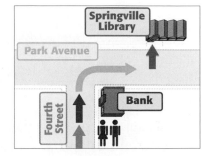

B **ROLE PLAY. PAIRS. Make your own conversations. Ask for and give directions from school to places in your community.**

1 GRAMMAR

A Imagine you are interested in renting an apartment. You want to know more about places in the neighborhood. Write questions with *Is there* and *Are there* and the words in parentheses.

1. (laundromat) _Is there a laundromat nearby?_____

2. (bank) _____

3. (restaurants) _____

4. (stores) _____

5. (gas stations) _____

6. (schools) _____

7. (post office) _____

8. (park) _____

B ROLE PLAY. PAIRS. Take turns. Ask the questions you wrote in Exercise A. Look at the neighborhood map. You are at the apartment for rent. Answer the questions. Tell where each place is located.

A: *Is there a laundromat nearby?*
B: *Yes, there is. There's a laundromat on First Avenue.*

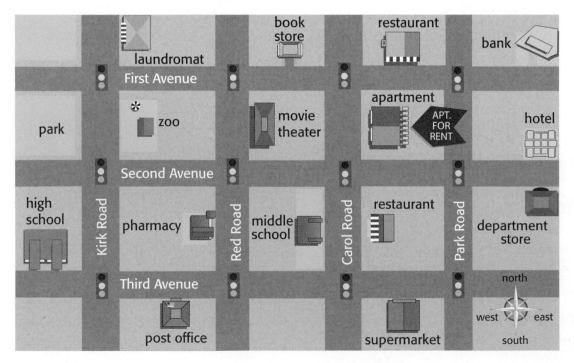

2   GRAMMAR

A WRITE. Look at the map on page 102. Write directions from one place on the map to another place.

> Start at the pharmacy. Go north on Red Road.

B PAIRS. Student A, read your directions from Exercise A. Student B, follow Student A's directions on the map on page 102. Where are you?

C Complete the conversations with the present continuous. Use contractions if possible.

1. **A:** I __'m looking for__ Dad. Is he home?
       (look for)

   B: Yes, he _____ the light in my bedroom.
                      (look at)

   It _____, and he _____ to fix it.
        (not work)   (try)

   A: But Dad isn't very good at fixing stuff.

   B: I know. Uncle Jerry is in my bedroom, too, and

   he _____ .
         (help)

   A: Does Uncle Jerry know how to fix a light?

   B: No. That's why Mom is on the phone right now.

   She's _____ an electrician!
            (call)

2. **A:** Hello?

   B: Hi, it's Alicia. Where are you?

   A: At home. Eddie and I _____ in the kitchen, and we _____
                               (sit)   (have)
   some coffee. I _____ a list of the things I need to do today.
                    (make)
   What about you?

   B: Well, I _____ coffee too. I'm at the coffee shop, and
                    (have)
   I _____ you to meet me.
      (wait for)

   A: Oh, no! I'm so sorry. I forgot! That's not on my list!

3 ACT IT OUT   What do you say?

STEP 1. CLASS. Review the Lesson 5 conversation between Paula and a landlady (CD 2 Track 10).

STEP 2. ROLE PLAY. PAIRS. Student A, you are talking to a landlord/landlady about an apartment. Ask questions about the apartment. Student B, you are the landlord/landlady. Answer Student A's questions. Make up the answers.

4 READ AND REACT   Problem-solving

STEP 1. Read about Anita's problem.

The lock on Anita's front door never worked well. Now the lock is broken. Anita calls the building manager. The building manager says it isn't his responsibility to fix the lock. He says "You break it. You fix it." She knows it is the building manager's responsibility.

STEP 2. PAIRS. What is Anita's problem? What can she do? Here are some ideas.

- She can pay a locksmith to fix the lock.
- She can pay a locksmith to fix the lock and take the money out of her rent check.
- She can call the city housing office and ask for help.
- She can _____.

5 CONNECT   For your Study Skills Activity, go to page 251. For your Team Project, go to page 278.

In the Past

Preview

Look at the picture.
What are the people
talking about?

UNIT GOALS

☐ Identify events
with family and
friends

☐ Talk about past
activities

☐ Recognize U.S.
holidays

☐ Talk about
milestones

☐ Talk about
something that
happened

☐ Write an absence
note to a teacher

1 WHAT DO YOU KNOW?

A CLASS. Look at the pictures. Which events with family and friends do you know?

B Look at the pictures and listen. Listen again and repeat.

2 PRACTICE

A PAIRS. Student A, point to a picture and ask about the event. Student B, answer the question.

A: *Where are the people?*
B: *They're at an anniversary party.*

B WORD PLAY. GROUPS OF 3. Look at the pictures. For which events do you dress formally in your country? For which do you dress casually? For which do you give gifts? Complete the chart.

Formal dress	Casual dress	Gift giving

C CLASS. Are the answers to Exercise B the same for events in the U.S.?

Events With Family and Friends

1. **a** birthday party
2. **a** wedding
3. **an** anniversary party
4. **a** funeral
5. **a** family reunion
6. **a** graduation party
7. **a** holiday meal
8. **a** baby shower
9. **a** barbecue
10. **a** retirement party
11. **a** potluck dinner
12. **a** surprise party

Learning Strategy
Personalize

Look at the list of events. Think of five events that you have attended. Make a card for each event. On one side of the card, write the vocabulary words. On the other side, write the date of the event and the names of some people who attended.

Show what you know!

STEP 1. Look at the list of events with family and friends. What is your favorite event?

_____

STEP 2. GROUPS OF 3. Talk about your favorite events. Explain your choices.

A: *What's your favorite event?*
B: *Weddings are my favorite event! Everyone is so happy. Everyone looks so beautiful.*

Listening and Speaking

1 BEFORE YOU LISTEN

CLASS. Look at the pictures. Which of these activities do you do with your family or friends?

listen to family stories

look at old photos

stay up late

dance all night

2 LISTEN

A **CLASS.** Look at the picture of Michelle and Sam. Guess: What are they talking about?

CD2 T16

B Listen to the conversation. Was your guess in Exercise A correct?

CD2 T16

C Listen again. Read the sentences. Circle *True* or *False*.

1. Michelle asks Sam about his weekend. True False

2. Sam was at a wedding last weekend. True False

3. Sam watched old movies last weekend. True False

4. Sam listened to family stories. True False

CD2 T17

D Listen to the whole conversation. What did Michelle do last weekend?

a.

b.

3 CONVERSATION

CD2 T18

A **Listen. Then listen and repeat.**

Extra syllable	**No extra syllable**	
invited	looked	listened
needed	dropped	showed

> **Pronunciation Watch**
>
> The -*ed* ending adds an extra syllable after the sound /t/ or /d/. It does not add an extra syllable after other sounds.

B **Say the words to yourself. For which verbs does -*ed* add a syllable? Circle the numbers.**

1. danced   2. visited   3. watched   4. wanted   5. talked   6. stayed

CD2 T19

C **Listen and check your answers.**

CD2 T20

D **Listen and repeat the conversation.**

Michelle: How was your weekend? How was the family reunion?
Sam: It was really nice, thanks. My whole family showed up.
Michelle: Sounds great.
Sam: Yeah, it was fun. We looked at old pictures and listened to family stories.

4 PRACTICE

A **PAIRS. Practice the conversation. Then make new conversations. Use the information in the boxes.**

A: How was your weekend? How was the ⬚⬚⬚⬚⬚⬚ ?

B: It was really nice, thanks. My whole family showed up.

A: Sounds great.

B: Yeah, it was fun. We ⬚⬚⬚⬚⬚⬚ and ⬚⬚⬚⬚⬚⬚ .

B **MAKE IT PERSONAL. PAIRS. Talk about a family event. What did you do?**

anniversary party
barbecue
wedding

watched family movies
cooked a lot of food
stayed up late

talked about old times
played games
danced all night

Grammar

Simple past: Regular verbs

Affirmative		
I She They	**looked**	at old pictures yesterday.

Negative		
I She They	**didn't cook**	dinner last night.

1 PRACTICE

A Complete the letter. Use the simple past of the words in parentheses.

Grammar Watch

For most regular verbs, add *-ed*.
For example: want → wanted

For verbs that end in *-e*, add *-d*.
For example: invite → invited

Hi, Sis!

How are you? I know you really (want) ___wanted___ to go to Josh's

birthday party last Saturday. We (miss) _____ you. Josh and Rebecca

(invite) _____ a lot of people, and almost everyone (show up) _____.

There was a lot of food and I (help) _____ in the kitchen. Then Josh

(play) _____ some music. We all (dance) _____ and

(not want) _____ to stop. We (not need) _____ to get up early the

next day, so everyone (stay) _____ late. It was a fun party. Talk to you soon!

Gina

B Complete the conversation. Use the past tense forms of the words in the box.

clean   ~~invite~~   not leave   stay up   visit   want   watch

A: You look a little tired this morning.

B: Yeah, I ___invited___ some friends over last night. They _____ until late

and then I _____ the house. It was a mess! You look a little tired, too.

A: I am. I _____ my cousin last night. We _____ a soccer game on TV.

I _____ to see the end so I _____ late.

A Read Kathy's to-do list. Then look at the pictures of the things she did after work today. Check the things Kathy did today on the list.

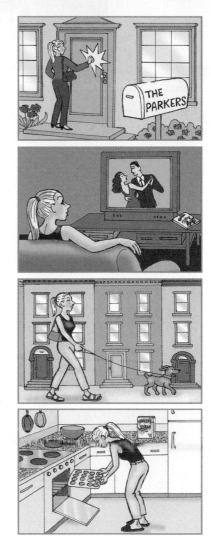

> Kathy's to-do list
>
> ☐ visit Mrs. Parker
> ☐ call Joe
> ☐ finish homework
> ☐ watch movie
> ☐ return movie to video store
> ☐ walk the dog
> ☐ go to the supermarket
> ☐ bake cookies

B PAIRS. Talk about what Kathy did and did not do after work.

A: *Kathy visited Mrs. Parker.*
B: *She didn't call Joe.*

C WRITE. On a separate piece of paper, write five sentences about what Kathy did and did not do after work.

Show what you know! Talk about past activities

STEP 1. Complete the sentence with true information. Use the simple past.

I _____ last week.

STEP 2. GROUPS OF 5. Play the Memory Game. Talk about what people did.

Talib: *I visited my sister.*
Minoru: *Talib visited his sister. I cooked dinner for my wife.*
Rita: *Talib visited his sister. Minoru cooked dinner for his wife. I watched three movies.*

Can you...talk about past activities? ☐

Recognize U.S. holidays

Life Skills

1   RECOGNIZE U.S. HOLIDAYS

A **PAIRS.** Look at the calendars. Write the name of each holiday on the correct line.

> Christmas Day   Columbus Day   Independence Day   Labor Day
> Martin Luther King Jr. Day   Memorial Day   ~~New Year's Day~~   Presidents' Day
> Thanksgiving Day   Veterans' Day

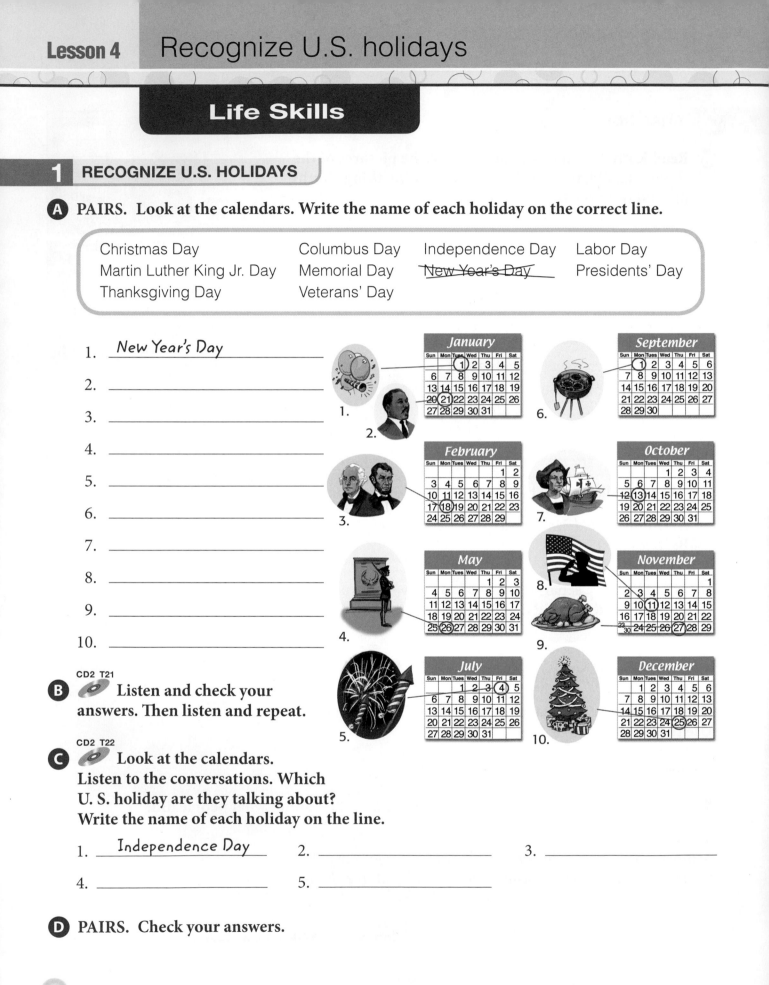

1. _New Year's Day_

2. _____

3. _____

4. _____

5. _____

6. _____

7. _____

8. _____

9. _____

10. _____

B CD2 T21   Listen and check your answers. Then listen and repeat.

C CD2 T22   Look at the calendars. Listen to the conversations. Which U. S. holiday are they talking about? Write the name of each holiday on the line.

1. _Independence Day_   2. _____   3. _____

4. _____   5. _____

D **PAIRS.** Check your answers.

A Read the article about national holidays.

What Do You Know About U.S. Holidays?

Take this quiz.

Q. How many national holidays are there in the United States?

A. There are ten national holidays, but most people don't know that because many businesses stay open on national holidays. Schools, banks, and government offices such as the post office are closed on all ten days. Many U.S. businesses observe only the "Big Six:" New Year's Day, Memorial Day, Independence Day, Labor Day, Thanksgiving Day, and Christmas Day.

Q. *Which holidays celebrate specific people?*

A. Presidents' Day, Martin Luther King Jr. Day, and Columbus Day celebrate specific people. Presidents' Day celebrates George Washington, the first president of the United States, and Abraham Lincoln, the sixteenth president. Martin Luther King Jr. Day celebrates Dr. King's work for the equality of all people. Columbus Day celebrates the day Columbus arrived in the Americas in 1492.

Q. *What's the difference between Veterans' Day and Memorial Day?*

A. Both holidays celebrate the U.S. military. On Veterans' Day, we celebrate all people in the U.S. military. On Memorial Day, we remember U.S. military personnel who died in wars.

B Read the article again. Read the sentences. Circle *True* or *False*. Correct the false information.

1. There are ten national holidays.	(True)	False
2. All businesses in the U.S. are closed on national holidays.	True	False
3. Government offices are closed on national holidays.	True	False
4. Presidents' Day celebrates the life of Martin Luther King Jr.	True	False
5. Columbus Day celebrates the day Columbus arrived in 1942.	True	False
6. Veterans' Day celebrates all people in the U.S. military.	True	False

Can you...recognize U.S. holidays? ☐

Talk about milestones

Listening and Speaking

1 BEFORE YOU LISTEN

CLASS. Look at the pictures of milestones.
What are some other important times in a person's life?

being born

growing up

graduating from school

getting a job

getting married

having children

2 LISTEN

CD2 T23

A 🔘 Listen to the interview on a radio show. Which milestones
do the people talk about?

☐ being born   ☐ growing up   ☐ going to school   ☐ getting married

CD2 T23

B 🔘 Listen again. Complete the sentences.

1. Daniel was born in _____.
   a. California   b. Colorado

2. Daniel wanted to be _____
   when he was a child.
   a. an actor   b. a plumber

3. Daniel _____ last night.
   a. went to a party   b. stayed home

3 CONVERSATION

CD2 T24

A Listen to the intonation of the sentences. Then listen and repeat.

> **Pronunciation Watch**
>
> To check our understanding, sometimes we repeat a statement as a question. The voice goes up at the end.

You were born in California?

Stella came to the U.S. last year?

Daniel always wanted to be an actor?

You got a job in a supermarket?

CD2 T25

B Listen to the sentences. Are they statements or questions? Add a period (.) to statements. Add a question mark (?) to questions.

1. Maria grew up in Houston

2. You came to the U.S. in 1995

3. Ali graduated from college two years ago

4. She got married last year

CD2 T26

C Listen and repeat the conversation.

Fred: So, tell me . . . Where are you from?

Chen: China. I was born in a small village, but I grew up in Beijing.

Fred: And you came to the U.S. five years ago?

Chen: Right. First my wife and I got an apartment in Long Beach. Then we moved to San Francisco.

Fred: Your English is very good. Did you study English in China?

Chen: Yes, I did, but I didn't practice speaking a lot.

4 PRACTICE

A PAIRS. Practice the conversation.

B MAKE IT PERSONAL. PAIRS. Ask your partner about events in his or her life.

Angela: *Where are you from?*
Ivan: *Russia . . .*

C Tell the class about your partner.

Ivan is from Russia. He came to the U.S. in 2007. He studied English in Russia.

Talk about milestones

Grammar

Simple past: Irregular verbs

Affirmative
I **came** to the U.S. ten years ago.

Negative
I **didn't come** to the U.S. last year.

Grammar Watch

Here are some examples of past tense forms.
See page 286 for more past tense forms.

Base form	Past tense form	Base form	Past tense form
have	**had**	begin	**began**
go	**went**	come	**came**
get	**got**	leave	**left**
take	**took**	make	**made**
grow	**grew**	do	**did**

1 PRACTICE

A Complete the sentences. Underline the correct words.

1. I **don't grow** / **didn't** grow up in the U.S. I **grow** / **grew** up in Haiti.

2. Rosa **meets** / **met** Ricardo in 2006 and they **get** / **got** married in 2008.

3. Yao **took** / **takes** some college classes last year but he didn't **graduated** / **graduate**.

4. Last year they **leave** / **left** Colombia and they **came** / **come** to the U.S.

5. Ho-Jin **goes** / **went** to Los Angeles and he **finds** / **found** a good job there.

6. My grandmother **have** / **had** three brothers but she didn't **have** / **had** any sisters.

B Complete the sentences. Write the simple past of the words in parentheses.

I __was born__ in Venezuela in 1987. I _____ up in Caracas. My
    (be born)   (grow)

family _____ a small store there. In 2005, my family left Venezuela, and
      (have)

we _____ to the U.S. I _____ find a job, but I _____ English
  (come)   (have to)   (not speak)

very well. So I _____ classes. A supermarket near my house needed
        (take)

cashiers. I _____ to the store, and I _____ an interview that day.
    (go)   (have)

I _____ the job. That was an important day for me. I still work at the
  (get)

supermarket, but I now I'm a manager.

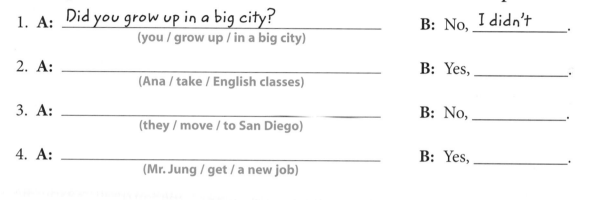

Simple past

Yes / No questions			
Did	you he she they	**grow up**	in Ecuador?

Short answers		
Yes,	I he she they	**did.**
No,		**didn't.**

··· **Grammar Watch**

Remember how to form past tense questions with *be*.

A: *Were you born in Poland?*
B: *Yes, I was.*

2 PRACTICE

Write questions and answers. Use the correct forms of the words in parentheses.

1. **A:** Did you grow up in a big city?
   (you / grow up / in a big city)
   B: No, I didn't.

2. **A:** _____
   (Ana / take / English classes)
   B: Yes, _____.

3. **A:** _____
   (they / move / to San Diego)
   B: No, _____.

4. **A:** _____
   (Mr. Jung / get / a new job)
   B: Yes, _____.

Show what you know! Talk about milestones

STEP 1. Write your name and four sentences about milestones in your life. Use a separate piece of paper.

> I grew up in Costa Rica.

STEP 2. GROUPS OF 5. Mix up the papers from Step 1. Student A, choose one paper. Other students, guess who wrote the paper. Take turns asking *Yes / No* questions.

B: *Did the person grow up in El Salvador?*
A: *No, she didn't.*
C: *Did she grow up in Costa Rica?*
A: *Yes, she did.*
D: *Did she come to the U.S. last year?*
A: *Yes, she did.*
E: *It's Patricia.*
A: *That's right!*

Can you...talk about milestones? ☐

Reading

CLASS. Scan the article. Who is Oprah Winfrey? When was she born?

CD2 T27

Listen. Read the article.

> **Reading Skill:**
> Scanning for Information
>
> Scanning an article means reading it quickly to find specific information. This is helpful when you need to find information such as names or dates quickly.

Oprah!

Oprah Winfrey is the host of *The Oprah Winfrey Show*. It is one of the most popular talk shows in the world. Oprah also has her own magazine, website, radio show, and book club.

Oprah was born in 1954. Her family was very poor, and her parents were not together. She had to move a lot. Her childhood was not easy. But Oprah was a fast learner and she did well in school. At the age of 17, Oprah got a job at a radio station as a newscaster. In 1973, she became the first African-American female television news anchor in Nashville, Tennesee. She was just 19.

In 1984, Oprah became the host of a talk show called *A.M. Chicago*. A year later, the TV network changed the name to *The Oprah Winfrey Show*. Today, millions of people in 132 countries watch the show every day.

But Oprah didn't stop there. In 1985, she acted in the movie *The Color Purple*. A year later she started a company, named Harpo Productions. It makes movies and TV specials. In 1996, she created Oprah's Book Club. It is now the largest book club in the world. In 2000, she started her first magazine, *O: The Oprah Magazine*.

These sucesses have made Oprah the richest African-American in the world. Oprah's charity, the Oprah Winfrey Foundation, gives millions of dollars to needy students and schools around the world. In 2007, Oprah spent $40 million to open the Oprah Winfrey Leadership Academy, a school for girls in South Africa.

Oprah on the set of *The Oprah Winfrey Show*

Oprah as Sofia in *The Color Purple*

A Read the article again. Complete the time line with the correct year or milestone.

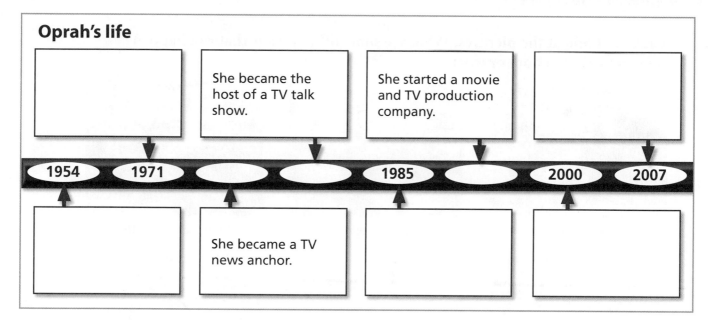

Oprah's life

	She became the host of a TV talk show.	She started a movie and TV production company.	

1954 — 1971 — ◯ — ◯ — 1985 — ◯ — 2000 — 2007

	She became a TV news anchor.		

B PAIRS. What is Oprah's greatest success? Why do you think so?

Show what you know!

PRE-WRITING. Write a time line of your life. Start with the year you were born and end with this year. Use the time line in Exercise A as a model.

My life

Birth   present

WRITE. Write a short autobiography. See page 270.

Talk about something that happened

Listening and Speaking

1 BEFORE YOU LISTEN

CLASS. Look at the pictures. What are some other things that can happen on your way to school or work?

I had car trouble.

I overslept.

I got stuck in traffic.

I forgot my lunch.

I lost my keys.

I took the wrong train.

2 LISTEN

CD2 T28

A Look at the picture of Maria and André having lunch. Listen to the conversation. Why does Maria ask, "Is everything OK?"

Because André looks _____.
a. sick   b. stressed out   c. nervous

CD2 T28

B Listen again. Put the events in the correct order.

_____ André got stuck in traffic.

_____ André got to work late.

_____ André lost his car keys.

C 🔘 **Listen to the whole conversation. Then answer the questions. Circle the correct answers.**

1. What day is it?
   a. Tuesday   b. Thursday

2. What mistake did André make?
   a. He went to work on his day off.   b. He didn't go to work.

3 | CONVERSATION

CD2 T30

🔘 **Listen and repeat the conversation.**

Maria: Is everything OK? You look stressed out.
André: Well, I had a rough morning.
Maria: Why? What happened?
André: First I lost my car keys.
Maria: Oh, no!
André: Then I got stuck in traffic.
Maria: When did you get to work?
André: At 10:00. I was really late.

4 | PRACTICE

A **PAIRS. Practice the conversation. Then make new conversations. Use the information in the boxes.**

A: Is everything OK? You look ░░░░░░░░░.

B: Well, I had a rough morning.

A: Why? What happened?

B: First I ░░░░░░░░░.

A: Oh, no!

B: Then I ░░░░░░░░░.

A: When did you get to work?

B: At 10:00. I was really late.

> upset
> unhappy
> exhausted

> lost my wallet
> overslept
> forgot my lunch

> had car trouble
> missed the bus
> took the wrong train

B **MAKE IT PERSONAL. PAIRS. Tell your partner about a bad morning you had.**

Talk about something that happened

Grammar

Simple past: Information questions

What		you	do?
Where	**did**	he	go?

Why		she	oversleep?
When	**did**	Angel	get to work?

1 PRACTICE

A Write questions about the past. Use the correct forms of the words in parentheses.

1. (What time / you / get up yesterday) _What time did you get up yesterday?_

2. (Where / you / go this morning) _____

3. (What / you / have for lunch yesterday) _____

4. (What time / you / get to school today) _____

5. (What / you / do last night) _____

B PAIRS. Ask and answer the questions in Exercise A.

A: *What time did you get up yesterday?*
B: *I got up at 7:00. I had to work at 8:00.*

C Complete the conversations. Read the replies. Write information questions about the underlined words.

1. **A:** _What did Saul forget?_

   B: Saul forgot <u>his wallet</u>.

2. **A:** _____

   B: Jane finished work <u>at 10:45</u>.

3. **A:** _____

   B: In-Ho missed the bus <u>because he overslept</u>.

4. **A:** _____

   B: Nadia found her car keys <u>in the kitchen</u>.

2 LIFE SKILLS WRITING

Write an absence note to a teacher. See page 261.

1 GRAMMAR

A Read the replies. Write questions about the underlined words.

1. **A:** _Did you go to Wilson Adult School?_

   B: <u>Yes</u>, I did. I went to Wilson Adult School.

2. **A:** _When did John and Ellen get married?_

   B: John and Ellen got married <u>last year</u>.

3. **A:** _____

   B: Samuel grew up <u>in Namibia</u>.

4. **A:** _____

   B: We moved <u>because we didn't like cold weather</u>.

5. **A:** _____

   B: <u>No</u>, we didn't. We didn't visit our aunt and uncle.

6. **A:** _____

   B: Todd got that job <u>in 2005</u>.

B Complete Nora's conversation with her grandmother, Jane. Write the correct past forms of the verbs in parentheses.

Nora: Grandma, you never _____told_____ me about your wedding day.
                                    (tell)

_____ married?
(where / you / get)

Jane: We _____ our wedding in a beautiful garden.
              (have)

Nora: _____ a lot of people?
         (you / invite)

Jane: No, we didn't. It was a small wedding.

Nora: _____ nervous?
              (you / feel)

Jane: Yes, I did. But I was really excited, too.

Nora: _____ that Grandpa was the right man for you?
         (how / you / know)

Jane: I just _____ it in my heart. And look at our life now—your
                (know)

grandfather and I have two children and five beautiful grandchildren.

Go to the CD-ROM for more practice.

2 ACT IT OUT   What do you say?

STEP 1. CLASS. Review the Lesson 5 conversation between Fred and Chen (CD 2 track 26).

STEP 2. PAIRS. Student A, tell your partner about the milestones of your life. Student B, ask questions about the milestones.

3 READ AND REACT   Problem-solving

STEP 1. Read about Yusef's problem.

Yusef started a new job at a hospital. Last night he had to clean the floors. His boss taught him how to use a floor cleaning machine. He used the machine, but then it stopped working. Yusef thinks he broke the machine.

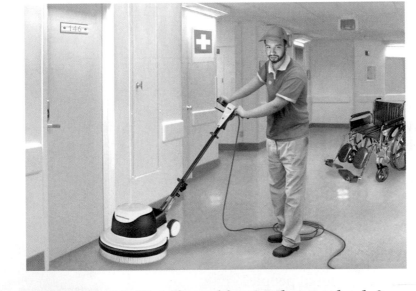

STEP 2. PAIRS. What is Yusef's problem? What can he do? Here are some ideas.

- He can tell his boss, "I'm sorry, I broke the machine."
- He can tell his boss, "Someone broke the machine."
- He can say nothing about the broken machine.
- He can _____.

4 CONNECT

For your Study Skills Activity, go to page 251.
For your Team Project, go to page 279.

Which goals can you check off? Go back to page 105.

Health Watch

Preview

**Look at the picture.
Where is the person?
What is she doing?
How does she feel?**

UNIT GOALS

☐ Identify health problems

☐ Make a doctor's appointment

☐ Read medicine labels

☐ Complete a medical history form

☐ Talk about an injury

☐ Call in when you have to miss work

1 WHAT DO YOU KNOW?

A CLASS. Look at the pictures. Which health problems do you know?

CD2 T31

B Look at the pictures and listen. Then listen and repeat.

2 PRACTICE

A WORD PLAY. Some expressions for health problems have the word *a* or *an* before them. Some have the word *the* before them. And some have no word before them.

CD2 T32

Listen and complete the chart. Write the health problems in the correct columns.

I have a _____.	I have _____.
headache	
I have the _____.	**I have an _____.**

B PAIRS. Point to the pictures. Ask and answer questions about the people.

A: *What's the matter?*
B: *She has a headache. What's the matter?*
A: *He has chest pains.*

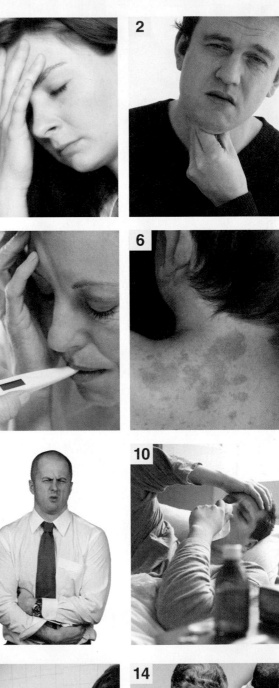

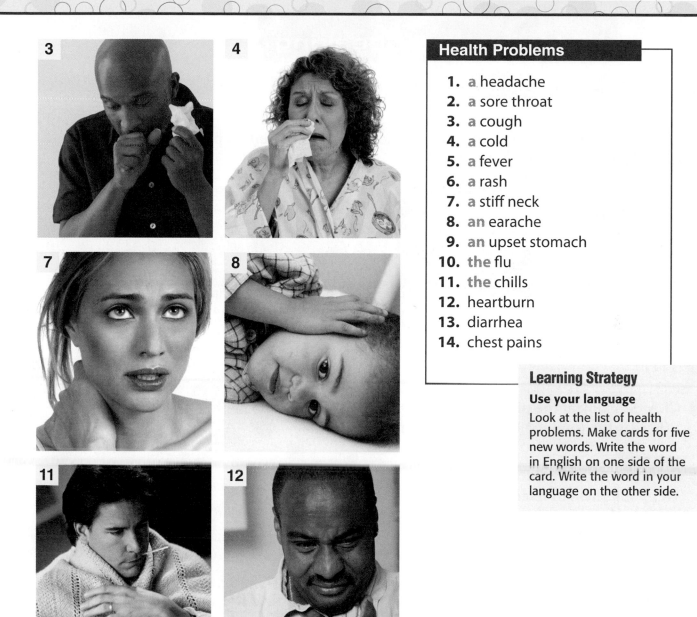

Health Problems

1. a headache
2. a sore throat
3. a cough
4. a cold
5. a fever
6. a rash
7. a stiff neck
8. an earache
9. an upset stomach
10. the flu
11. the chills
12. heartburn
13. diarrhea
14. chest pains

Learning Strategy

Use your language

Look at the list of health problems. Make cards for five new words. Write the word in English on one side of the card. Write the word in your language on the other side.

Show what you know!

STEP 1. Do you go to the doctor? When? Complete the sentence.

I go to the doctor when I _____.

STEP 2. GROUPS OF 3. Talk to your classmates. When do you go to the doctor?

Listening and Speaking

1 BEFORE YOU LISTEN

CLASS. Look at the pictures and read the symptoms. When do people have these symptoms?

She's dizzy.

He's nauseous.

It's itchy.

It's swollen.

2 LISTEN

A **CLASS.** Look at the pictures. Guess: Where is the woman? Where is the man?

CD2 T33

B 🔘 Listen to the conversation. Was your guess in Exercise A correct?

CD2 T33

C 🔘 Listen again. What is the matter with Roberto? Check all of his symptoms.

☐ He has a fever.   ☐ He's nauseous.

☐ He has heartburn. ☐ He's dizzy.

CD2 T33

D 🔘 Listen again. Complete the information on the appointment card. Check the day and write the time of the appointment.

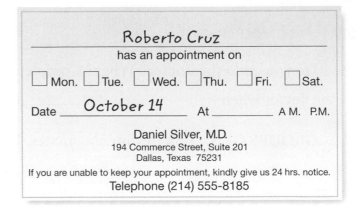

Roberto Cruz
has an appointment on

☐ Mon. ☐ Tue. ☐ Wed. ☐ Thu. ☐ Fri. ☐ Sat.

Date ___*October 14*___ At _____ A M. P.M.

Daniel Silver, M.D.
194 Commerce Street, Suite 201
Dallas, Texas 75231
If you are unable to keep your appointment, kindly give us 24 hrs. notice.
Telephone (214) 555-8185

3 CONVERSATION

CD2 T34

A Listen to the sentences. Notice how we link a consonant sound to a vowel sound. Then listen and repeat.

Pronunciation Watch

We often link words together without a break when we speak.

I have a fever.

Can I make an appointment?

Can you come at eight?

We close at noon on Friday.

CD2 T35

B Listen and repeat the conversation.

Receptionist: Hello. Westview Clinic.
Roberto: Hi. This is Roberto Cruz. I need to make an appointment, please.
Receptionist: All right. What's the matter?
Roberto: I have a fever and I'm nauseous.
Receptionist: OK. Can you come on Tuesday morning? How about at 9:00?
Roberto: Yes, that's fine.

4 PRACTICE

A PAIRS. Practice the conversation. Then make new conversations. Use your own names and the information in the boxes.

A: Hello. Westview Clinic.

B: Hi. This is _____. I need to make an appointment, please.

A: All right. What's the matter?

B: I have a _____ and _____.

A: OK. Can you come _____? How about at _____?

B: Yes, that's fine.

cough	my throat is swollen	on Thursday	noon
headache	I'm dizzy	this afternoon	3:00
rash	my leg is itchy	first thing tomorrow	8:30

B ROLE PLAY. PAIRS. Make your own conversations. Use your own names and different information.

Make a doctor's appointment

Grammar

Prepositions of time: *on / at / by / in / from ... to*		
Can you come	**on**	Tuesday morning?
Roberto's appointment is	**at**	9:00 A.M.
Please get here	**by**	5:00 today.
I'm going to see the doctor	**in**	an hour.
The pharmacy is open	**from**	8:00 A.M. **to** 9:00 P.M.

Grammar Watch

- Use *on* with a day or date.
- Use *at* with a specific time on the clock.
- Use *by* with a specific time in the future.
- Use *in* with an amount of time in the future, with a month or year, or with *the morning/afternoon/evening.*
- Use *from ... to* with a starting time and an ending time.

1 PRACTICE

A Underline the correct word.

1. Can you come **on / <u>at</u>** 9:15 A.M. on April first?

2. You need to get here **by / in** 5:00.

3. The clinic is open from 8:00 A.M. **at / to** 5:00 P.M.

4. The office is closed **on / in** Saturday and Sunday.

5. The doctor can see you **from / in** an hour.

6. Dr. Evans has openings **at / from** 3:40 to 5:00 P.M.

7. My appointment is **at / in** 2:30 this afternoon.

B Complete the sentences. Write *on, at, by, in,* or *from ... to.*

1. The dentist has appointments available __on__ June 6 and 7.

2. The doctor can call you back _____ a few minutes.

3. My son's appointment is _____ 4:30 today.

4. The clinic has openings _____ 3:30 _____ 5:00 tomorrow afternoon.

5. The doctor's office closes _____ noon for lunch.

6. Can I come _____ Monday?

7. The doctor wants to see you again _____ a week.

8. The drugstore is open _____ 9:00 A.M. _____ 7:00 P.M.

9. You need to call _____ 5:00 P.M. because the office closes then.

10. Is the office open _____ Saturdays?

A Look at the appointment card. Answer the questions. Complete the sentences with *on*, *at*, *by*, *in*, or *from . . . to*.

John R. Medeiros, M.D.
114 Main St., Springfield, IL 62702
Office hours: M–F 8:00–5:00   (909) 555-1234

APPOINTMENT

FOR: ___Ms. Elizabeth Ruiz___

DATE: ___Wed., Oct. 6___   TIME: ___10:15 A.M.___

Please arrive at least 10 minutes before the time of your appointment.

1. What day is Elizabeth's appointment?

   It is ___on Wednesday___.

2. What time is her appointment?

   It is _____.

3. When is the doctor's office open?

   It is open _____.

4. It is now 8:15 A.M. on October 6. How soon is Elizabeth going to see the doctor?

   She is going to see him _____.

5. What time does Elizabeth need to arrive at the doctor's office?

   She should be there _____.

B PAIRS. Compare your answers.

Show what you know!   Make a doctor's appointment

PAIRS. Student A, look at the notes on this page. Student B, look at the notes on page 247.

Read the notes about the Lee family's appointments. Some information is missing. Take turns. Ask questions with *When* and *What time*. Write the missing information.

A: *When is Walter's dentist appointment?*
B: *On Friday at . . .*

Walter —
dentist, on
_____ at
_____ P.M.

Gloria's checkup with Dr. Rosen, 9:30 A.M., Jan. 10

Jack — blood test at the hospital, 2:30 P.M. on Thurs. (Get there by 2:15.)

Olivia! You need to make an appointment to see Dr. Jay in ___ weeks.

Sue — call the Dr. tomorrow; his office is open from _____ to _____.

Can you... make a doctor's appointment? ☐

Read medicine labels

Life Skills

1 READ OTC MEDICINE LABELS

A CLASS. What over-the-counter medicine do you buy?

B PAIRS. Read the definitions. Then read the medicine label. Find words that have the same meaning as the definitions. Write the words on the lines.

> You can buy over-the-counter (OTC) medicine such as aspirin from any drugstore. For other medicine, you need to get a prescription from a doctor first.

1. for a short time: _temporarily_

2. make better: _____

3. because of: _____

4. make less: _____

5. do not use after this date: _____

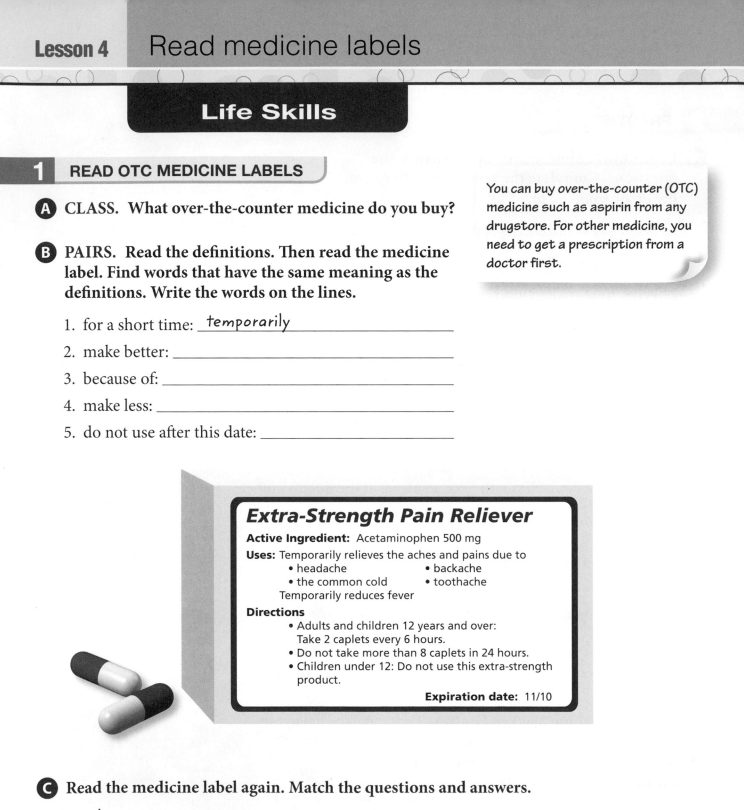

Extra-Strength Pain Reliever

Active Ingredient: Acetaminophen 500 mg

Uses: Temporarily relieves the aches and pains due to
- headache
- backache
- the common cold
- toothache

Temporarily reduces fever

Directions
- Adults and children 12 years and over: Take 2 caplets every 6 hours.
- Do not take more than 8 caplets in 24 hours.
- Children under 12: Do not use this extra-strength product.

Expiration date: 11/10

C Read the medicine label again. Match the questions and answers.

1. _b_ What is this medicine for?   a. November 2010.

2. ____ Who can take this medicine?   b. Aches and pains, and fever.

3. ____ How much do I take?   c. Two caplets every six hours.

4. ____ Who cannot use this product?   d. Children under 12.

5. ____ What is the expiration date?   e. Adults and children over 12.

A CLASS. Look at the prescription and the medicine label. Answer the questions.

Who wrote the prescription?
Who is it for?
Who do you give a prescription to?
Where can you get this medicine?
What information is on the label?

Leora Fishman, M.D.
Greenville Clinic
1123 W. Main St., Ft. Lauderdale, FL 33312
(954) 555-8732

Name _Kate Reed_ Age _36_
Address _25 Scenic Drive, Apt. 21B,_
Fort Lauderdale, FL 33312
Date _06/05/10_
R
Milacam 15 MG

Signature _Leora Fishman_

Bio-Med Pharmacy
Doctor: Leora Fishman
Patient: Kate Reed
Dosage: Take 2 tablespoons by mouth once a day. Take with food.
Warning: Do not take with aspirin.

Milacam 15 MG

2 Refills   Exp: 10/05/12

B Read the medicine label in Exercise A again. Match the questions and answers.

1. __e__ What is the name of the medicine?   a. Two.

2. ____ How often do I take it?   b. Two tablespoons.

3. ____ What is the dosage?   c. October 2012.

4. ____ What is the expiration date?   d. Once a day.

5. ____ How many refills can I get?   e. Milacam.

CD2 T36

C Listen and check your answers. Then listen and repeat.

3 PRACTICE

PAIRS. Take turns being the customer and the pharmacist. Ask and answer the questions in Exercise B about the prescription medicine.

Bio-Med Pharmacy

Doctor: Mark Smith   Patient: Bill Lake

Dosage: Put one drop in each eye every 4 to 6 hours for seven days.

Warning: For the eyes only.

Polymazin B Eyedrops

No Refills   Exp: 08/12/11

Bio-Med Pharmacy

Doctor: Paul Jones   Patient: Mei-Yu Sun

Dosage: Apply to affected skin 3 times a day for seven days.

Warning: For external use only. Do not eat. Do not put in eyes.

Bactobane 2% Ointment

1 Refill   Exp: 12/02/11

4 LIFE SKILLS WRITING   Complete a medical history form. See page 262.

Can you...read medicine labels?

Listening and Speaking

1 BEFORE YOU LISTEN

A Look at the pictures. Match each picture with a sentence from the box.
Write the sentences on the lines.

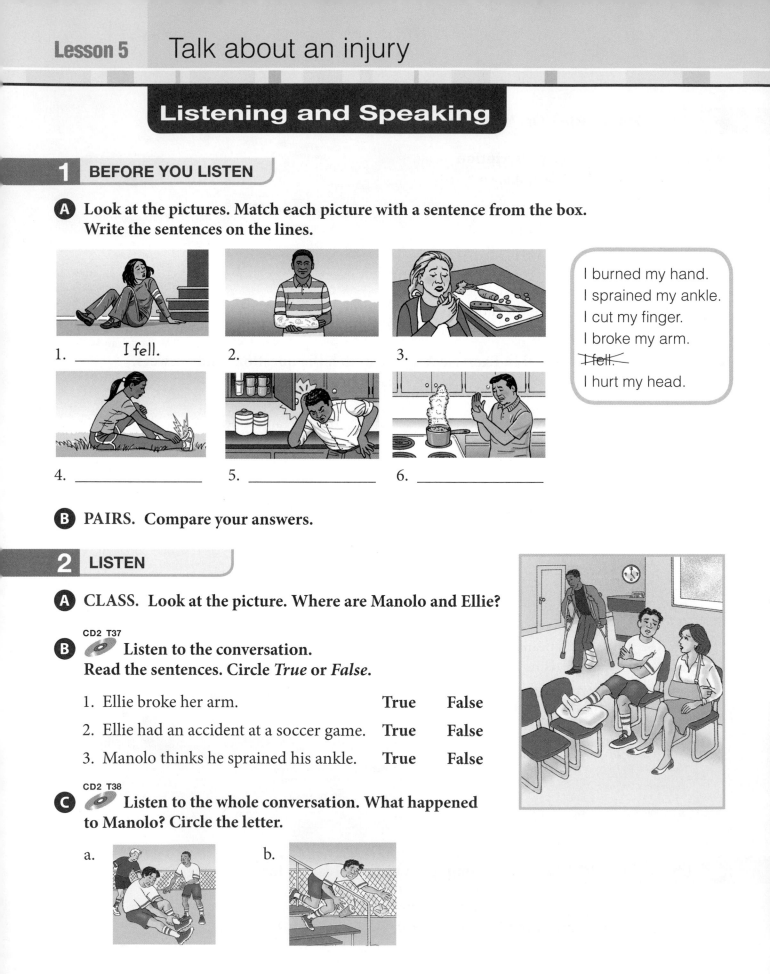

1. _____I fell._____   2. _____   3. _____

I burned my hand.
I sprained my ankle.
I cut my finger.
I broke my arm.
~~I fell.~~
I hurt my head.

4. _____   5. _____   6. _____

B PAIRS. Compare your answers.

2 LISTEN

A CLASS. Look at the picture. Where are Manolo and Ellie?

B CD2 T37 Listen to the conversation.
Read the sentences. Circle *True* or *False*.

1. Ellie broke her arm.   **True   False**

2. Ellie had an accident at a soccer game. **True   False**

3. Manolo thinks he sprained his ankle.   **True   False**

C CD2 T38 Listen to the whole conversation. What happened
to Manolo? Circle the letter.

a.   b.

3 CONVERSATION

Pronunciation Watch

When the letter *t* is between two vowel sounds, it often sounds like a quick /d/ in North American English.

A CD2 T39  **Listen to the sentences. Notice the pronunciation of the underlined *t*'s. Then listen and repeat.**

Wha<u>t</u> are you doing here?
I was a<u>t</u> a soccer game.
What's the ma<u>tt</u>er?

B CD2 T40  **Listen to the sentences. Which underlined *t*'s have the sound /d/? Circle the numbers.**

1. Wha<u>t</u> about you?
2. I hur<u>t</u> my ankle.

3. Tha<u>t</u>'s too bad.
4. See you la<u>t</u>er.

C CD2 T41  **Listen and repeat the conversation.**

Manolo: Hi, Ellie. What are you doing here?
Ellie: Oh, hi, Manolo. I had an accident. I broke my arm.
Manolo: Oh, no! I'm sorry to hear that.
Ellie: Thanks. What about you?
Manolo: I hurt my ankle at a soccer game. I think I sprained it.
Ellie: That's too bad.

4 PRACTICE

A **PAIRS. Practice the conversation. Then make new conversations. Use your own names and the information in the boxes.**

A: Hi, _____. What are you doing here?
B: Oh, hi, _____. I had an accident. _____
A: Oh, no! I'm sorry to hear that.
B: Thanks. What about you?
A: I hurt my _____ at a soccer game. I think I sprained it.
B: That's too bad.

I cut my hand.
I burned my finger.
I fell.

foot
wrist
back

B **ROLE PLAY. PAIRS. Make your own conversations. Use your own names and different information.**

Talk about an injury

Grammar

Simple past: Irregular verbs

Affirmative		
Ellie	**had**	an accident.
She	**broke**	her arm.
Manolo	**got**	hurt.
He	**hurt**	his ankle.

Grammar Watch

Common irregular verbs

Base form	Past-tense form	Base form	Past-tense form
break	**broke**	get	**got**
cut	**cut**	have	**had**
fall	**fell**	hurt	**hurt**

• See page 286 for more past-tense forms.

1 PRACTICE

A Complete the sentences. Underline the correct verbs.

1. I don't want my son to play soccer. Sometimes players **get** / got hurt.

2. Oh, no! I think I **break / broke** my leg.

3. Pilar **cuts / cut** her finger and went to the hospital.

4. He **hurts / hurt** his ankle on the stairs yesterday.

5. My grandfather sometimes **falls / fell** in the house. I'm worried.

6. They **have / had** an accident last Saturday.

7. My son **breaks / broke** his foot and went to the emergency room.

8. My daughter is sick today. She **has / had** a sore throat.

B Write sentences about the past. Use a verb from the box.

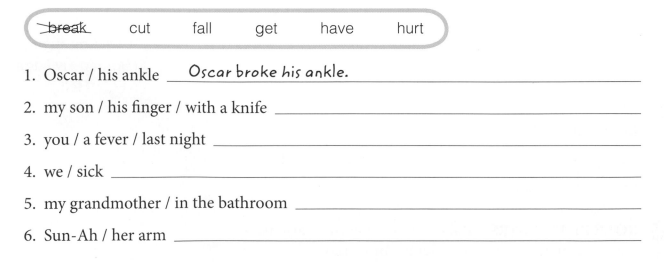

~~break~~   cut   fall   get   have   hurt

1. Oscar / his ankle ___Oscar broke his ankle.___

2. my son / his finger / with a knife _____

3. you / a fever / last night _____

4. we / sick _____

5. my grandmother / in the bathroom _____

6. Sun-Ah / her arm _____

A PAIRS. Look at the pictures. What happened last weekend? Decide together.

Jessica had an accident in the kitchen. She . . .

1. Jessica

2. David

3. EMERGENCY — Emery

4. Denise

B WRITE. On a separate piece of paper, write two sentences about each picture in Exercise A. Write about what happened.

Show what you know! Talk about an injury

STEP 1. Complete the questions.

Did you ever hurt _____?

Did you ever break _____?

Did you ever have _____?

STEP 2. GROUPS OF 5. Ask your partners your questions. Take notes.

A: *Did you ever break your toe?*
B: *No, but I broke my finger at work last year.*

STEP 3. Tell the class about your partners.

Can you . . . talk about an injury? ☐

Reading

1 BEFORE YOU READ

A CLASS. What is stress? When do you feel stressed?

B PAIRS. Scan the article. Look at the words and sentences in color. Answer the questions.

1. What two questions does the article answer?

2. What are four causes of stress?

Reading Skill: Using Formatting Clues

Authors sometimes use formatting such as boldface type, bullets, and color to help readers find the main points.

2 READ

CD2 T42

Listen. Read the article.

STRESS

Everyone feels stress sometimes. But some people have so much stress that they become sick.

What causes stress?

Change   The biggest source of stress is change. It may be a bad change, like losing a job or getting divorced. But even a good change, like going on vacation, causes stress!

Loss of Control   You also feel stress in situations that are out of your control. Maybe you are stuck in traffic or your kids are sick. When you can't change the bad things in your life, you feel stress.

Negative Attitudes   The way you think can cause stress. For example, you worry a lot or you think too much about the bad things in your life. These kinds of negative attitudes cause stress.

Unhealthy Habits   Finally, the way you live can cause stress. Do you eat too much junk food? Do you work too many hours? These kinds of unhealthy habits add stress to your life.

How can you manage stress?

• Find out what causes stress in your life. Pay attention to the times you feel stressed out.

• Think about ways to change the things that cause you stress.

• Accept the things you can't change. Sometimes you can't avoid a stressful situation. You need to find a way to live with it.

• Talk about it. Sometimes you need help. Talk about your stress with a family member, friend, counselor, or doctor.

A Read the article again. Circle *True* or *False*.

1. Even good changes, like getting married, can cause stress.	**True**	**False**
2. Being in a situation you can't control causes stress.	**True**	**False**
3. Eating too much junk food is an example of a negative attitude.	**True**	**False**
4. You can always avoid stressful situations.	**True**	**False**
5. Talking with someone can help you manage stress.	**True**	**False**

B Take the stress quiz. Then count your points. How much stress do you have?

Stress Quiz

Circle the number that is true for you.

	Never		Sometimes		Every day
1. I get headaches.	1	2	3	4	5
2. I get stomachaches.	1	2	3	4	5
3. I have trouble sleeping.	1	2	3	4	5
4. I can't concentrate.	1	2	3	4	5
5. I worry about small things.	1	2	3	4	5
6. I get angry easily.	1	2	3	4	5
7. I want to be alone.	1	2	3	4	5
8. I argue with my friends and family.	1	2	3	4	5

Total Score ___ + ___ + ___ + ___ + ___ = ___

Not Much Stress 8–18   Some Stress 19–29   A lot of Stress 30–40

C PAIRS. Compare your scores. Talk about how stress affects your life.

My score is 30. I get headaches at work and have trouble sleeping . . .

Show what you know!

PRE-WRITING. Write a list of things in your life that cause stress.

NETWORK. Find classmates with the same causes of stress. Form a group. Talk about ways you can manage stress.

WRITE. Write about the stress in your life. See page 271.

Listening and Speaking

1 BEFORE YOU LISTEN

A READ. CLASS. Look at the picture and read about Hugo. Then answer the questions.

> Hugo is at the dental clinic. He woke up with a bad toothache this morning. He was supposed to work from 10:00 A.M. to 6:00 P.M. today. At 9:30, he called his supervisor and explained his problem. He had to miss work today.

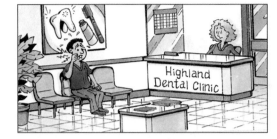

1. What is Hugo's problem?

2. Why did Hugo call his work supervisor?

B CLASS. Have you ever had to miss work or school?

2 LISTEN

CD2 T43

A Look at the pictures of Soo-Jin calling her work supervisor. Listen to the conversation. Answer the questions.

1. Why is Soo-Jin calling?
   a. She's going to be late.
   b. She's going to miss work.

2. Where is Soo-Jin going?
   a. to the hospital
   b. to the doctor's office
   c. to the dentist's office

CD2 T44

B Listen to the whole conversation. What is Soo-Jin going to do later?

a. call her supervisor
b. go to work
c. call the doctor

3 | CONVERSATION

CD2 T45

A **Listen to the sentences. Notice the thought groups. Then listen and repeat.**

I'm sorry / to hear that.
Do you think / you'll be in / tomorrow?
I have to / take my son / to the clinic.

Pronunciation Watch

We use pauses to break sentences into smaller thought groups. These pauses make sentences easier to say. They also organize the meaning of the sentence. This helps the listener understand.

CD2 T46

B **Listen and repeat the conversation.**

Paula: Hello. Paula Charles speaking.

Soo-Jin: Hi, Paula. This is Soo-Jin. I can't come in today because I have to go to the doctor. I don't feel well.

Paula: Sorry to hear that. Thanks for calling, and take care of yourself.

Soo-Jin: Thanks.

4 | PRACTICE

A PAIRS. Practice the conversation. Then make new conversations. Use your own names and the information in the boxes.

A: Hello. _____ speaking.

B: Hi, _____. This is _____. I can't come in today because

I have to _____. _____

A: Sorry to hear that. Thanks for calling, and _____.

B: Thanks.

take my son to the clinic	He has a fever.	I hope he feels better
take care of my mother	She's sick.	I hope she gets well soon
go to the dentist	I broke my tooth.	good luck

B ROLE PLAY. PAIRS. Make your own conversations. Use your own names and different information.

Call in when you have to miss work

Grammar

Ways to express reasons		
Soo-Jin missed work yesterday	**because**	she didn't feel well.
She went to the doctor	**for**	a prescription.

Grammar Watch

- Use *because* + a subject and a verb.
- Use *for* + a noun.

PRACTICE

A Complete the sentences. Write *because* or *for*.

1. I can't go to school __because__ I have a cold.

2. I have to go to the drugstore _____ some medicine.

3. My wife is going to the doctor _____ a blood test.

4. Carlo went to the clinic _____ he hurt his back.

5. I went to the store _____ some cold medicine.

6. I was absent yesterday _____ I had a fever.

B Look at the words. Where do the people have to go? Why? Write one sentence with *because* and one sentence with *for*.

1. Jack / the pharmacy / some medicine

   Jack has to go to the pharmacy because he needs some medicine.

   _____

2. Janelle / the doctor / a flu shot

   _____

   _____

3. Gladys / the dentist / a checkup

   _____

   _____

1 GRAMMAR

A Complete the sentences. Use the simple past of a verb from the box.

> break   cut   fall   get   ~~have~~

1. I ___had___ a cold for three weeks, but now I feel fine.

2. Poor Rosa! She _____ down the stairs and hurt her back.

3. Henry had an accident at work and _____ a bone in his foot.

4. Be careful with that knife. Jim _____ his hand with it yesterday.

5. I went to the doctor's office, and I _____ a prescription.

B Complete the conversations. Use the words in the boxes.

> at   by   for   ~~on~~

1. **A:** What are you doing ___on___ Wednesday afternoon?

   B: I'm going _____ a checkup.

   A: When is your appointment?

   B: It's _____ 4:30, but I need to go early. They want me to
   be there _____ 4:15.

> at   because   by   from   in   to

2. **A:** I need to see a doctor _____ I think I have an infection.

   B: Can you be here _____ an hour?

   A: I'm sorry, I can't. I work _____ 3:00 _____ 11:00.

   B: How about tomorrow? We have an opening _____ 9:00.

   A: That's fine. Thank you.

   B: OK. Please be here _____ 8:45.

2 ACT IT OUT   What do you say?

STEP 1. CLASS. Review the Lesson 2 conversation between the receptionist and Roberto (CD 2 track 33).

STEP 2. ROLE PLAY. PAIRS. Student A, you are the patient. Student B, you are the receptionist at the doctor's office.

> **Student A:**
> • Call the doctor's office and ask for an appointment.
> • Explain your medical problem.
> • Agree on a time you can come.

> **Student B:**
> • Ask about the patient's health problem.
> • Suggest a time for the appointment.

3 READ AND REACT   Problem-solving

STEP 1. Read about Ramona's problem.

Ramona has a coworker named Mike. Mike often calls in late or sick to work. Tonight he calls in sick again. Ramona knows that he is not sick. She knows that Mike plans to attend a baseball game tonight. Ramona's boss asks her to cover Mike's hours. Ramona doesn't want to work late tonight.

STEP 2. PAIRS. What is Ramona's problem? What can she do? Here are some ideas.

- She can work late.
- She can tell her boss that Mike is not really sick.
- She can say, "I'm sorry, I can't work late tonight."
- She can _____.

4 CONNECT   For your Goal-setting Activity, go to page 252.
For your Team Project, go to page 280.

Which goals can you check off? Go back to page 125.

Job Hunting

Preview

Look at the title of the unit and the picture. What are the people doing?

UNIT GOALS

- ☐ Identify job duties
- ☐ Talk about your skills at a job interview
- ☐ Read help-wanted ads
- ☐ Complete a job application
- ☐ Answer questions about work history
- ☐ Answer questions about availability

1 WHAT DO YOU KNOW?

A CLASS. Look at the pictures. Which jobs do you know? Use words from the box.

> computer system administrator
> food service worker
> manager
> nurse assistant
> receptionist
> sales associate
> stock clerk
> warehouse worker

B CLASS. Look at the pictures. What are some duties, or things you have to do, for each job?

C CD2 T47 Listen to the job duties. Then listen and repeat.

2 PRACTICE

A PAIRS. Student A, say a job from *What do you know?* Student B, say two job duties for that job.

A: *Manager.*
B: *Plan work schedules. Supervise employees.*

B WORD PLAY. GROUPS OF 3. Look at the list of job duties. On a separate piece of paper, write another job duty for each job.

1A

1B

3A

3B

5A

5B

7A

7B

2A

2B

4A

4B

6A

6B

Job Duties

1A. install computer hardware
1B. help with computer problems

2A. take care of patients
2B. record patient information

3A. receive shipments
3B. unload materials

4A. assist customers
4B. stock shelves

5A. greet visitors
5B. handle phone calls

6A. prepare food
6B. clean kitchen equipment

7A. supervise employees
7B. plan work schedules

Learning Strategy

Make connections

Look at the list of job duties. Make cards for five new words. Write a job duty on one side of the card. Write a job that matches that duty on the other side.

Show what you know!

STEP 1. Think of your dream job. What is the title of your job? What are the duties?

Job title: _____

Job duties: _____ _____ _____

STEP 2. GROUPS OF 3. Tell your classmates about your dream job.

Listening and Speaking

1   BEFORE YOU LISTEN

CLASS. Look at the job skills. Which skills do you have?

operate a forklift

use a word-processing program

use a cash register

order supplies

type

speak Spanish

2   LISTEN

A   CLASS. Look at the picture of Albert and Manny. Guess: What is happening?

CD2 T48
B   Listen to the conversation. Was your guess in Exercise A correct?

CD2 T48
C   Listen again. Complete the sentences.

1. _____ is a store manager.
   a. Manny   b. Albert

2. _____ is looking for a job.
   a. Manny   b. Albert

3. Manny assists customers and _____ at his job.
   a. stocks shelves   b. orders supplies

4. Manny _____ use a cash register.
   a. can   b. can't

3 CONVERSATION

CD2 T49

A 💿 Listen. Then listen and repeat the sentences.

I can't use a cash register.   I can learn.
Can you speak Chinese?   Yes, I can.

CD2 T50

B 💿 Listen and repeat the conversation.

Albert: Manny? Hi, I'm Albert Taylor, the store manager.
Please have a seat.

Manny: Thank you. It's nice to meet you.

Albert: I have your application here. I see that you are working now.
What are your job duties?

Manny: Well, I assist customers and stock shelves.

Albert: OK. Tell me about your skills. Can you use a cash register?

Manny: No, I can't, but I can learn.

Pronunciation Watch

Can often has a weak pronunciation with a short, quiet vowel when another word comes after it. It sounds like "c'n." *Can* has a strong pronunciation at the end of a sentence. *Can't* always has a strong pronunciation.

4 PRACTICE

A PAIRS. Practice the conversation. Then make new conversations. Use your own names and the information in the boxes.

A: _____? Hi, I'm _____, the store manager.
Please have a seat.

B: Thank you. It's nice to meet you.

A: I have your application here. I see that you are working now.
What are your job duties?

B: Well, I _____ and _____.

A: OK. Tell me more about your skills. Can you _____?

B: No, I can't, but I can learn.

receive shipments	unload materials	operate a forklift
greet visitors	handle phone calls	type
prepare food	clean equipment	order supplies

B ROLE PLAY. PAIRS. Make your own conversations. Use different information.

Grammar

Can to express ability

Affirmative		
You Manny We	**can**	stock shelves.

Negative		
I They She	**cannot** **can't**	**speak** Chinese.

Yes/No questions		
Can	you	**use** a cash register?

Short answers				
Yes,	I	**can.**	**No,** I	**can't.**

1 PRACTICE

A Look at the pictures. Write one question with *can* for each picture.

1. Can Nadia lift heavy boxes?
_____

2. _____
_____

3. _____
_____

B PAIRS. Ask and answer the questions in Exercise A.

A: *Can Nadia lift heavy boxes?*
B: *No, she can't.*

2 PRACTICE

A **PAIRS.** Look at Luisa's job application. Ask and answer questions about Luisa's skills. Use *can*.

A: *Can Luisa use a computer?*
B: *No, she can't.*

Luisa Ruiz

Please check the skills you have.

Office skills
- ❑ use a computer
- ☑ answer the phone
- ☑ record information

Warehouse skills
- ❑ operate a forklift
- ☑ sort materials
- ❑ lift up to 50 lbs.

B **WRITE.** Write sentences about Luisa's skills. Use *can* and *can't*.

1. Luisa can't use a computer.
2. _____
3. _____
4. _____
5. _____
6. _____

C **WRITE.** Look at the skills on the application in Exercise A. Write sentences about things you can and can't do.

1. _____
2. _____
3. _____
4. _____

Show what you know!   Talk about your skills at a job interview

STEP 1. Write three questions to ask your group about their job skills.

Question	Name	Answer
Can you use a computer?	Paola	Yes
1. Can you		
2. Can you		
3. Can you		

STEP 2. GROUPS OF 4. Interview each member of your group. Ask one of your questions. Complete the chart in Step 1.

STEP 3. Tell the class about your group's job skills.

Paola can use a computer. Juan can . . .

Can you...talk about your skills at a job interview? ❑

Life Skills

1 **READ HELP-WANTED ADS**

A **CLASS.** Look at the help-wanted ads. Where can you find these ads? Where else can people find out about jobs?

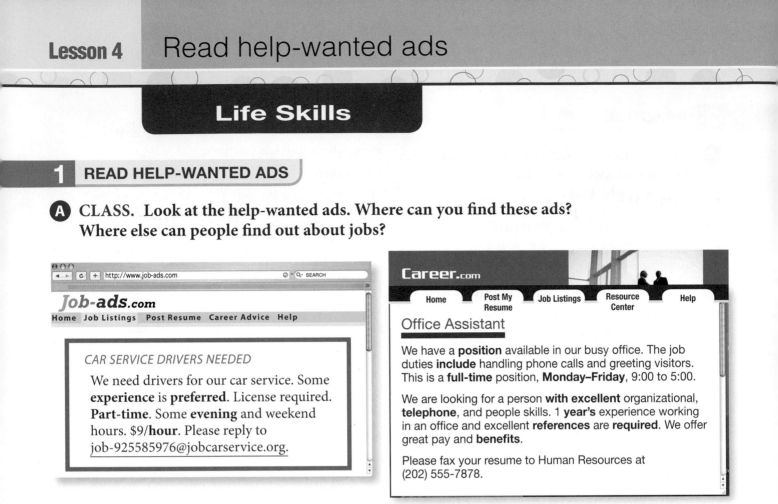

Job-ads.com
http://www.job-ads.com

Home   Job Listings   Post Resume   Career Advice   Help

CAR SERVICE DRIVERS NEEDED

We need drivers for our car service. Some **experience** is **preferred**. License required. **Part-time**. Some **evening** and weekend hours. $9/**hour**. Please reply to job-925585976@jobcarservice.org.

Career.com

Home   Post My Resume   Job Listings   Resource Center   Help

Office Assistant

We have a **position** available in our busy office. The job duties **include** handling phone calls and greeting visitors. This is a **full-time** position, **Monday–Friday**, 9:00 to 5:00.

We are looking for a person **with excellent** organizational, **telephone**, and people skills. 1 **year's** experience working in an office and excellent **references** are **required**. We offer great pay and **benefits**.

Please fax your resume to Human Resources at (202) 555-7878.

B Read the help-wanted ads. Look at the words in bold.
Match the words and the abbreviations. Write the full words.

1. hr.   _hour_
2. M–F   _____
3. PT   _____
4. FT   _____
5. excel.   _____
6. yr.   _____
7. tel.   _____
8. pos.   _____

9. bnfts.   _____
10. req.   _____
11. pref.   _____
12. exp.   _____
13. ref.   _____
14. incl.   _____
15. w/   _____
16. eve.   _____

C **PAIRS.** Compare your answers.

D **PAIRS.** Read the help-wanted ads again. Student A, describe the car service driver job. Student B, describe the office assistant job.

A Read the help-wanted ads. Then read the sentences. Write the letter of the job.

HELP WANTED		
RECEPTIONIST FT pos. M-F in busy medical office. 2 yr. exp. req. Need good computer and tel. skills. Great pay and bnfts. FAX resume to (802) 555-2149 or send to gmoss@HealthPractice.com.	**STORE MANAGER** FT pos. avail. Duties incl. supervise employees, plan work schedule, assist customers. Looking for a person w/ excel. people skills. 1 yr. manager exp. req. Exp. in office supply stores pref. Excel. ref. req. Some weekend hrs. Call Manuel for an interview at (802) 555-9814.	**SALES ASSOCIATE AT JOE'S COOL CLOTHES** PT. eve. and weekend hrs. $10/hr. No exp. necessary. Apply in person at store. Liberty Mall. No calls, please.
a	b	c

1. __c__ This is a part-time job.

2. _____ This job has good benefits.

3. _____ This job pays $10 an hour.

4. _____ Go to the store to apply for this job.

5. _____ Call the store to apply for this job.

6. _____ Send a résumé to apply for this job.

7. _____ You need excellent people skills for this job.

8. _____ You need excellent references to get this job.

9. _____ You need two years' experience for this job.

10. _____ You don't need experience for this job.

B PAIRS. Compare your answers.

C GROUPS OF 3. Look at the ads on this page and on page 152. Which job are you interested in? Why?

I'm interested in the receptionist job because I need a full-time job.

3 LIFE SKILLS WRITING Complete a job application. See page 263.

Can you... read help-wanted ads? ☐

Listening and Speaking

1 BEFORE YOU LISTEN

A CLASS. Look at the people. Read the reasons they changed jobs. What are some other reasons people change jobs?

B PAIRS. Have you ever changed jobs? What was the reason?

I'd like to make more money.

I'd like a different schedule.

I'd like a job closer to home.

I'd like to do something different.

2 LISTEN

CD2 T51

A Listen to more of Manny's job interview. Put the events in the order they happened.

1. _____ Manny got a job as a stock clerk.

2. _____ Manny came to the U.S.

3. _____ Manny got a job as a gardener.

CD2 T51

B Listen again. Why does Manny want to change jobs?

CD2 T52

C Listen to the whole conversation. Manny says he was unemployed. What does *unemployed* mean?

CD2 T52

D Listen to the whole conversation again. Answer the questions.

1. When was Manny unemployed?
   a. two months ago   b. two years ago

2. Why was Manny unemployed?
   a. His mother was sick.   b. He was sick.

3. How long was Manny unemployed?
   a. for two years   b. for two months

CD2 T53

Listen and repeat the conversation.

Albert: So, tell me more about your work experience.

Manny: Well, I came to the U.S. three years ago. First, I got a job as a gardener. Then last year I got a job as a stock clerk.

Albert: OK. So now you're a stock clerk. Why are you looking for another job?

Manny: Things in my life have changed, and now I'd like to do something different.

4 PRACTICE

A **PAIRS.** Practice the conversation. Then make new conversations. Use the information in the boxes.

A: So, tell me more about your work experience.

B: Well, I came to the U.S. _____ ago. First, I got a job as a _____ . Then last year I got a job as a _____ ,.

A: OK. So now you're a _____ . Why are you looking for another job?

B: Things in my life have changed, and now I'd like _____ .

a year	warehouse worker	truck driver	to make more money
a few years	nurse assistant	receptionist	a different schedule
ten months	food service worker	cook	a job closer to home

B **ROLE PLAY. PAIRS.** Make your own conversations. Use different information.

Grammar

Time expressions with *ago*, *last*, *in*, and *later*

I came to the U.S.	three years 10 months	ago.	One month		I started school.
I got a job	last	year. week.	Two days	later,	I got a better job.
I changed jobs	in	July. the fall.	A week		I was unemployed.

1 PRACTICE

A   Complete the sentences. Use the words in the boxes.

1.
> ~~ago~~
> in
> last

Teresa came to the U.S. two years ___ago___. She studied

English _____ year. She got a job _____ December.

2.
> ago
> last
> later

Six months _____, Mei-Li came to the U.S. She started work in a

factory one month _____. She left that job _____ week

because she got a better job.

3.
> in
> last
> later

_____ 2004, Mohammed came to the U.S. One year _____,

he got a job in a supermarket. He got a new job in a warehouse

_____ month.

B   Write each statement a different way. Use *ago* or *in*.

1. Tina got a new job last month.   _Tina got a new job a month ago._

2. Inez learned to use a computer in 2001. _____

3. Frank got his job a year ago. _____

4. Walter left his job in January. _____

5. Louise started school six months ago. _____

6. Beatriz changed jobs last week. _____

A **WRITE.** Look at the time line. Write a short paragraph about Aram. Use *in*, *ago*, and *later*. There is more than one correct answer.

May, 2005
came to the U.S.

June, 2005
started English classes

January, 2006
got his first job

July, 2007
got a better job

December, 2009
became a supervisor

Aram came to the U.S. in May, 2005.
_____

_____

B **PAIRS.** Compare your paragraphs.

Show what you know! Answer questions about work history

STEP 1. Answer the questions about yourself. Use *in*, *ago*, or *later*.

1. When did you come to this country?_____
2. When did you start school here? _____

STEP 2. GROUPS OF 5. Take turns asking *When did you come here?*
Draw a time line to show when each person in the group came here.

Viktor: *I came here in July.*
Indira: *I came here four months ago.*

Viktor   Indira

July   September

STEP 3. Draw your time line on the board. Explain it to the class.

Can you... answer questions about work history? ☐

Reading

1 BEFORE YOU READ

A CLASS. Look at the pictures. Talk about the job market for these fields of employment in your area. Which fields have many jobs available?

agriculture technology health care manufacturing

B CLASS. Look at the title of the article and the pictures. Predict: What do you think is the topic of the article?

Reading Skill: Predicting the Topic

You can often guess what an article is about by looking at the title and any pictures. This will prepare you to understand what you read.

2 READ

CD2 T54

Listen. Read the article. Was your guess in Exercise B correct?

Today's Hot Jobs

The U.S. job market is changing fast. In 1900, 41 percent of workers had jobs on farms. Now only 2 percent of workers have agricultural jobs. In 1950, 25 percent of workers had jobs in manufacturing. Now only 12.5 percent have manufacturing jobs. So what fields of employment are growing today?

Health Care
Many of the fastest-growing jobs are in health care. The U.S. population is getting older. These older Americans need medical care and help with daily living. The greatest need is for home health aides

and physician assistants. Home health aides take care of patients in their homes. Physician assistants help doctors in a clinic or hospital.

Technology
As the field of technology changes, the jobs change, too. In the 1980s, most technology workers

were computer programmers. Now there is more need for network analysts, web designers, and software engineers. Network analysts make sure e-mail and Internet communications are working well. Web designers create Internet sites. Software engineers develop software like games and word-processing programs.

Today's jobs are in health care and technology. The job market continues to change quickly. Where will tomorrow's jobs be?

Source: U.S. Department of Labor

A Read the article again. What is the main idea?

    a. The number of jobs in the U.S. is growing.

    b. The U.S. job market is changing fast.

    c. Many of the fastest-growing jobs are in health care.

B Read the sentences. Circle *True* or *False*.

1. In 1900, 2 percent of workers in the U.S. had agricultural jobs.	True	False
2. Today, 12.5 percent of workers have jobs in manufacturing.	True	False
3. The field of health care is growing because people are getting older.	True	False
4. The number of home health aides is increasing.	True	False
5. Employers need workers with Internet skills.	True	False
6. Network analysts plan and make Internet sites.	True	False
7. Most technology workers are computer programmers now.	True	False

C What are the fastest-growing jobs in the following fields? Complete the chart.

Health Care		
Technology		

Show what you know!

PRE-WRITING. What job do you want to have in five years? What do you need to do to get that job? Write notes.

> *nurse assistant — learn English, . . .*

NETWORK. Find classmates who want to have the same job in five years. Form a group. Talk about the things you need to do to get the job.

WRITE. Write about the job you want in five years. See page 271.

Answer questions about availability

Listening and Speaking

1 BEFORE YOU LISTEN

A PAIRS. Read the information about job interviews. Look at the words in boldface. What do the words mean?

At a job interview, the interviewer asks you about your **availability**. For example, "Which **shift** can you work, day or night? and "Can you work on weekends?" The interviewer may ask if your hours are **flexible**. For example, "Can you work different hours if the schedule changes?" The interviewer also asks when you can start. If you are working, you should give your boss one or two weeks' **notice** that you are leaving your job. This will help your boss find a new employee to fill your position when you leave.

B CLASS. Do you work? What are your work hours? Do you like your work schedule?

2 LISTEN

CD2 T55

A 💿 Listen to the end of Manny's interview. When does Manny prefer to work? Check all the correct answers.

☐ mornings   ☐ afternoons

CD2 T55

B 💿 Listen again. When can Manny start work?

a. tomorrow   b. in two weeks   c. in two days

CD2 T56

C 💿 Listen to the whole conversation. Answer the questions.

1. Manny asks, "When can I expect to hear from you?" What does this mean?

2. At the end of the interview, does Manny know if he got the job?

3 CONVERSATION

A 💿 **Listen to the questions. Then listen and repeat.**

Pronunciation Watch

Some questions with *or* ask the listener to make a choice. In these questions, the voice goes up on the first choice and down on the last choice.

Do you prefer mornings or afternoons?

Can you work first shift or second shift?

Do you work days or nights?

CD2 T58

B 💿 **Listen and repeat the conversation.**

Albert: Let me ask you a few questions about your availability. Do you prefer mornings or afternoons?

Manny: Well, I prefer mornings, but I'm flexible.

Albert: All right. Can you work on weekends?

Manny: Yes, I can.

Albert: Great. And when could you start?

Manny: In two weeks. I need to give two weeks' notice at my job.

4 PRACTICE

A PAIRS. Practice the conversation. Then make new conversations. Use the information in the boxes and your own information.

A: Let me ask you a few questions about your availability.

Do you prefer   ?

B: Well, I prefer   , but I'm flexible.

A: All right. Can you work on   ?

B: Yes, I can.

A: Great. And when could you start?

B: In two weeks. I need to give two weeks' notice at my job.

first or second shift	first shift	Saturdays
days or nights	days	Sundays

B ROLE PLAY. PAIRS. Make your own conversations. Use different information.

Answer questions about availability

Grammar

Ways to express alternatives: *or*, *and*

He can work mornings	**or**	afternoons.
They can work Saturdays	**and**	Sundays.
I can't work Mondays	**or**	Tuesdays.

> **Grammar Watch**
>
> Use *or* (not *and*) in negative statements.

PRACTICE

A Complete the conversations. Write *and* or *or*.

1. **A:** Which shift do you prefer?

   B: I'm flexible. I can work first shift _____or_____ second shift.

2. **A:** Can you work weekends?

   B: Sure! I can work both Saturday _____ Sunday. I want a lot of hours.

3. **A:** Can you work both Saturday and Sunday?

   B: I'll be happy to work Saturday _____ Sunday, but I can't work both days.

4. **A:** Can you take classes in the morning _____ in the evening?

   B: In the morning. I can't take classes in the evening because I work second shift.

B Look at Carlos's and Nadia's job applications. Write two sentences about each person's availability. Use *or* with *can* and *can't*.

1. Carlos can work second shift or third shift.

2. _____

___Carlos Hernandez___

When can you work? Check the boxes.

first shift ☐ second shift ☑ third shift ☑ weekends ☐

3. _____

4. _____

___Nadia Perez___

When can you work? Check the boxes.

first shift ☑ second shift ☑ third shift ☐ weekends ☐

C WRITE. Write two sentences about your own work availability. Use *or* with *can* and *can't*.

1 GRAMMAR

A Complete the parts of a job interview. Use *can* and *can't*. Use the words in parentheses.

Manager: _____*Can you use*_____ a cash register?
                   (you / use)

Terry: No, I _____, but _____.
                                        (I / learn)

Manager: OK, well, maybe _____ shelves at first.
                              (you / stock)

Terry: Sure. _____ that.
                  (I / do)

Manager: Do you prefer afternoons or evenings?

Terry: _____ in the afternoon or in the evening. I'm flexible.
            (I / work)

Manager: _____ on weekends?
              (you / work)

Terry: Sure. On the weekend, _____ mornings, afternoons,
                                  (I / work)
or evenings.

Manager: _____ tomorrow?
              (you / start)

Terry: Yes, _____.

B Complete the sentences. Use *ago, and, in, last, later,* and *or*.

Ali Osman came to the U.S. _____*in*_____ 2005. One month _____,
                                1.   2.
he started school. He got his first job _____ 2006. It was in a hospital, and
                                          3.
he worked nights. Ali didn't like his work schedule. A few weeks _____, his
                                                                    4.
boss asked, "Ali, do you prefer days _____ nights?" Ali said, "I prefer days."
                                        5.
A week _____, he changed his hours.
         6.

Ali continued to go to school. _____ year, he had classes three nights a
                                 7.
week: on Monday, Tuesday, _____ Thursday. This year, he's going to school
                            8.
_____ the morning. He changed jobs a few weeks _____ . He has a
    9.   10.
better job at a different hospital. But now he works from 12:00 P.M. to 8:00 P.M., so
he can't go to class in the afternoon _____ the evening.
                                        11.

Go to the CD-ROM for more practice.

2 | ACT IT OUT — What do you say?

STEP 1. CLASS. Review Albert and Manny's job interview in Lessons 2, 5, and 8 (CD 2 tracks 48, 51, and 55).

STEP 2. PAIRS. Student A, you are a job interviewer. Student B, you are applying for a job.

> **Student A:** ask about the applicant's:
> • job skills
> • work history
> • availability

> **Student B:** answer the interviewer's questions about your skills, work experience, and availability.

3 | READ AND REACT — Problem-solving

STEP 1. Read about Marco's problem.

Marco is unemployed. He has a job interview tomorrow. At his last job, he had a problem. He made a mistake and his boss fired him. Marco does not think his boss was right. Marco is worried that the interviewer will ask, "Why did you leave your last job?" He doesn't know how to answer the question.

STEP 2. PAIRS. What is Marco's problem? What can he do? Here are some ideas.

- He can say, "I left my last job because I wanted a different schedule."
- He can say, "I was fired" and then explain what he learned.
- He can say, "I was fired" and explain why his boss was not fair.
- He can _____.

4 | CONNECT

For your Community-building Activity, go to page 252.
For your Team Project, go to page 281.

Which goals can you check off? Go back to page 145.

Parents and Children

Preview

**Look at the picture.
Who are the people?
What are they doing?**

UNIT GOALS

- ☐ Identify school subjects

- ☐ Make plans for school events

- ☐ Take a phone message

- ☐ Complete a school enrollment form

- ☐ Talk about progress in school

- ☐ Discuss your child's behavior in school

1 WHAT DO YOU KNOW?

A CLASS. Look at the pictures. Which school subjects do you know?

B CD3 T2 Look at the pictures and listen. Then listen and repeat.

2 PRACTICE

A WORD PLAY. PAIRS. Choose a school subject from the vocabulary list. Don't tell your partner. Write three clues for the word. Your partner will guess the word.

> art: paint, draw, color

Student A, read your clues. Student B, guess after each clue. Take turns.

A: *Paint.*
B: *Art?*
A: *Right!*

B What schools are in your community? Find out and write the names of schools you know. Talk about your list with the class.

School	Name of school
preschool	
elementary school	
middle school	
high school	

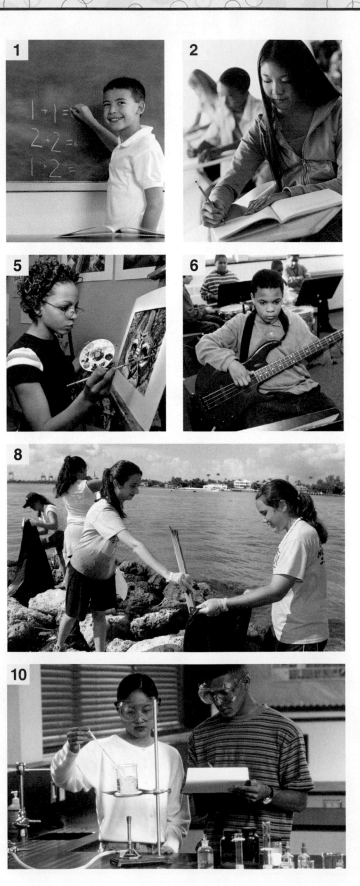

4

7

9

School Subjects

1. math
2. language arts/English
3. P.E. (physical education)
4. social studies/history
5. art
6. music
7. technology
8. community service
9. world languages
10. science

Learning Strategy

Use your language

Look at the list of school subjects. Make cards for five new words. Write the word in English on one side of the card. Write the word in your language on the other side.

Show what you know!

STEP 1. GROUPS OF 3. What are the three most important subjects for students to learn? Why?

_____   _____   _____

STEP 2. Tell the class your ideas.

Make plans for school events

Listening and Speaking

1 BEFORE YOU LISTEN

READ. CLASS. Look at the pictures and read the information. Then answer the questions.

A parent-teacher conference is a meeting between a student's teacher and his or her parents. The teacher and parents discuss the child's progress in school.

PTO stands for Parent-Teacher Organization. A PTO is a group of teachers and parents of students in a school. They work together to improve the school.

parent-teacher conference

parent-teacher organization (PTO)

1. What is the purpose of a parent-teacher conference?

2. What is the purpose of a PTO?

2 LISTEN

A CLASS. Look at the picture. Mr. and Mrs. Duval have a notice from their son's school. Guess: What is the notice about?

B CD3 T3 Listen to the conversation. Was your guess in Exercise A correct?

C CD3 T3 Listen again. Answer the questions.

1. When is the parent-teacher conference?
   a. Tuesday the 19th at 6:00
   b. Thursday the 19th at 6:00
   c. Thursday the 19th at 9:00

2. What does Mr. Duval have to do on the day of the conference?
   a. go to work   b. go to class   c. watch the kids

D CD3 T4 Listen to the whole conversation. What is Mr. Duval going to do on Monday the 23rd?

a. go to work   b. go to the parent-teacher conference   c. go to a band concert

3 | CONVERSATION

A **Listen to the sentences. Then listen and repeat.**

CD3 T5

I'll try.
We'll both go.
He'll be at work.
She'll meet him there.
My mother will watch the kids.

Pronunciation Watch

The word *will* usually has a short, weak pronunciation. After a pronoun (such as *I* or *we*), we usually use the contraction *'ll*.

B **Listen and repeat the conversation.**

CD3 T6

Mrs. Duval: Carlo brought a notice home from school today. There's a parent-teacher conference in two weeks.

Mr. Duval: Oh, yeah? What day?

Mrs. Duval: Thursday the 19th at 6:00. My mother will watch the kids. That way we can both go.

Mr. Duval: Oh, I have to work that day until 9:00, but I'll try to change my shift.

4 | PRACTICE

A **PAIRS. Practice the conversation. Then make new conversations. Use the information in the boxes.**

A: Carlo brought a notice home from school today. There's a ⬚ in two weeks.

B: Oh, yeah? What day?

A: Thursday the 19th at 6:00. My mother will watch the kids. That way we can both go.

B: Oh, I have to be at work that day until 9:00, but I'll ⬚ .

school play
PTO meeting
science fair

switch hours with someone
ask if I can leave early
change my schedule

B **ROLE PLAY. PAIRS. Make your own conversations. Use different information.**

Make plans for school events

Grammar

Future with *will*

Affirmative			
My mother She	**will** **'ll**	**watch**	the kids.

Negative			
Frank They	**will not** **won't**	**go**	to the PTO meeting.

1 PRACTICE

Grammar Watch

- Use *will* + the base form of a verb.
- *won't* = *will not*.
- Use contractions with *will* for speaking and informal writing.

A **Complete the sentences. Use *will* for the future.**

1. Anwar ___will work___ the evening shift this week.
   (work)
   He changed his schedule.

2. Laura _____ on the soccer team next year.
   (play)

3. The PTO _____ a bake sale in October.
   (have)

4. Raphael _____ home until 5:30. He gets help with his homework after school.
   (not / be)

5. The Technology Club _____ this week because Monday is a holiday.
   (not / meet)

6. Andre _____ late for dinner. He has football practice today.
   (be)

7. The kids _____ school on Friday because the teacher has a conference all day.
   (not / have)

B **Complete the conversation. Use *will* for the future and the words in the box. Use contractions if possible.**

> play   go   ~~be~~   check

A: Can you go to Jimmy's baseball game this Thursday night?

B: I'm sorry, I can't. I have to work.

A: That's too bad. Jimmy ___will be___ sad. He wanted you to come.

B: Well, they _____ again next week, right?

A: I think there's a game next Friday. I _____ the schedule.

B: OK. I _____ to the next game. I promise.

Complete the e-mail. Use the future with *will* and the words in parentheses.

✉ invitation

To: jane@abc.com
Subject: Invitation

Hi Jane,

Thank you for inviting us to Sue's school play next Friday night. Unfortunately, Jack has a

class, so he ___won't be___ there. But the kids and I _____. I usually get out of
    (1. not / be)   **(2. come)**

work at around 6:30, but I _____ early if I can. The kids and I _____
                (3. leave)   **(4. eat)**

a quick dinner, and we _____ to the school around 8:00. Don't worry—we
            (5. get)

_____ late! I'm going out now, so I _____ you tonight. I _____
    (6. not / be)   **(7. not / call)**   **(8. call)**

you on Sunday, and we _____ some more then.
                (9. talk)

Anita

Show what you know!   Make plans for school events

**STEP 1. GROUPS OF 5. Look at the pictures.
Choose one event. Look at the event tasks in the chart.
Decide who will do each task. Complete the chart.**

A: *Who wants to get permission from the school?*
B: *I'll call the principal tomorrow.*

a school bake sale

Event:	
Event task	**Group member**
get permission from the school	
design a flyer	
decide who will bring what	
set up before the event	
clean up after the event	

STEP 2. Tell the class about your plans.

an international party

Can you…make plans for school events? ☐

Life Skills

1 TAKE A PHONE MESSAGE

A PAIRS. Look at the picture. Guess: Why is the woman calling the school?

Winter Hill Elementary School.

OFFICE

B CD3 T7 Listen to the conversation. Was your guess in Exercise A correct?

C CD3 T7 Read the phone messages. Listen to the conversation again. Circle the number of the correct message.

1.

Date __3/9__ Time __1:15__

To __Mr. Taylor__

While You Were Out

From __Elsa Vega (Maria's teacher)__

Phone __(718) 555-4343__

Message: __Will call back.__

_____

2.

Date __3/9__ Time __1:15__

To __Mr. Taylor__

While You Were Out

From __Elsa Vega (Maria's mom)__

Phone __(718) 555-4343__

Message: __Please call back.__

_____

D CD3 T8 Listen. Mr. Taylor is returning Ms. Vega's call. Ms. Vega's son Beto answers the phone and takes a message. Complete the message.

E PAIRS. Compare your answers.

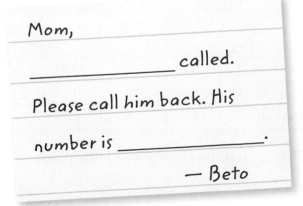

Mom,

_____ called.

Please call him back. His

number is _____.

— Beto

A Complete the conversation with words from the box.

> available   call me back   give him
> take a message   ~~This is~~

A: Winter Hill Elementary School.

B: Hello. _____*This is*_____ Elsa Vega. May I speak to Mr. Taylor please?

A: I'm sorry. He's not _____ right now. May I _____?

B: Yes, please. I have a question about my daughter Maria's math homework.

Please ask him to _____.

A: Sure. What's your number?

B: It's (718) 555-4343.

A: OK. I'll _____ the message.

B: Thank you.

B PAIRS. Compare your answers.
Then practice the conversation.

C PAIRS. Make your own conversations.

Student A: You are the parent. Call
Mr. Taylor at the Winter Hill Elementary
School. Leave a message with the secretary.

Student B: You are the secretary. Take the
message. Use today's date and time.

Date _____ Time _____

To _____

While You Were Out

From _____

Phone _____

Message: _____

_____

3 **LIFE SKILLS WRITING**   Complete a school enrollment form. See page 264.

Can you...take a phone message?   ☐

Listening and Speaking

1   BEFORE YOU LISTEN

READ. CLASS. Look at the picture. Read the information. What are some ways students can get extra help with school?

Sometimes students have trouble in their classes. Students can get help from their parents and older brothers and sisters. Sometimes they can get extra help from teachers or older students before or after school. Most local libraries also have programs to help students with their schoolwork.

2   LISTEN

A CLASS. Look at the picture. Guess: Where is Carlo's mother? Who is she talking to?

CD3 T9
B Listen to the conversation. Was your guess in Exercise A correct?

CD3 T9
C Listen again. Answer the questions.

1. What subject is Carlo doing well in?

_____

2. What subject *isn't* Carlo doing well in?

_____

CD3 T10
D Listen to the whole conversation. What does Carlo's teacher suggest?

a. help from older students
b. extra homework
c. help from his parents

3 CONVERSATION

CD3 T11

Listen and repeat the conversation.

Mr. Thomson: Hi, I'm Harold Thompson, Carlo's teacher. Nice to meet you.

Mrs. Duval: I'm Carlo's mother, Annette Duval. Nice to meet you, too. So, how's Carlo doing?

Mr. Thomson: Carlo's a good student. I enjoy having him in class.

Mrs. Duval: That's good to hear.

Mr. Thomson: He does very well in math. He works carefully.

Mrs. Duval: He likes math a lot. What about social studies?

Mr. Thomson: Well, he's having a little trouble in that class. He needs to do his homework.

Mrs. Duval: OK. I'll talk to him.

4 PRACTICE

A PAIRS. **Practice the conversation. Then make new conversations. Use the information in the boxes.**

A: Hi, I'm _____, Carlo's teacher. Nice to meet you.

B: I'm Carlo's _____, _____. Nice to meet you, too. So, how's Carlo doing?

A: Carlo's a good student. I enjoy having him in class.

B: That's good to hear.

A: He does very well in _____. He _____.

B: He likes _____ a lot. What about _____?

A: Well, he's having a little trouble in that class.

He needs to _____.

B: OK. I'll talk to him.

science
social studies
language arts

learns quickly
studies hard
writes well

language arts
science
math

ask more questions
spend extra time on it
study a little more

B MAKE IT PERSONAL. **PAIRS. Talk about your English ability. What do you do well? What do you have trouble in? Suggest ways your partner can improve his or her English.**

A: *My pronunciation is good. I have trouble with writing.*

B: *How about writing a journal in English?*

Grammar

Adverbs of manner

Adjective		
Carlo is a	**careful** **quick** **good**	worker.

Adverb		
Carlo works	**carefully**. **quickly**. **well**.	

Grammar Watch

- For most adverbs of manner, add -*ly* to the adjective. See page 287 for more spelling rules.

- A few adverbs of manner are irregular:
  good → well
  hard → hard
  fast → fast

1   PRACTICE

A   **Complete the sentences. Look at the underlined adjective. Write the adverb of manner.**

1. Sonia is a <u>careless</u> writer. She writes ___carelessly___ .

2. Vahan's pronunciation is <u>clear</u>. He speaks _____.

3. Amadi is a <u>fast</u> learner. He learns _____.

4. Your children are <u>good</u> students. They do _____ in school.

5. My son is a <u>hard</u> worker. He works _____ on his homework.

6. May-Ling is very <u>quiet</u> in class. She plays _____ with the other children.

7. Meng's handwriting is <u>neat</u>. He writes _____.

B   **Change the adjectives in the box to adverbs of manner. Use the adverbs to complete the sentences.**

> careful   creative   good   hard   ~~poor~~   quick

1. Darren never practices the piano. He plays ___poorly___ .

2. Nuncia gets good grades. She does _____ in school.

3. We don't have much time. Please work _____.

4. Amina works fast, but she makes mistakes. She needs to work _____.

5. Ernesto had a lot of great ideas for his science project. He always thinks _____.

6. John has a test tomorrow. He needs to study _____.

Object pronouns

Singular	
Can you help	**me**?
I need to see	**you.** **him.** **her.**
You can do	**it.**

Plural	
Come with	**us.**
I am proud of all of	**you.** **them.**

······· **Grammar Watch**

An object pronoun takes the place of a noun:

*I need to call <u>Bill</u>. I need to call **him**.*

Use an object pronoun:

- after a verb: *Call **me**. I know **her**.*
- after a preposition: *Talk to **me**. He's standing next to **her**.*

2 PRACTICE

Complete the sentences. Write the correct object pronoun.

1. Ms. Carson was at the parent-teacher conference. I met _____*her*_____.

2. There is a PTO meeting on Friday. We can't attend _____.

3. Emily and Mary are doing very well in school. We're proud of _____.

4. My daughter is not doing well in science. I am worried about _____.

5. My son needs help in math class. Can you help _____?

6. Are you busy? I need to talk to _____.

7. When we don't understand something, our teacher helps _____.

8. Art class is hard for me. I don't like _____.

9. My son does his homework every day. I never have to remind _____.

Show what you know!   Talk about progress in school

STEP 1. WRITE. Think of three students you know. How are they doing in school? Write a sentence about each person on a separate piece of paper. Use an adverb of manner.

My daughter is doing well in school because she works hard.

STEP 2. GROUPS OF 3. Read your sentences. Talk about the people.

STEP 3. Tell the class about the students you talked about.

Can you...talk about progress in school? ☐

Reading

1 BEFORE YOU READ

CLASS. Read the chart. What types of colleges are there in your community?

	Community college	College	University
Degrees offered	Associate's Degree (2 years)	Bachelor's Degree (4 years)	Bachelor's Degree (4 years)
			Master's Degree (2 more years)
			Doctor of Philosophy (4–7 more years)

2 READ

CD3 T12

Listen. Read the article.

Going to College

Thinking of going to college? Here are some things you should know.

Rising College Enrollment

According to the U.S. Census Bureau, 49 percent of high school graduates in 1980 went to college. Fifty-nine percent went to college in 1990. In 2007, over 66 percent of high school graduates went to college. Every year more and more Americans decide that going to college is a way to a better future.

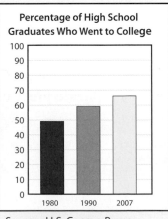

Percentage of High School Graduates Who Went to College

Source: U.S. Census Bureau

The Cost of College

But going to college costs a lot. Today, the average cost of tuition is between $2,000 and $22,000 a year. This does not include the cost of books, housing, and food. These can cost between $8,000 and $16,000 more a year.

Average Cost of Tuition	
Private College	$22,000
Public College	$ 6,000
Community College	$ 2,000

Paying for College

How do people pay for tuition? Many students get financial aid—scholarships, grants, and loans. Many students get loans. Some students get scholarships because their grades are good. Some students get grants because their income is low. Scholarships and grants are the best kind of financial aid because you don't have to pay them back. You do have to pay back student loans after you graduate. Most students use a combination of scholarships, grants, and loans to pay the high cost of college.

A PAIRS. Read the article again. What are the three main points of the article?

B Look at the graph about high school graduates in the article. Answer the questions.

1. What do the numbers on the left side of the graph mean?

   a. the percentage of high school graduates who went to college
   b. the number of high school graduates who went to college

2. What percentage of high school graduates went to college in 1980?

   a. 50   b. 60

3. How many high school graduates went to college in 2007?

   a. 65,000   b. the graph doesn't say

> **Reading Skill:**
> Use Information in Charts and Tables
>
> Authors sometimes use graphs and tables to present information. This information supports the author's main ideas.

C Read the statements. Circle *True* or *False*.

1. Today, fewer high school graduates go to college than in the past.	True	False
2. The cost of books, housing, and food for one year can be between $8,000 and $16,000.	True	False
3. One year of tuition at a community college is $6,000.	True	False
4. Three types of financial aid are scholarships, grants, and loans.	True	False
5. You have to pay back grants and loans.	True	False

D PAIRS. Compare your answers. Correct the false statements.

Show what you know!

PRE-WRITING. PAIRS. Is going to college one of your goals? Explain your answer.

WRITE. Write about your educational goals. See page 272.

Listening and Speaking

1 BEFORE YOU LISTEN

CLASS. Look at the pictures. Do students in your country behave in this way?

☐ bully other kids

☐ not pay attention

☐ not get along with others

☐ fool around in class

☐ be disrespectful

Where is Steve?

☐ skip class

2 LISTEN

A CD3 T13 Listen to the conversation. Mr. and Mrs. Herrera got a call from their son Luis's teacher. What trouble is Luis having in school? Check the boxes in Before You Listen.

B CD3 T13 Listen again. What are Luis's parents going to do?

a. talk to Luis
b. call the principal
c. go to a parent-teacher conference

C CD3 T14 Listen to the whole conversation. Underline the correct words.

Luis usually **does well / has problems** in school.

3 CONVERSATION

Pronunciation Watch

The **'s** or **s'** possessive ending adds an extra syllable after the sounds at the end of *Luis, Liz, Josh, Mitch* and *George*. It does not add an extra syllable after other sounds.

CD3 T15

A 💿 **Listen to the possessive nouns. Then listen and repeat.**

my boss**'s** name

Alex**'s** friend

George**'s** class

his friend**'s** house

Sue**'s** homework

her parent**'s** car

CD3 T16

B 💿 **Listen again. Underline the possessive nouns that add a syllable.**

CD3 T17

C 💿 **Listen and repeat the conversation.**

Mrs. Herrera: Where's Luis?

Mr. Herrera: He's at a friend's house. Why? What's up?

Mrs. Herrera: Well, his teacher called. He's having some trouble at school.

Mr. Herrera: Uh-oh. What kind of trouble?

Mrs. Herrera: She said he's not paying attention and skipping class.

Mr. Herrera: What? Well, we need to talk to him right away.

Mrs. Herrera: Definitely. Let's all talk tonight after dinner.

4 PRACTICE

A **PAIRS.** Practice the conversation. Then make new conversations. Use the information in the boxes.

A: Where's Luis?

B: He's at a friend's house. Why? What's up?

A: Well, his teacher called. He's having some trouble at school.

B: Uh-oh. What kind of trouble?

A: She said he's ▒▒▒▒▒ and ▒▒▒▒▒.

B: What? Well, we ▒▒▒▒▒ right away.

A: Definitely. Let's all talk tonight after dinner.

> not getting along with others
> getting to school late
> being disrespectful to his teachers

> bullying some other kids
> not doing his homework
> fooling around in class

> need to find out what's going on
> have to have a talk with him
> need to have a family meeting

B **MAKE IT PERSONAL.** **GROUPS OF 3.** What should Luis's parents do?

Discuss your child's behavior in school

Grammar

Possessive nouns

Singular	Plural
Their son**'s** name is Luis.	Their son**s'** names are Minh and Sang.
	The children**'s** classroom is down the hall.

Grammar Watch

To form a possessive noun:

- Add *'s* to most singular nouns: *a boy's name*.

- Add only an apostrophe to plural nouns that end in *-s*: *my parents' car*.

- Add *'s* to plural nouns that do not end in *-s*: *the men's hats*

- See page 287 for more spelling rules.

PRACTICE

A Underline the correct word.

1. Who is your **daughters / <u>daughter's</u>** teacher?

2. My **sons / son's** are in the first and second grades.

3. The **teachers / teacher's** first name is Alex.

4. Sometimes a teacher calls a **students / student's** parents.

5. I know the names of all my **classmates / classmates'**.

6. My **daughter's / daughters'** names are Alicia and Rita.

7. The guidance **counselor's / counselors'** name is Ms. White.

B Find and correct the error in each sentence.

1. My ~~sons~~ son's grades are poor, so I need to talk to his teacher.

2. The new teacher's names are Ms. Trudeau and Ms. Appleton.

3. Where is the school nurse' office?

4. My daughters report card was good, but my son is having a hard time.

5. The principal will try to answer all the parents's questions.

6. Teachers like to meet their students parents.

C PAIRS. Check your answers.

1   GRAMMAR

A Complete the school newsletter. Use the future with *will*.

March Events   Oak Grove Middle School

Bake Sale

The fourth grade (1. have) _will have_ a bake sale on March 6 at 12:30 P.M. in the cafeteria. Students (2. sell) _____ cookies, cupcakes, and other baked goods.

PTO Meeting

The Oak Grove PTO (3. meet) _____ on March 9. Members (4. discuss) _____ new school programs for this year. Please join us!

B Complete the conversations. Write the possessive forms of the nouns in parentheses. Change the adjectives in parentheses to adverbs of manner.

1. **A:** How are my (son) _____son's_____ grades in math?

   B: Fine. He's doing very (good) _____well_____.

2. **A:** How were the (children) _____ grades?

   B: Great! They're working (hard) _____ in school.

3. **A:** I didn't hear the (little girl) _____ name.

   B: I think she said, "Mimi." She speaks (quiet) _____.

4. **A:** I can't read the (student) _____ handwriting.

   B: I know. He writes (sloppy) _____.

C Cross out the underlined nouns and write object pronouns.

1. Do you know Mr. Jones? I like ~~Mr. Jones~~ *him* a lot.

2. My daughter Eliza is having a hard time. Can you help <u>Eliza</u>?

3. Brad's homework is hard. He doesn't understand <u>his homework</u>.

4. Asha's schoolbooks are heavy. It's hard for her to carry <u>her schoolbooks</u>.

5. I want to meet my children's teachers. I want to talk to <u>the teachers</u>.

Go to the CD-ROM for more practice.

2   ACT IT OUT — What do you say?

STEP 1. CLASS. Review the Lesson 2 conversation between
Mr. and Mrs. Duval (CD 3 track 3).

STEP 2. ROLE PLAY. PAIRS. You are the parents of two children.
Your daughter Sandra is in the seventh grade. Your son
Kyle is in the ninth grade. Read the school events notices.
Make plans to attend your children's events.

Lincoln Middle School LMS

January Events

January 24
PTO Meeting 6–7 P.M.
Parent-teacher conferences 7–9 P.M.

January 25
Science Fair 8:30 A.M.–4:30 P.M.

Melrose High School MELROSE
This week's school events

January 24
Band Concert 7–8 P.M.

January 25
PTO Meeting 5–6 P.M.
Parent-teacher conferences 6–9 P.M.

3   READ AND REACT — Problem-solving

STEP 1. Read about Mai's problem.

Mai's daughter Kalaya is twelve years old. Mai received a note from Kalaya's
teacher. The teacher wrote that Kalaya is misbehaving in class. She is not
getting along with another student. Kalaya says that the other student is
bullying her. Mai believes Kalaya. She doesn't think that the teacher is
being fair.

STEP 2. PAIRS. What is Mai's problem? What can she do?
Here are some ideas.

- She can talk to the teacher.
- She can talk to the school principal.
- She can talk to the other student's parents.
- She can _____.

4   CONNECT

For your Study Skills Activity, go to page 253.
For your Team Project, go to page 282.

Which goals can you check off? Go back to page 165.

Let's Eat!

Preview

**Look at the picture.
Where are the people?
What are they doing?**

UNIT GOALS

- ☐ Identify food containers and quantities

- ☐ Ask for quantities of food

- ☐ Read nutrition information

- ☐ Complete a healthy eating log

- ☐ Compare information in food ads

- ☐ Read a menu

- ☐ Order food in a restaurant

1 WHAT DO YOU KNOW?

A CLASS. Look at the pictures. Which foods do you know? Which containers and quantities do you know?

CD3 T18
B Look at the pictures and listen. Then listen and repeat.

2 PRACTICE

CD3 T19
A Look at the pictures and listen. Check the pictures of the words you hear.

B PAIRS. Check your answers.

C WORD PLAY. GROUPS OF 3. Which foods come in these containers? Use the foods in the pictures and your own ideas.

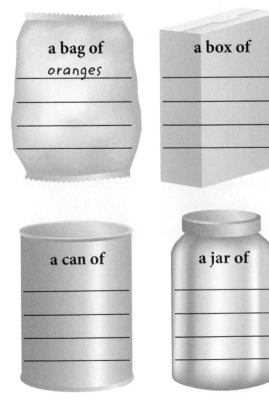

a bag of
oranges

a box of

a can of

a jar of

1

6

8

9

12

13

14

2 ☐

3

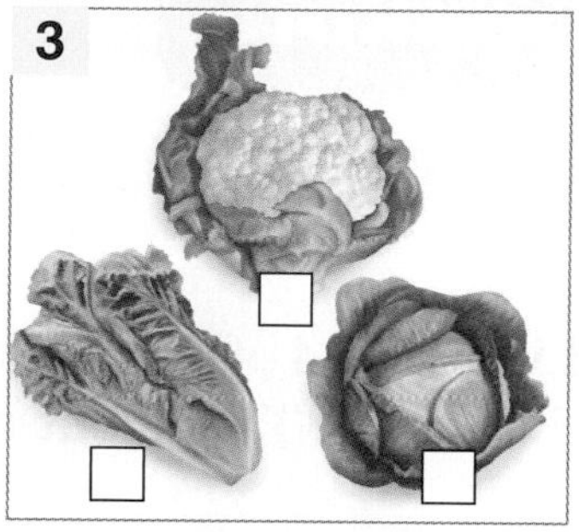

4

5

Cookies

Tomatoes SOUP
Tuna

7

MAYONNAISE   Grape JELLY   PICKLES
☐   ☐   ☐

Food Containers and Quantities

1. bag	8. bottle
2. bunch	9. container
3. head	10. pint
4. box	11. quart
5. can	12. half-gallon
6. dozen	13. gallon
7. jar	14. pound

10

Milk   SALSA   COTTAGE CHEESE
☐   ☐   ☐

11

Orange JUICE   Milk   Chocolate Milk   ICED TEA
☐   ☐   ☐   ☐

Learning Strategy

Draw pictures

Look at the list of food containers. Make cards for three or four food containers. On one side, write the word. On the other side, draw a picture of the container.

Show what you know!

STEP 1. Think about the food you have at home. Write a list of ten food items. Use container and quantity words.

a gallon of milk
a head of lettuce

STEP 2. GROUPS OF 4. Compare your lists. Circle the foods that everyone in your group has at home.

STEP 3. Tell the class about the food your group has at home.

We all have a gallon of milk and . . .

Listening and Speaking

1 BEFORE YOU LISTEN

CLASS. Where do you go food shopping? What kind of store is it? Find classmates who shop at the same kind of stores. Talk about why you shop there.

a supermarket

a convenience store

an outdoor market

2 LISTEN

A CLASS. Look at the picture of two roomates, Agnes and Yuka. Guess: What are they talking about?

CD3 T20
B Listen to the conversation. Was your guess in Exercise A correct?

CD3 T20
C Listen again. What does Agnes need from the grocery store? What does Yuka need? Write *A* for Agnes and *Y* for Yuka.

  ___

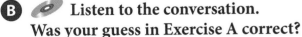

CD3 T21
D Listen to the whole conversation. Complete the sentence.

Agnes needs to _____.

a. find her purse   b. get something from the refrigerator   c. write the things down

3 CONVERSATION

CD1 T26

Listen and repeat the conversation.

Agnes: Hi, Yuka. I'm going to the grocery store for some milk. Do you need anything?

Yuka: Uh, let me see. Could you get a can of tomatoes?

Agnes: A can of tomatoes? Sure, no problem.

Yuka: Oh, and I need some onions.

Agnes: How many onions?

Yuka: Two.

Agnes: All right. A can of tomatoes and two onions. I'll be back in a little while.

4 PRACTICE

A PAIRS. Practice the conversation. Then make new conversations. Use your own names and the information in the boxes.

A: Hi, _____. I'm going to the grocery store for some _____. Do you need anything?

B: Uh, let me see. Could you get a can of _____?

A: A can of _____? Sure, no problem.

B: Oh, and I need some _____.

A: How many _____?

B: Two.

A: All right. A _____ and two _____. I'll be back in a little while.

B ROLE PLAY. PAIRS. Make your own conversations. Talk about the food you need.

Ask for quantities of food

Grammar

Count nouns/Non-count nouns

Singular count nouns	Plural count nouns	Non-count nouns	
an onion a sandwich	two onions some sandwiches	bread fish	milk rice

	Yes/No questions			*Affirmative/Negative answers*			
Are		onions?	**Yes,**		**are**	**some**	on the counter.
	there **any**		**No,**	there	**aren't**	**any**.	Sorry.
Is		milk?	**Yes,**		**is**	**some**	in the fridge.
			No,		**isn't**	**any**.	Sorry.

Grammar Watch

- There is = there's
- See page 288 for spelling rules for plurals.
- See page 289 for more examples of non-count nouns.

1 PRACTICE

A Complete the questions with *Is/Are there any*. Complete the answers with *There's/There are* or *There isn't/aren't*.

1. **A:** _____Is there any_____ bread?

   B: Yes, _____there's_____ some on the counter.

2. **A:** _____ tomatoes?

   B: No, _____ any.

3. **A:** _____ coffee?

   B: Yes, _____ some in the pot.

4. **A:** _____ carrots?

   B: Yes, _____ some in the refrigerator.

5. **A:** _____ butter?

   B: No, _____ any, but we have margarine.

6. **A:** _____ bananas?

   B: No, _____. I ate the last one.

B PAIRS. Practice the conversations in Exercise A.

How much / How many

How	**much**	chicken oil	do we need?
	many	eggs cans of soup	

A Complete the conversation. Underline the correct words.

Ana: How **much** / <u>**many**</u> potatoes do we have? Do we need more?

Beatriz: Yes. I'll get a five-pound bag at the store.

Ana: OK. Are you going to get **cheese** / **cheeses**?

Beatriz: Yeah. But how **much** / **many** cheese do we need?

Ana: Oh, a pound is fine. We need some **fruit** / **fruits**, too.

Beatriz: OK. I'll get three **orange** / **oranges**.

Ana: How **much** / **many** milk do we have?

Beatriz: None. I'll get a half gallon.

Ana: Could you get some **sugar** / **sugars**, too?

Beatriz: Sure. How **much** / **many** sugar do you want?

Ana: One pound is enough.

Shopping List

5 lbs. of potatoes

_____

_____

_____

_____

_____

B WRITE. Write Beatriz's shopping list.

Show what you know! Ask for quantities of food

STEP 1. What food do you like to take on a picnic? Write a list.

STEP 2. GROUPS OF 5. Plan a picnic. Decide where to go and what food you will take.

A: *Let's go to Central Park.*
B: *OK. Let's take some chicken sandwiches.*
C: *Good idea. How many do we need? I think . . .*

Can you...ask for quantities of food? ☐

Life Skills

1 READ FOOD LABELS

A **CLASS.** Do you eat a healthy diet? How do you know the foods you eat are healthy?

B Scan the article. What is a nutrient?

What's in My Food?

Carbohydrates, cholesterol, fiber, protein, sodium, and sugar are some of the nutrients in food. All of these nutrients are good for you, but only in the right amounts.

Carbohydrates give you energy for several hours. Foods such as pasta, bread, and potatoes have a lot of carbohydrates.

Cholesterol is only in animal fat. Foods such as butter, mayonnaise, red meat, and eggs have a lot of cholesterol. Too much cholesterol is not good for you.

Fiber is from plants. Foods such as vegetables, fruits, and grains all have lots of fiber. Fiber is good for you. It helps your stomach digest food.

Protein makes your body strong. Foods such as chicken, fish, and beans have a lot of protein.

Sodium is another word for salt. Foods such as potato chips, canned soups, and olives have a lot of sodium. Too much sodium is not good for you.

Sugar gives you quick energy. Candy, cookies, and soda have a lot of sugar. Too much sugar is not good for you. Watch out! Sometimes sugar has a different name, such as high-maltose corn syrup or high-fructose corn syrup.

How do you find out what's in your food?

Read the ingredient and nutrition labels on your food packages. An ingredient label lists all the ingredients in the food. The ingredients are listed in the order of amount. The first ingredient on the list is the main (or largest) ingredient. The last ingredient is the smallest one. A nutrient label lists the amount of each nutrient in one serving of the food. To eat a healthy diet, you need to ask, "What's in my food?" and make sure you eat the right amounts of each nutrient.

C Read the article. Write the missing food item for each nutrient category.

1. **carbohydrates:** bread, potatoes, _____pasta_____

2. **cholesterol:** butter, mayonnaise, red meat, _____

3. **fiber:** vegetables, grains, _____

4. **protein:** chicken, beans, _____

5. **sodium:** potato chips, olives, _____

6. **sugar:** candy, soda, _____

D Read the nutrition labels for a gallon of whole milk and a gallon of non-fat milk. Read the sentences. Circle *True* or *False*.

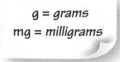

g = grams
mg = milligrams

Nutrition Facts
Serving Size 1 Cup
Servings Per Container 16

Amount Per Serving

Calories 160 Calories from Fat 71

Total Fat 8 g

Cholesterol 35 mg

Sodium 125 mg

Total Carbohydrate 13 g
  Dietary Fiber 0 g
  Sugar 12 g

Protein 8 g

whole milk

Nutrition Facts
Serving Size 1 Cup
Servings Per Container 16

Amount Per Serving

Calories 90 Calories from Fat 0

Total Fat 0 g

Cholesterol 5 mg

Sodium 130 mg

Total Carbohydrate 13 g
  Dietary Fiber 0 g
  Sugar 12 g

Protein 8 g

non-fat milk

1. There are 16 servings in a gallon of milk.   (True)   False

2. The whole milk has 160 calories per serving.   True   False

3. The whole milk has zero grams of total fat per serving.   True   False

4. The non-fat milk has 5 milligrams of cholesterol per serving.   True   False

5. The whole milk has 125 milligrams of sodium per serving.   True   False

6. Non-fat milk has 12 grams of dietary fiber per serving.   True   False

7. Both kinds of milk have 12 grams of sugar per serving.   True   False

8. The non-fat milk has zero grams of protein per serving.   True   False

E PAIRS. Check your answers.

2 PRACTICE

A GROUPS OF 3. Look at the two nutrition labels in Exercise D again. Which milk do you think is better for your health? Why?

I think non-fat milk is better because . . .

B PAIRS. Look at the labels. Circle the main ingredient. Underline the sugar ingredients.

PEANUT ENERGY BAR

Ingredients: peanuts, high-maltose corn syrup, sugar, rolled oats, high-fructuse corn syrup.

SUNSHINE ORANGE DRINK

Ingredients: water, high-fructose corn syrup, sugar, 2% or less of each of the following juices — orange, apple, lime, grapefruit.

3 LIFE SKILLS WRITING

Complete a healthy eating log. See page 265.

Can you...read nutrition information? ☐

Listening and Speaking

1 BEFORE YOU LISTEN

CLASS. Look at the people.
Read the reasons that they buy food.
What's important to *you* when you
buy food?

Convenience is important to me. I buy food that's easy to prepare.

I buy food that **tastes good**. That's all I care about.

I think about **price**. I get store brands and things on sale.

I buy **healthy** food like low-fat milk and whole wheat bread.

I like **fresh** fruits and vegetables. I don't buy frozen or canned food.

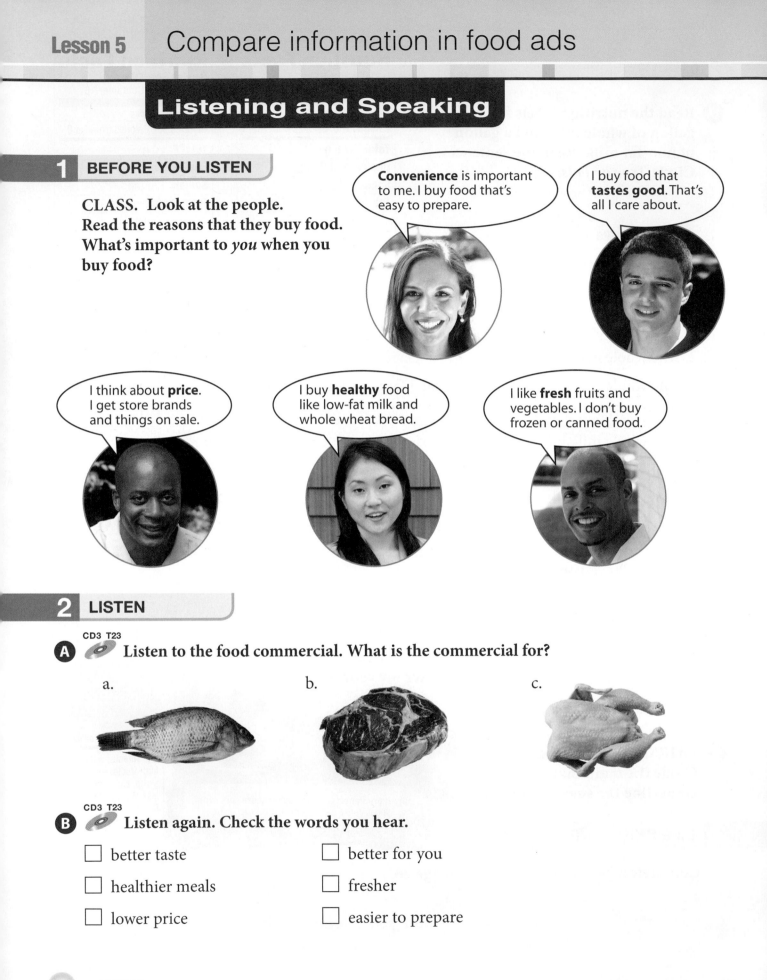

2 LISTEN

A CD3 T23 Listen to the food commercial. What is the commercial for?

a.

b.

c.

B CD3 T23 Listen again. Check the words you hear.

☐ better taste   ☐ better for you

☐ healthier meals   ☐ fresher

☐ lower price   ☐ easier to prepare

3 CONVERSATION

A CLASS. Look at the picture of Lucy and her mother, Estela, in the supermarket. Guess: What are they talking about?

CD3 T24

B  Listen to the conversation. Was your guess in Exercise A correct?

CD3 T25

C Listen and repeat the conversation.

Lucy: Oh, you buy Franklin brand coffee. Is it good?

Estela: Yes, it's excellent. I think it's better than all the other brands.

Lucy: Really? Why?

Estela: It tastes great and it's not expensive.

4 PRACTICE

A PAIRS. Practice the conversation. Then make new conversations. Use the information in the boxes.

A: Oh, you buy _____ brand _____ . Is it good?

B: Yes, it's excellent. I think it's better than all the other brands.

A: Really? Why?

B: _____ and it's not expensive.

Sunshine	orange juice	It tastes good
Captain Cook	fish	It's always fresh
Dairy Glenn	ice cream	It's low-fat

B MAKE IT PERSONAL. GROUPS OF 3. Talk about a product you like. Explain why you like it.

Grammar

Comparative adjectives with *than*

| This coffee is | fresh.
tasty.
expensive. | It's | **fresher**
tastier
more expensive | **than** | the other brands. |

1 PRACTICE

A **Write the comparative forms with *-er* or *more*.**

1. fresh   *fresher*

2. fast   _____

3. good   _____

4. delicious   _____

5. sweet   _____

6. expensive   _____

7. healthy   _____

8. fattening   _____

9. salty   _____

Grammar Watch

To form comparative adjectives:

- from one-syllable adjectives, add *-er*.

- from two-syllable adjectives ending in *y*, change *y* to *i* and add *-er*.

- from adjectives of two or more syllables, use *more* + an adjective.

- Some comparative adjectives are irregular. For example: *good* → *better*.

- See page 289 for more spelling rules.

B **Complete the sentences. Write the comparative form of the adjective in parentheses. Add *than*.**

1. Bananas are (sweet) ___*sweeter than*___ apples.

2. Margarine is (cheap) _____ butter.

3. Fresh orange juice tastes (good) _____ frozen orange juice.

4. I think homemade meals are (tasty) _____ fast food.

5. Fresh fruit is (nutritious) _____ canned fruit.

6. Canned soup is (convenient) _____ homemade soup.

7. Vegetables are (good for you) _____ cookies.

8. Sandwiches are (easy to make) _____ hamburgers.

A PAIRS. Compare the food in the supermarket ad. Use adjectives from the box or other adjectives.

A small salad is cheaper than a large salad.

cheap
delicious
expensive
fattening
fresh
good
nutritious
salty

B On a separate piece of paper, write six sentences comparing the food in the supermarket ad.

Super prices this week!

14" Ready-to-bake pizza
$5⁹⁹ each
2 for $10⁹⁹

Try our salads!
$2⁹⁹ small
large $4⁹⁹

Super Salty potato chips
89¢
12-oz. bag

Hart's fat-free, low-sodium pretzels
$1⁸⁹
12-oz. box

Show what you know!   Compare information in food ads

STEP 1. GROUPS OF 3. You are the owners of a food company. Think of a food or drink you will sell. Write three reasons why your product is better than other brands.

> Old South fried chicken is more delicious than other brands. It is . . .

STEP 2. WRITE. SAME GROUPS OF 3. Write a radio commercial for your product.

> Are you hungry? Then try Old South fried chicken. Old South fried chicken is more delicious than other brands . . .

STEP 3. Read your commercial to the class. As a class, vote on the best product.

Can you . . . compare information in food ads? ☐

Reading

1 BEFORE YOU READ

A CLASS. What do you know about the drug caffeine?
How does it make people feel? Is it good for you or bad for you?

B Look at the products. Check the products that have caffeine.
Circle the product that has the most caffeine.

☐ Cola   ☐ Chewing gum   ☐ Coffee   ☐ Tea   ☐ Chocolate   ☐ Headache medicine   ☐ Lemon/lime soda

CD3 T26
C Listen and check your answers. Are you surprised by this information?

2 READ

CD3 T27
Listen. Read the article.

Caffeinated Nation

You have a cup of coffee for breakfast. Later in the day, you have a cola with your lunch. After work, you take some pain reliever for a headache. You may not know it, but each of these products **contains** caffeine. Almost everyone **consumes** caffeine. Ninety percent of people living in the U.S. **consume** caffeine every day. Most people get caffeine from coffee, but others get it from tea, cola, chocolate, or even some medicines.

What is caffeine?
Caffeine is a chemical found in coffee beans, tea leaves, cocoa beans, and other plants.

What are the effects of caffeine?
Fifteen minutes after caffeine enters your body, you start to feel changes. Your heart beats faster. You may have more energy and feel more awake. You feel happier. These **effects** can last for several hours. When they go away, you may feel a little tired and sad.

Is caffeine bad for you?

For most people, caffeine in average amounts does not cause health problems. Research shows that drinking two to three cups of coffee a day is not **harmful**. However, too much caffeine can be bad for your health. It can make you feel nervous and **irritable**. It may give you a headache or an upset stomach. If you **consume** caffeine too late in the day, you may find it difficult to sleep at night. It's a good idea to read the labels on medicines, foods, and **beverages** to find out if they **contain** caffeine.

3 CHECK YOUR UNDERSTANDING

A Look at the words in bold in the article. Guess the meaning of the words from context. Match the words and the definitions.

1. _____ contain	a. a drink	
2. _____ consume	b. eat or drink something	
3. _____ effect	c. causing a health problem or injury	
4. _____ harmful	d. the way that something changes a person	
5. _____ irritable	e. have something inside it	
6. _____ beverage	f. getting a little angry quickly and easily	

Reading Skill:
Getting Meaning from Context

You can sometimes guess the meaning of a word from the words or sentences around it.

B Read the article again. Complete the statements.

1. Almost all Americans consume _____ every day.

2. Some medicine such as _____ has caffeine.

3. There is caffeine in beverages such as _____ and _____.

4. Drinking more than _____ cups of coffee a day can affect your health.

5. Too much caffeine can give you a _____ or an _____.

6. If you consume caffeine late in the day, you may find it difficult to _____.

C PAIRS. Check your answers.

Show what you know!

PRE-WRITING. PAIRS. Is caffeine bad for you? Explain your answer.

WRITE. Keep a caffeine journal. See page 272.

Listening and Speaking

1   BEFORE YOU LISTEN

**CLASS. Look at the menu. Which foods do you know?
Which foods look good?**

Mom's Café

Main Dishes

Main dishes are served with a house
salad and your choice of one side.

meatloaf   roast chicken   pork chops

All Main Dishes $9.95

Asian noodles   hamburger   fish sandwich   macaroni and
cheese

Sides

coleslaw   French fries

mixed
vegetables   onion rings

mashed potatoes

Drinks

soda   bottled water
apple juice   iced tea

2   LISTEN

CD3 T28

A   Ernesto and Angela are ordering lunch in a
restaurant. Listen to the conversation. Look at the
guest check. Complete their order.

CD3 T29

B   Listen to the whole conversation.
Why is the waitress surprised?

a. The woman wants to change her order.
b. The man ordered a lot of food.
c. The people decide to leave the restaurant.

Guest Check

TABLE   SERVER
3   Sally   CHECK #
                            088207
2   iced teas

1
            with
     mixed vegetables
1
            with
onion rings

            TAX
            TOTAL

3 CONVERSATION

A CD3 T30

Listen to the sentences. Notice the pronunciation of *to*, *the*, *a*, and *of*. Then listen and repeat.

Are you ready to order?

I'd like the meatloaf.

A side of mixed vegetables.

Pronunciation Watch

The words *to*, *the*, *a*, and *of* usually have a weak pronunciation. The vowel sound is short and quiet.

B CD3 T31

Listen to the sentences. Complete each sentence with *to*, *the*, *a* or *of*.

1. I'd like _____ soda.

2. I'm ready _____ order now.

3. I'll have _____ roast chicken.

4. Could I have a side _____ coleslaw?

C CD3 T32

Listen and repeat the conversation.

Waitress: Here are your iced teas. Are you ready to order?

Ernesto: Yes. I'd like the meatloaf.

Waitress: And what would you like with that?

Ernesto: A side of mixed vegetables.

Waitress: OK. Meatloaf with mixed vegetables.

Ernesto: And a hamburger with a side of onion rings.

Waitress: A hamburger with onion rings.

Ernesto: Oh, and could we have some sugar?

Waitress: Sure. Here you go. I'll be right back with your salads.

4 PRACTICE

A PAIRS. Practice the conversation.

B ROLE PLAY. GROUPS OF 3. Make your own conversations. Students A and B, you are the customers. Order food from the menu on page 200. Student C, you are the waiter or waitress. Take the customers' orders.

Grammar

Quantifiers with plural nouns

	Affirmative			Negative	
We have	**many** **a lot of** **some** **a few**	apples.	We don't have	**many** **a lot of** **any**	apples.

Quantifiers with non-count nouns

	Affirmative			Negative	
We have	**a lot of** **some** **a little**	sugar.	We don't have	**a lot of** **any** **much**	sugar.

PRACTICE

A **Underline the correct words.**

1. Apple juice has **many** / <u>**a lot of**</u> sugar.

2. You should eat **some** / **a few** fruit every day.

3. Vegetables have **a lot of** / **many** fiber.

4. Athletes eat **much** / **a lot of** carbohydrates to get energy.

5. There aren't **a few** / **many** nutrients in a bag of candy.

6. There is usually **a lot of** / **much** salt and fat in cheese.

> **Grammar Watch**
>
> Don't use *much* + a non-count noun in affirmative statements.
> **Example:** *We eat a lot of rice.*
> (**Not:** *We eat ~~much rice~~.*)

B **Complete the conversations. More than one answer may be possible.**

1. **A:** Do you eat ____a lot of____ eggs? You know, they have a lot of cholesterol.

   B: No, not really. I eat only _____ eggs a week.

2. **A:** I really like fish. Do you eat _____ fish?

   B: Yes, I love it! It's good for you.

3. **A:** What would you like to drink?

   B: I'd like _____ water, please.

1 GRAMMAR

A Complete the conversation. Underline the correct words.

Cook: Do we have enough <u>meat</u> / meats for tomorrow?

Assistant: I think so. There's **much** / **a lot** of meat in the refrigerator. But there isn't **much** / **many** fish.

Cook: OK. Put it on the list. What about vegetables? Are there **much** / **many** potatoes?

Assistant: About 100 pounds. But there are only **a little** / **a few** carrots.

Cook: How **much** / **many** onions?

Assistant: Onions? There aren't **any** / **some**.

Cook: OK. Then we need **any** / **some** carrots and onions. Put **rice** / **rices** on the list, too.

Assistant: OK. How **much** / **many** pounds of rice?

Cook: Fifty. And how about **fruit** / **fruits**? I need **much** / **a lot of** apples for tomorrow's apple pies.

Assistant: I'll put them on the list. We have **some** / **any**, but only **a little** / **a few**. I think we need some **sugar** / **sugars** for the pies, too.

B Compare two foods. Write four sentences. Use the comparative forms of adjectives from the box or other adjectives.

| delicious | easy to cook | fattening | good for you | sweet | tasty |

Apples are better for you than candy bars.

1. _____

2. _____

3. _____

4. _____

Go to the CD-ROM for more practice.

2 ACT IT OUT   What do you say?

PAIRS. Read the nutrition labels. Compare the brands.
Use the words in the box. Tell the class which brand you would buy.
Explain your answer.

| fattening | good for you | nutritious | salty | tasty |

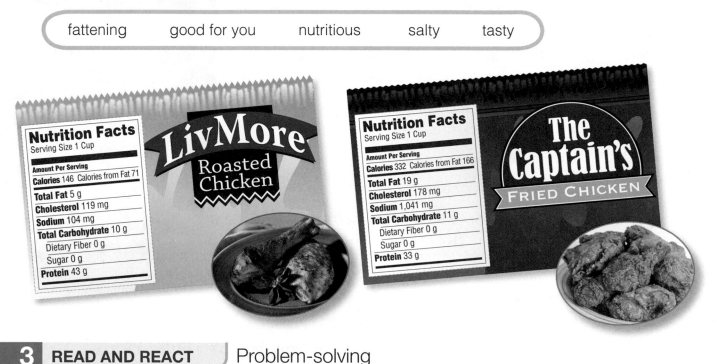

Nutrition Facts
Serving Size 1 Cup

Amount Per Serving
Calories 146 Calories from Fat 71

Total Fat 5 g
Cholesterol 119 mg
Sodium 104 mg
Total Carbohydrate 10 g
  Dietary Fiber 0 g
  Sugar 0 g
Protein 43 g

LivMore Roasted Chicken

Nutrition Facts
Serving Size 1 Cup

Amount Per Serving
Calories 332 Calories from Fat 166

Total Fat 19 g
Cholesterol 178 mg
Sodium 1,041 mg
Total Carbohydrate 11 g
  Dietary Fiber 0 g
  Sugar 0 g
Protein 33 g

The Captain's FRIED CHICKEN

3 READ AND REACT   Problem-solving

STEP 1. Read about Amalya's problem.

Amalya has a full-time job. After work, she also has to cook for
her family and do the housework. Often she does not have enough
time to prepare a healthy meal for her family. Also, fresh fruit and
vegetables are expensive in her neighborhood.

**STEP 2. PAIRS. What is Amalya's problem? What can she do?
Here are some ideas.**

- She can buy inexpensive frozen vegetables.
- She can ask her family to help with shopping, cooking, and washing dishes.
- She can shop at a farmer's market for fresh fruits and vegetables.
- She can _____.

4 CONNECT   For your Community-building Activity, go to page 253.
For your Team Project, go to page 283.

Which goals can you check off? Go back to page 185.

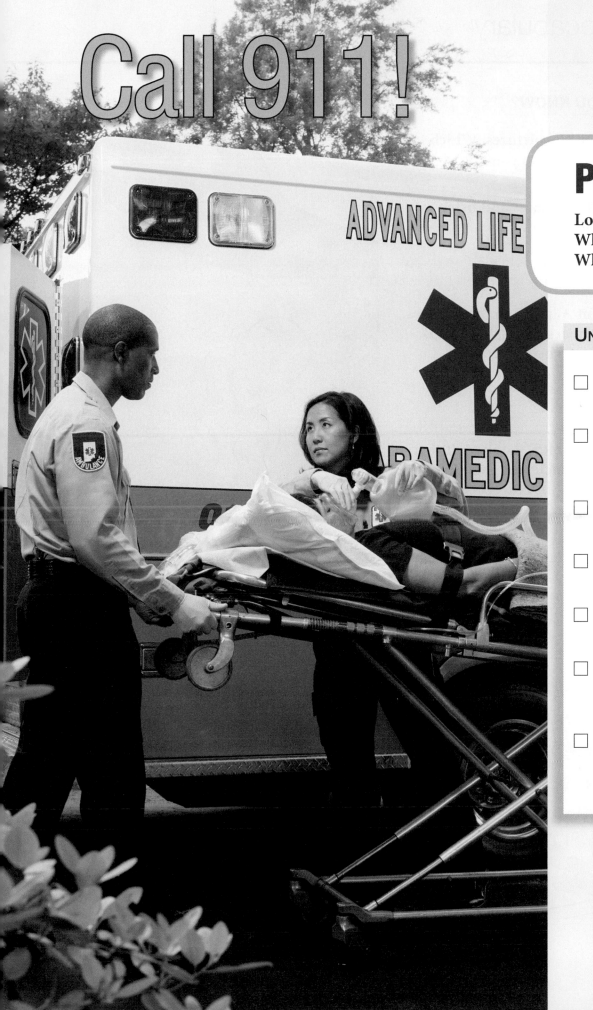

Call 911!

Preview

Look at the picture.
Who are the people?
What is happening?

UNIT GOALS

☐ Identify medical emergencies

☐ Call 911 to report a medical emergency

☐ Talk about medical emergencies

☐ Understand fire safety procedures

☐ Describe an emergency

☐ Respond to a police officer's instructions

☐ Complete an employee accident report

1　WHAT DO YOU KNOW?

A CLASS.　Look at the pictures. Which medical emergencies do you know?

B CD3 T33　Look at the pictures and listen. Listen again and repeat.

2　PRACTICE

A PAIRS.　Student A, point to the pictures. Ask about the emergencies. Student B, identify the emergencies.

A: *What's the emergency?*
B: *She's unconscious.*

B WORD PLAY.　PAIRS.　Look at the list of medical emergencies on page 207. Write the words in the correct column.

Happening right now	Happened in the past
She's bleeding.	

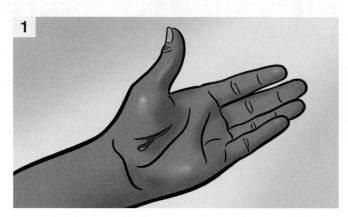

2

3

5

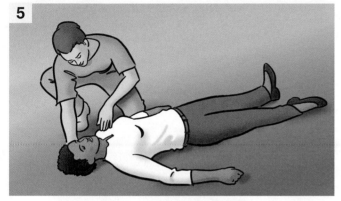

7

Medical Emergencies

1. **She's** bleeding.
2. **He's** choking.
3. **She's** having trouble breathing.
4. **He's** having a heart attack.
5. **She's** unconscious.
6. **He's** having an allergic reaction.
7. **He** swallowed poison.
8. **She** burned herself.
9. **He** fell.

Learning Strategy

Use your language

Look at the list of medical emergencies. Make cards for four or five new medical emergencies. Write the sentence in English on one side of the card. Write the sentence in your language on the other side.

Show what you know!

GROUPS OF 3. Have you or someone you know ever had a medical emergency? What happened? What did you do?

Call 911 to report a medical emergency

Listening and Speaking

1 BEFORE YOU LISTEN

READ. CLASS. Read about 911 emergency calls. Then look at each picture. What is the situation? Should you call 911?

> Call 911 when there is an emergency situation. Calling 911 is free from any telephone in the U.S.

2 LISTEN

A CLASS. Look at the picture. Guess: What is happening?

CD3 T34
B Listen to the conversation. Was your guess in Exercise A correct?

CD3 T34
C Listen again. What does the 911 operator ask? Check the questions.

- ☐ What's your emergency?
- ☐ Where are you?
- ☐ What's the location of the emergency?
- ☐ What are the cross streets?
- ☐ What are you doing?
- ☐ What's your name?

CD3 T34
D Listen again. Where is the emergency?

Write the names of the cross streets. _____

CD3 T35
E Listen to the whole conversation. How is the man going to get to the hospital? Circle the letter.

a. an ambulance   b. a taxi

3 CONVERSATION

Pronunciation Watch

CD3 T36

A 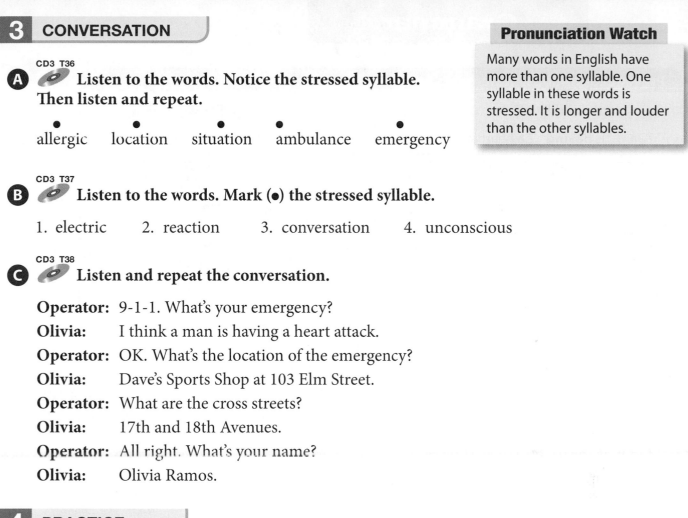 Listen to the words. Notice the stressed syllable. Then listen and repeat.

Many words in English have more than one syllable. One syllable in these words is stressed. It is longer and louder than the other syllables.

  •   •   •   •   •

allergic   location   situation   ambulance   emergency

CD3 T37

B Listen to the words. Mark (•) the stressed syllable.

1. electric   2. reaction   3. conversation   4. unconscious

CD3 T38

C Listen and repeat the conversation.

Operator: 9-1-1. What's your emergency?

Olivia: I think a man is having a heart attack.

Operator: OK. What's the location of the emergency?

Olivia: Dave's Sports Shop at 103 Elm Street.

Operator: What are the cross streets?

Olivia: 17th and 18th Avenues.

Operator: All right. What's your name?

Olivia: Olivia Ramos.

4 PRACTICE

A PAIRS. Practice the conversation.

B ROLE PLAY. PAIRS. Make new conversations. Use different emergencies and locations.

A: 9-1-1. What's your emergency?

B: _____.

A: OK. What is the location of the emergency?

B: _____.

A: What are the cross streets?

B: _____ and _____.

A: All right. What's your name?

B: _____.

Grammar

Present continuous: Statements and questions

Affirmative		
A man	**is having**	a heart attack.

Negative			
He	**is**	not	**breathing**.

Yes / No questions		
Is	he	**bleeding**?

Short answers					
Yes,	he	**is**.	**No**,	he	**'s not**.

Information questions			
What	**are**	they	**doing**?
Where		you	**going**?
What	**is**	**happening**	now?
Who		**calling**	911?

Answers		
They	**'re waiting**.	
I	**'m going**	to the clinic.
He	**'s talking**	to the police.
The driver	**is calling**.	

1 PRACTICE

Complete the sentences. Use the correct present continuous form of the verb in parentheses.

1. Help! Call 911! My mother __is choking__ !
   (choke)

2. A man just fell down in the parking lot. He _____.
   (not breathe)

3. _____ you _____ to the 911 operator now?
   (talk)
   Tell him we need an ambulance right away.

4. A woman _____ on the ground. I think she's unconscious.
   (lie)

5. They are taking Frank to the hospital. Who _____ with him?
   (go)

6. The police _____. Where _____ they _____?
   (leave)   (go)

7. What _____? There are a lot of fire trucks in the street.
   (happen)

8. I fell off my bicycle and hurt my knee. It's sore, but it _____.
   (not bleed)

9. I'm taking Mike to the emergency room. I think he _____
   (have)
   an allergic reaction to some food he ate.

Grammar Watch

- You can use contractions in the present continuous.

  She's bleeding.
  They aren't breathing.
  What's happening?

- See page 290 for spelling rules for *-ing* verbs.

Complete the phone conversation between two friends. Use the correct present continuous form of the verb in parentheses.

A: You won't believe this. There was an accident in front of my house!

B: Oh, no! What _'s happening_ ?
　　　　　　　　　(happen)

A: Well, one man is ＿＿＿＿＿＿ 911. Wait … Now I see an ambulance.
　　　　　　　　　(call)
　　It ＿＿＿＿＿＿ down the street. And a fire truck.
　　　(come)

B: Is anyone hurt?

A: I'm not sure. A man ＿＿＿＿＿＿ a woman. He ＿＿＿＿＿＿ to her
　　　　　　　　　　　(help)　　　　　　　　**(talk)**
　　and she ＿＿＿＿＿＿ her head. I think she ＿＿＿＿＿＿ .
　　　　　(hold)　　　　　　　　　**(bleed)**

Show what you know!　Talk about medical emergencies

STEP 1. PAIRS. Student A, look at the picture on this page. Student B, look at the picture on page 247.

Student A, study the picture. What are the people doing? Write six sentences.

　A baby is crying.

STEP 2. SAME PAIRS. Talk about your pictures. What is different? Find at least six differences.

A: *In my picture, a baby is crying.*
B: *In my picture, a baby is sleeping.*

Can you…talk about medical emergencies? ☐

Life Skills

1 IDENTIFY FIRE HAZARDS

PAIRS. Look at the picture. Match the fire hazards to their descriptions.

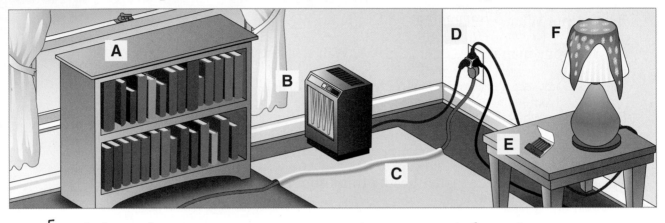

1. __F__ cloth on a lamp

2. ____ too many plugs in an electrical outlet

3. ____ an electrical cord under a rug

4. ____ no window exit

5. ____ matches available to children

6. ____ a heater close to a curtain

2 IDENTIFY FIRE SAFETY WORDS

A What fire safety words do you know? Write the words from the box.

> an escape plan   exits   a fire escape   ~~a fire extinguisher~~   a smoke alarm

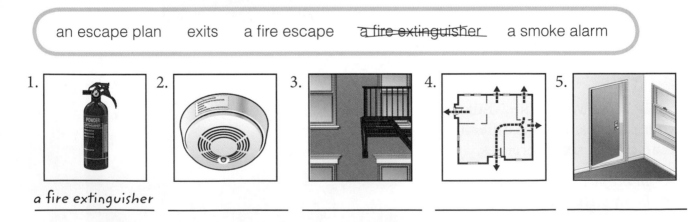

1. a fire extinguisher

2. _____

3. _____

4. _____

5. _____

CD3 T39

B Listen and check your answers. Then listen and repeat.

C GROUPS OF 3. What are other home fire hazards? What can people do to make their home safer?

3 LEARN FIRE SAFETY TIPS

CD3 T40

A Listen to the fire safety tips. Then listen again. Complete the tips.

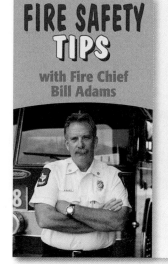

FIRE SAFETY TIPS

with Fire Chief
Bill Adams

1. Leave your _____ immediately. Do not take anything with you.

2. Don't stop to call _____. Call from a neighbor's house outside of your building.

3. Don't use an _____ to exit your building. Use the stairs.

4. Feel every closed _____ before opening it. Do not open a door that is hot. Try to find another exit.

5. If you smell _____, stay close to the floor. Cover your mouth and nose with a wet cloth.

6. When you get outside, do not go back into your home for any reason. Tell _____ about anyone still inside the building.

B READ. PAIRS. Read about Carmen. Which of the fire safety tips from Exercise A did she follow? Did she make any mistakes?

Last night there was a fire in Carmen's apartment building. First, she called 911. Then she got her wallet and keys from her bedroom. she touched the front door to her apartment, but it was not hot. She opened the door. She smelled smoke so she ran to the stairs. She didn't take the elevator. She waited across the street from the building until the firefighters said it was OK to go back inside.

4 TALK ABOUT FIRE ESCAPE PLANS

PAIRS. Look at the Pierre family escape plan. Answer the questions.

1. How many bedrooms are there?

2. How many people live there?

3. How many windows are there?

4. How many exits are there in each bedroom? Where are they?

5. Where is the family meeting place?

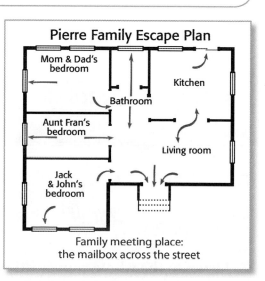

Pierre Family Escape Plan

Mom & Dad's bedroom

Kitchen

Bathroom

Aunt Fran's bedroom

Living room

Jack & John's bedroom

Family meeting place: the mailbox across the street

Can you...understand fire safety procedures? ☐

Listening and Speaking

1 BEFORE YOU LISTEN

CLASS. Look at the dangerous situations. What are some other dangerous situations?

a construction accident

a car accident

a robbery

an explosion

2 LISTEN

A CLASS. Look at the picture. Guess: What are Mr. and Mrs. Novak talking about?

a. traffic   b. the news   c. the weather

CD3 T41

B Listen to the conversation. Was your guess in Exercise A correct?

CD3 T41

C Listen again. Which story are they talking about?

a.
MORNING HERALD
Fire Destroys Hotel,
No Injuries Reported

b.
Greenville Times
Route 52 Car Accident
Leaves Two Hospitalized

c.
Village News
Gas Explosion Injures Two

d.
Journal News
First Federal Bank Robbed, No One Hurt

CD3 T42

D Listen to the whole conversation.

What problem did the emergency situation cause? _____

3 CONVERSATION

CD3 T43

A Listen to the pairs of words. Notice the sound /h/ at the beginning of the second word in each pair. Then listen and repeat.

1. ear   hear   3. art   heart

2. I   high   4. ow   how

CD3 T44

B Listen to each pair of words. Are the two words the same (*S*) or different (*D*)? Write *S* or *D*.

1. _____   2. _____   3. _____   4. _____   5. _____   6. _____

CD3 T45

C Listen and repeat the conversation.

Mr. Novak: Did you hear what happened yesterday?

Mrs. Novak: No. What happened?

Mr. Novak: There was a gas explosion downtown.

Mrs. Novak: Oh my gosh. That's terrible. Was anybody hurt?

Mr. Novak: Yes. Two people went to the hospital.

4 PRACTICE

A PAIRS. Practice the conversation. Then make new conversations. Use the information in the boxes.

A: Did you hear what happened yesterday?

B: No. What happened?

A: There was a _____ downtown.

B: Oh my gosh. That's terrible. Was anybody hurt?

A: _____

> robbery
> car accident
> construction accident

> No one was hurt.
> There were no injuries.
> Four people were hurt.

B MAKE IT PERSONAL. PAIRS. Make your own conversations. Talk about an emergency situation you have heard about.

Grammar

There was / There were

Affirmative			
There	**was**	a gas explosion	yesterday.
	were	two car accidents	last week.

Negative		
There	**wasn't**	a fire.
	was no	fire.
	weren't	any injuries.
	were no	injuries.

Yes / No questions		
Was	**there**	a fire?
Were		any injuries?

Short answers					
Yes,	**there**	**was.**	No,	**there**	**wasn't.**
		were.			**weren't.**

1 PRACTICE

Complete the conversations. Use *there* and *was* or *were*.

1. **A:** What happened downtown last night?

   B: _____There was_____ a robbery at the jewelry store.

   A: _____ any customers there?

   B: Yes, _____. But no one was hurt.

2. **A:** _____ a problem at the high school last night.

   B: I know. _____ a fight after the basketball game.

   A: Wow! Did the police come?

   B: Yes, _____ five police cars in the parking lot.

3. **A:** _____ an explosion at the factory yesterday.

   B: Was anybody hurt?

   A: No, luckily _____ no injuries.

4. **A:** _____ an accident on Main Street this morning?

   B: Yes, _____. I heard about it on the radio.

   A: I thought so. _____ a lot of traffic and I was late to work.

A WRITE. Look at the pictures of emergency situations from the news last night. Write two sentences to describe each picture. Use *there was* or *there were* and words from the box or your own ideas.

> a lot of smoke   a traffic jam   a crowd of people   lots of police

There was a fire last night. There was a lot of smoke.

1.

2.

3.

4.

B PAIRS. Compare your answers.

Show what you know!   Describe an emergency

STEP 1. GROUPS OF 3. Student A, tell about an emergency situation you have heard about. Students B and C, ask questions to get more information.

A: *I watched the news on TV last night. There was a fire on Center Street.*
B: *Was anybody hurt?*
A: *Some people went to the hospital.*

STEP 2. Tell the class about an emergency situation.

Can you...describe an emergency? ☐

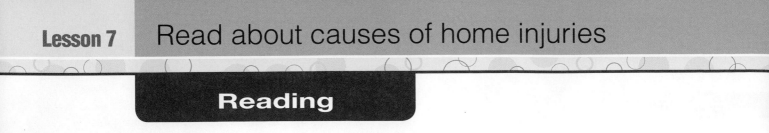

Reading

1 BEFORE YOU READ

CLASS. Look at the pictures of everyday objects in the home. Which of these objects can be dangerous?

candy

cleaning supplies

a bathtub

a stove

a balloon

medicine

2 READ

CD3 T46

Listen. Read the article. Were your guesses in Before You Read correct?

Accidents Will Happen

What do you think of when you think of home? Do you think of comfort and safety? Well, think again! Every four seconds a person in the U.S. gets injured in the home. In fact, one-third of all injuries happen at home. Every year about 10 million people visit hospital emergency rooms because of household accidents.

What are the most common causes of home injuries?

❶ **Falls** are the most common cause of home injuries. More than 5 million people are injured by falls each year. Falls are especially dangerous for people age 65 and older.

Safety tips: Make sure halls and stairs have enough light. Keep your floors clear of clothes, toys, and other things. Put nonslip rubber mats in bathtubs and showers.

❷ **Poisonings** are the second most common cause of home injuries. There are 2.3 million poisonings every year. Poisonings can happen to people of all ages.

Safety tips: Keep all medicine and cleaning supplies away from children. Keep all your medicines in their original containers so you don't take the wrong medicine.

3 **Burns** are the third leading cause of home injuries. There are 261,000 fire and burn injuries every year. Most burns happen in the kitchen while cooking or eating food.

Safety tips: Stay in the kitchen while food is cooking. Turn pot handles inward, so they don't stick out from the stove. Don't wear loose clothes while cooking.

4 **Choking** accidents are the fourth leading cause of home injuries. Children—especially those younger than five—can easily choke on food and small objects. Candy causes 20 percent of all childhood choking accidents. Any object that can fit inside a paper towel roll can cause choking.

Safety tips: Don't give young children small pieces of candy. Keep small objects like coins, jewelry, balloons, and toys with small parts out of their reach. Be sure to read toy labels for warnings.

Source: www.homesafetycouncil.org

3 CHECK YOUR UNDERSTANDING

A GROUPS OF 3. Look at paragraphs 2, 3, and 4. Each person choose a paragraph. Say which sentence in each paragraph gives the main idea. Say which sentences contain supporting details.

In paragraph one, the main idea sentence is Falls are the most common cause of home injuries. *The supportive details are . . .*

B GROUPS OF 3. Read the safety tips for each kind of home injury. Which of the tips do you do?

I have rubber mats in my bathtub.

Reading Skill:
Identifying Supporting Details

Supporting details are reasons, examples, steps, or other kinds of information. Authors use supporting details to help explain the main ideas.

Show what you know!

PRE-WRITING. PAIRS. How safe is your home? What can you do to make it safer?

WRITE. Write about the safety of your home. See page 273.

Listening and Speaking

1 BEFORE YOU LISTEN

A **CLASS.** Do you know what to do if you are pulled over by the police?

B Take the quiz. Check *True* or *False*.

Do you know...
**what to do if you
get pulled over?**

1. You should always pull over to the left. ☐ True ☐ False

2. After you pull over, you should get out of your car. ☐ True ☐ False

3. Keep your hands on the steering wheel when
   the police officer talks to you. ☐ True ☐ False

4. Give the police officer your driver's license, registration,
   and proof of insurance. ☐ True ☐ False

5. Don't argue with the police officer. ☐ True ☐ False

6. If a police officer gives you a ticket, you need to pay
   the police officer immediately. ☐ True ☐ False

2 LISTEN

CD3 T47

A Listen to the police officer talking about what to do if you're
pulled over. Then check your answers on the quiz.

B **PAIRS.** Discuss the quiz. Did any of the answers surprise you?
What did you learn from the police officer's talk?

3 CONVERSATION

A CLASS. Look at the traffic violations. What are some other violations you know of?

running a red light

tailgating

not wearing a seat belt

speeding

CD3 T48

B Listen and repeat the conversation.

A: I need to see your license, registration, and proof of insurance.

B: OK. My license is in my pocket. The other things are in the glove compartment.

A: That's fine. You can get them.

B: Here you go.

A: I'll be back in a moment. Please turn off your engine and stay in your car.

[a few minutes later]

A: Do you know why I pulled you over?

B: I'm not sure.

A: I pulled you over for speeding.

B: I see.

4 PRACTICE

A PAIRS. Practice the conversation. Then make new conversations. Use different traffic violations.

B MAKE IT PERSONAL. GROUPS OF 3. Talk about a time you or someone you know was pulled over.

Grammar

Compound imperatives				
Affirmative				
Turn off	your engine	**and**	**stay**	in your car.
Negative				
Don't get out	of your car	**or**	**take off**	your seat belt.

Grammar Watch

- Connect two affirmative imperatives with *and*.
- Connect two negative imperatives with *or*.

PRACTICE

A Read the driving rules. Complete each sentence with *and* or *or*.

1. Drive carefully __and__ obey all traffic laws.

2. Be sure to wear your seat belt _____ use car seats for young children.

3. Don't use your cell phone _____ read a map while driving.

4. Drive more slowly _____ put on your headlights in bad weather.

5. Don't tailgate _____ change lanes without signaling.

B Read the advice about what to do during a traffic stop. Rewrite each pair of sentences as two imperatives with *and* or *or*.

1. You should use your turn signal. You should pull over to a safe spot.

   Use your turn signal and pull over to a safe spot.

2. You should wait for the police officer. You should roll down your window.

   _____

3. You should be polite. You should follow the officer's instructions.

   _____

4. You should not argue with the officer. You should not offer money to the officer.

   _____

5. You should not start your car. You should not leave until the officer gives you permission to go.

   _____

1 GRAMMAR

Complete the phone conversations. Use the correct present continuous form of the verb in parentheses, or use the correct form of *there be* in the past.

1. **Bill:** Hi, Ann. Listen, I'm going to be late. I ___*am sitting*___ in my car.
(sit)

    I'm stuck in a traffic jam. _____ an accident near Lakeland.
    (there be)

    Ann: Oh, no! Was anyone hurt?

    Bill: I'm not sure. _____ an ambulance
    (there be)
    here a few minutes ago.

    Ann: _____ you _____?
    (move)

    Bill: Actually, a police officer _____
    (direct)
    traffic now. Got to go. I'll see you soon.

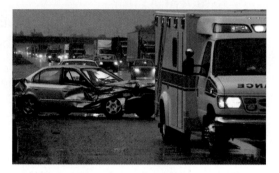

2. **Sue:** Hi, Rita. I hope I _____ at a bad time?
(not call)

    Rita: No, I _____ today. The factory is closed.
    (not work)
    _____ an explosion yesterday.
    (there be)

    Sue: You're kidding!

    Rita: No, it's true. Luckily, _____ no injuries.
    (there be)

    Sue: That's amazing. _____ a fire?
    (there be)

    Rita: Yeah, a big one. _____ ten or twelve fire trucks there.
    (there be)

    Sue: Wow.

2 LIFE SKILLS WRITING Complete an employee accident report. See page 266.

3 ACT IT OUT — What do you say?

STEP 1. CLASS. Review the Lesson 2 conversation between the 911 operator and Olivia (CD 3 track 34).

STEP 2. ROLE PLAY. PAIRS. Student A, you see an emergency situation. Student B, you are the 911 operator.

Student A:
- Think of an emergency situation.
- Role-play calling 911. Describe the emergency.
- Answer the 911 operator's questions.

Student B:
- Ask about the emergency.
- Ask about the location of the emergency.
- Ask for the caller's name.

4 READ AND REACT — Problem-solving

STEP 1. Read about Fahad's problem.

Fahad had an accident at work. He burned himself and he is in a lot of pain. Fahad went to a clinic and the doctor said he should not work for one week. Fahad is afraid to tell his boss about the accident. He doesn't want to lose his job.

STEP 2. PAIRS. What is Fahad's problem? What can he do? Here are some ideas.

- He can report his accident to his boss.
- He can say nothing and continue working.
- He can ask a co-worker to cover his hours for the week.
- He can _____.

5 CONNECT

For your Study Skills Activity, go to page 254.
For your Team Project, go to page 284.

Which goals can you check off? Go back to page 205.

The World of Work

Preview

Look at the picture.
Where is the woman?
What is she doing?

UNIT GOALS

- [ ] Identify job responsibilities
- [ ] Ask about policies at work
- [ ] Talk about responsibilities
- [ ] Read a pay stub
- [ ] Ask a co-worker to cover your hours
- [ ] Ask about work schedules
- [ ] Request a schedule change
- [ ] Complete a vacation request form

1 WHAT DO YOU KNOW?

A CLASS. Look at the pictures. What are the people doing? Which job responsibilities do you know?

CD3 T49

B Look at the pictures and listen. Listen again and repeat.

2 PRACTICE

A PAIRS. What are the job responsibilities for each of the following jobs?

computer system administrator	nurse assistant
sales assistant	warehouse worker

A: *What are the responsibilities of a nurse assistant?*
B: *Wash hands, wear latex gloves . . .*

B WORD PLAY. GROUPS OF 3. Look at the categories of job responsibilities. Complete the chart with job responsibilities from the list on page 227. There may be more than one correct answer.

Category	Job responsibility
Wear the right clothing	*wear a uniform*
Follow health and safety rules	
Be on time	
Communicate with others	
Use equipment correctly	

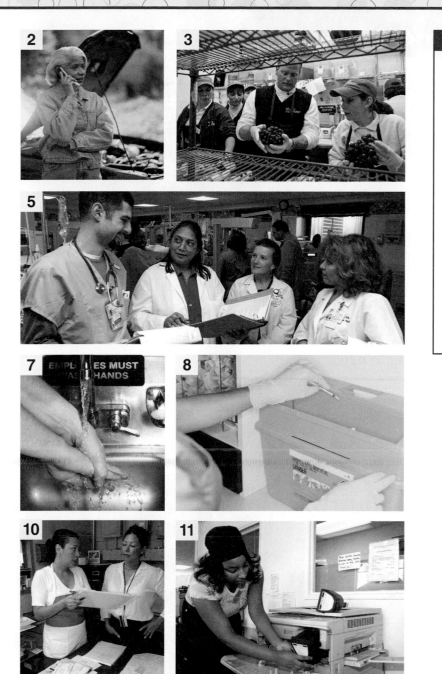

Job Responsibilities

1. clock in/out
2. call in late
3. follow directions
4. report problems with the equipment
5. work as a team
6. wear a uniform
7. wash hands
8. wear latex gloves
9. wear safety gear
10. ask questions
11. maintain the equipment
12. store the equipment

Learning Strategy

Learn words that go together

Choose six job responsibilities from the vocabulary list. Make vocabulary cards. Write the verb on the front of the card and the other words on the back. For example, *wear / a uniform.*

Show what you know!

STEP 1. Look at the list of job responsibilities. Think of a job you have or want. List the responsibilities for that job.

STEP 2. PAIRS. Tell your partner about the job and the responsibilities.

Ask about policies at work

Listening and Speaking

1 BEFORE YOU LISTEN

A CLASS. Look at the picture of a customer and an employee at the Greenville Hotel. Imagine you are the manager of the hotel. What is the employee doing wrong?

B CLASS. What other things are employees usually not allowed to do at work?

2 LISTEN

CD3 T50

A Listen to Michelle Rivera talking to new employees at their orientation meeting. What does Michelle talk about?

☐ wearing the right clothing

☐ wearing safety gear

☐ being on time

☐ working as a team

CD3 T50

B Listen again. Complete the sentences. Write the words you hear.

1. You must wear your _____ badge during your work shift.

2. Employees in housekeeping and food service must _____.

3. During your 6-hour shift you must take a 30-minute _____.

4. You must not _____ or _____ for another employee.

New employee orientation

3 CONVERSATION

A 🔘 Listen to the questions. Then listen and repeat.

Can I ask you a few questions?

Do we have to clock out?

Are we allowed to wear sneakers?

Pronunciation Watch

In *Yes / No* questions, the voice usually goes up at the end.

B 🔘 Monica is a new employee at the Greenville Hotel. She's asking Michelle Rivera a question. Listen and repeat the conversation.

Monica: Hi, Michelle. Can I ask you a question?

Michelle: Sure. What do you want to know?

Monica: Am I allowed to wear sneakers?

Michelle: No, you aren't. You have to wear black shoes.

Monica: OK. Thanks. I'm glad I asked.

4 PRACTICE

A PAIRS. Practice the conversation. Then make new conversations. Use your partner's name and the information in the boxes.

A: Hi, _____. Can I ask you a question?

B: Sure. What do you want to know?

A: Am I allowed to _____?

B: No, you aren't. You have to _____.

A: OK. Thanks. I'm glad I asked.

eat at my desk	eat in the break room
park anywhere	park in the back
trade shifts	talk to a manager

B ROLE PLAY. PAIRS. Make your own conversations. Use different information.

Grammar

Expressions of necessity: *must / have to*

You	have to must		
He	has to must	wear	black shoes.

Expressions of prohibition: *must not / can't*

You	must not can't	wear	sneakers.

· · · · · · · · · · · ·

Grammar Watch

We almost never use *must* for questions. Use *have to* for questions.

Do we have to wear a uniform?

---

1   PRACTICE

Complete the conversations. Use *must*, *must not*, *have to*, or *can't* and a verb. There may be more than one correct answer.

1. **A:** Are you going to the orientation meeting today?

   B: Yes. All new employees ___*have to go*___ to the meeting.

2. **A:** Can we smoke in the break room?

   B: No, we _____ anywhere in the building.

   There's a smoking area outside.

3. **A:** What's the uniform for front desk employees?

   B: Front desk employees _____ dark suits and black shoes.

4. **A:** How do I take a sick day?

   B: You just call your manager. But you _____ your

   manager at least 30 minutes before the start of your shift.

5. **A:** I'm going to eat lunch at my desk.

   B: Sorry, it's not allowed. You _____ at your desk.

   You _____ in the break room.

A READ. Read the information.
Answer the questions.

1. Who is the information for?

2. What is the information about?

B Complete the statements
about Jack's responsibilities.
Use the correct form of
have to, must, must not,
or *can't.*

Your Duties as an Employee

To make your work more successful, here is a list of reminders:

- Be on time. This is very important.
- Call your supervisor if you are going to be late.
- Begin and end your breaks at the scheduled times.
- Don't forget to clock in and out.
- Don't clock in or out for other employees.
- Don't make personal calls at work.

1. Jack *has to be* _____ on time for work.

2. He _____ if he's going to be late.

3. He _____ his breaks on time.

4. He _____ in and out.

5. He _____ for other employees.

6. He _____ personal calls at work.

C PAIRS. Compare your answers.

Show what you know! Talk about responsibilities

STEP 1. NETWORK. Are you an employee? A student? A parent? Form three
groups. If you are a member of more than one of these three groups, choose one.

STEP 2. SAME GROUPS. What responsibilities do members of your group
have? Write at least five responsibilities using *have to* and *can't.*

> Students have to be on time for class.

STEP 3. CLASS. Write three lists of responsibilities on the board.
Which group has the most responsibilities: employees, students, or parents?

Can you...talk about responsibilities? ☐

Life Skills

1 READ A PAY STUB

A **PAIRS.** Look at Frank's pay stub. How much money did he earn? How much money did he get?

Frank Martin	**Pay Date** 10/29	**Pay Period** 10/17–10/23	**Rate of Pay** $10.00	

Description	Hours	Earnings	Deductions	Amount
Regular	40	$400.00	Federal tax	$40.00
			State tax	$20.00
			Social Security	$30.00
			Medicare	$7.20
			State Disability Insurance (SDI)	$6.00

Total Gross Pay	$400.00	Total Deductions	$103.20	**Net Pay** $296.80

1 — days you worked for this paycheck
2 — amount of money you get per hour
3 — amount of money you get *before* deductions
4 — money taken out to pay for taxes and insurance
5 — amount of money you get *after* deductions

B Look at Frank's pay stub again. Match the deductions with the definitions.

1. ___e___ Federal tax   a. tax you pay the state government

2. _____ State tax   b. money for older people not working now

3. _____ Social Security   c. money for workers who are disabled and can't work

4. _____ Medicare   d. money for health care for older people

5. _____ SDI   e. tax you pay the U.S. government

C Look at Frank's pay stub again. Correct the incorrect statements.

1. Frank's pay stub is for ~~two weeks~~ *one week* of work.

2. Frank's company paid him on 10/23 for this pay period.

3. Frank gets paid $40 per hour.

4. Four deductions were taken out of Frank's paycheck.

5. Frank paid the U.S. government $20 in taxes.

6. Frank got $400 after all deductions were taken out.

A Read Alex's pay stub. Answer the questions.

Note: When you work more than 40 hours a week, you get a special overtime rate of pay. It is one and a half times your regular rate.

Alex Simon			Pay Date 12/22	Pay Period 12/02–12/16	Rate of Pay $12.00
Description	**Hours**	**Earnings**	**Deductions**		**Amount**
Regular	80	$960.00	Federal tax		$114.00
Overtime	10	$180.00	State tax		$57.00
			FICA ┌Social Security		$85.50
			└Medicare		$20.50
Total Gross Pay		$1,140.00	**Total Deductions**	$277.00	**Net Pay** $863.00

1. How long is the pay period? *From December 2 to December 16*

2. On what day did the company pay Alex for this pay period? _____

3. How many overtime hours did Alex work? _____

4. How many total hours did Alex work? _____

5. What is Alex's regular rate of pay? _____

6. What is Alex's gross pay? _____

7. How much money was taken out in deductions? _____

8. What is Alex's net pay? _____

B PAIRS. Check your answers.

C PAIRS. Look at the pay stub in Exercise A. Look at Alex's overtime earnings. How much did Alex get paid per hour for overtime?

Can you...read a pay stub? ☐

Ask a co-worker to cover your hours

Listening and Speaking

1 BEFORE YOU LISTEN

A **READ. Look at the picture. Read the information about Ron and Jim. Answer the questions.**

> Ron is a manager at Discount Music. One of his employees, Jim, calls the store. He can't work his shift because he has to baby-sit his niece. It is only an hour before his shift starts. Ron can't find anyone to cover Jim's shift. There are a lot of customers and Ron has to work very hard.

1. Why can't Jim work his shift?

2. What problems does this cause?

B **GROUPS OF 3. What should employees do if they are going to miss work?**

2 LISTEN

A **CLASS. Luis and Rachel are co-workers. Look at the picture. Guess: What are they talking about?**

CD3 T53

B **Listen to the conversation. Was your guess in Exercise A correct?**

CD3 T53

C Listen again. Answer the questions.

1. Luis asks Rachel for a favor. What's the favor?

2. Does Rachel agree to do the favor?

CD3 T54

D **Listen to the whole conversation. Answer the question.**

Luis and Rachel check the schedule. What do they want to know?
a. who is working that day   b. what time the shift starts   c. what time the shift ends

3 CONVERSATION

CD3 T55

A 🔘 **Listen to the sentences. Then listen and repeat.**

What's up?   I have to study.

What time do you start?   I start at 9:30.

CD3 T56

B 🔘 **Listen and repeat the conversation.**

Luis: Hi, Rachel. Can I ask you a favor?

Rachel: Sure. What is it?

Luis: I'm on the schedule for Monday, but I can't come in.

Rachel: Oh. What's up?

Luis: I have to study for a test. Can you take my shift for me?

Rachel: What time do you start?

Luis: 9:30.

Rachel: No problem.

> **Pronunciation Watch**
>
> Information questions and statements usually end with falling intonation. The voice jumps up on the most important word in the sentence and then goes down at the end.

4 PRACTICE

A **PAIRS. Practice the conversation. Then make new conversations. Use your partner's name and the information in the boxes.**

A: Hi, _____. Can I ask you a favor?

B: Sure. What is it?

A: I'm on the schedule for Monday, but I can't come in.

B: Oh. ▮

A: I have to ▮. Can you take my shift for me?

B: What time do you start?

A: 9:30.

B: No problem.

> What's going on?
> What's happening?
> Why not?

> baby-sit my niece
> go to the dentist
> pick up my in-laws at the airport

B **ROLE PLAY. PAIRS. Make your own conversations. Use different reasons for missing work.**

Grammar

Information questions with *Who*

	Who = subject		Answers
Who	**works** **wrote**	on Mondays? the schedule?	Luis and I work on Mondays. Mary wrote the schedule.
	Who = object		Answers
Who	**do** I **give** **did** she **see**	my timesheet to? yesterday?	Give your timesheet to your supervisor. She saw Jeff.

Grammar Watch

- To ask about the subject, use *Who* + a verb.
- To ask about the object, use *Who* + a helping verb + a subject + a verb.

1 PRACTICE

A Put the words in order. Write questions. Capitalize the first word.

1. who / extra hours / needs ___Who needs extra hours?___

2. I / ask / who / do / about sick time _____

3. the schedule / makes up / who _____

4. I / call / do / who / about trading shifts _____

5. goes / on break / who / at 10:45 A.M. _____

B Write questions with *Who* to ask for the underlined information.

1. **A:** ___Who needs a favor?___
   B: <u>Bill</u> needs a favor.

2. **A:** _____
   B: I usually work with <u>Jung-Su</u>.

3. **A:** _____
   B: Jim needs to call <u>his supervisor</u>.

4. **A:** _____
   B: They need to see <u>Fran</u>.

5. **A:** _____
   B: <u>Jose and Carlos</u> helped me out.

Information questions with *What / Which / When / Where*					Answers
What time	**does**	my shift	**begin**?		At 3:00 P.M.
Which days	**do**	I	**have off**	this week?	Thursday and Friday.
When	**did**	you	**start**	your break?	Five minutes ago.
Where	**do**	we	**go**	to clock in?	The break room.

2 PRACTICE

Complete the conversations. Write information questions. Use *What time,*
Which, When, Where and the words in parentheses.

1. **A:** (day / you / have off) _Which day do you have off?_

   B: Tuesday.

2. **A:** (my shift / start) _____

   B: At 3:00 P.M.

3. **A:** (I / get / a vacation) _____

   B: After six months on the job.

4. **A:** (I / clock in) _____

   B: Outside the employee break room. The time clock is on the wall.

5. **A:** (we / get / breaks) _____

   B: At 10:15 A.M. and 2:30 P.M. Check with your supervisor.

Show what you know! Ask about work schedules

GROUPS OF 3. Look at the
work schedule. Student A,
choose one employee.
Students B and C, guess the
employee. Ask questions with
What, Which, and *When.*

A: *OK, I'm ready.*
B: *What does the employee do?*
A: *He's a cashier.*
C: *What time does he start work?*

	Mon.	Tues.	Wed.	Thu.	Fri.	Sat.	Sun.
Eduardo, stock clerk	OFF	OFF	6–2 Break: 11–11:30	6–2 Break: 11–11:30	6–2 Break: 11–11:30	6–2 Break: 11–11:30	6–2 Break: 11–11:30
Stan, stock clerk	OFF	OFF	6–1 Break: 11–11:30	6–1 Break: 11–11:30	6–1 Break: 11–11:30	6–2 Break: 11–11:30	6–2 Break: 11–11:30
Deng, stock clerk	6–2 Break: 12–12:30	6–2 Break: 12–12:30	6–1 Break: 12–12:30	6–1 Break: 12–12:30	OFF	OFF	6–2 Break: 12–12:30
Ivan, cashier	OFF	OFF	8–2 Break: 11–11:30	8–2 Break: 11–11:30	8–2 Break: 11–11:30	8–2 Break: 11–11:30	8–2 Break: 11–11:30
Marco, cashier	8–2 Break: 12–12:30	8–2 Break: 12–12:30	8–2 Break: 12–12:30	8–2 Break: 12–12:30	OFF	OFF	8–2 Break: 12–12:30
Will, cashier	OFF	9–2 Break: 12–12:30	9–2 Break: 12–12:30	9–2 Break: 12–12:30	9–2 Break: 12–12:30	OFF	9–2 Break: 12–12:30

Can you…ask about work schedules? ☐

Reading

1   BEFORE YOU READ

A READ. PAIRS. Look at the pictures. Read about Fran and Al. Why did they stop working?

Fran   Al

> Fran is 70 years old. She is retired. She stopped working in 2007.
>
> Al can't work. He was in an accident and now he is disabled.

B CLASS. Social Security is a government program. What do you know about it?

Reading Skill:
Think About What You Know

Before you read, think about what you already know about the topic. This information will help you understand the article.

2   READ

CD3 T57

 Listen. Read the FAQ (Frequently Asked Questions).

Social Security FAQ

Home   Contact Us   Help   Search

What is Social Security?
Social Security is a U.S. government program. It pays money (benefits) to people age 62 or older who have retired. It also provides money for people who can't work because of a disability.

How did Social Security start?
The U.S. government created Social Security in 1935 to help needy Americans. At that time, many Americans were poor. People had to work their whole lives. People who were too old or too sick to work had to get help from family members. People without families had a difficult time.

How does Social Security work?
Workers pay a Social Security tax. The money is automatically taken out of each paycheck. This money is used to pay the benefits of people who are retired or disabled today.

How much do people pay?
Workers pay 6.2 percent of their earnings. Their employers pay another
6.2 percent. Self-employed workers pay 12.4 percent of their earnings.

Can everyone get Social Security benefits?
No. To get Social Security payments, you have to work and pay Social
Security taxes for a total of ten years.

Can a noncitizen of the United States get Social Security benefits?
Yes. Any person who works legally in the U.S. and pays Social Security
taxes for ten years can get benefits.

Does everyone get the same amount?
No. People who work longer and pay more Social Security taxes get a
bigger retirement benefit. The average Social Security payment is now
over $1,000 a month.

Top of page

3 CHECK YOUR UNDERSTANDING

A Read the FAQ again. Read the statements. Circle *True* or *False*.

1. The U.S. government created the Social Security   **True**   **False**
   program in 1935.

2. Every retired person in the U.S. gets   **True**   **False**
   Social Security benefits.

3. You have to work a total of twenty years to get   **True**   **False**
   Social Security benefits.

4. Only U.S. citizens can get Social Security benefits.   **True**   **False**

5. Everyone gets the same Social Security payment.   **True**   **False**

B PAIRS. Look at the boldfaced questions in the FAQ. Ask and answer
the questions in your own words.

Show what you know!

PRE-WRITING. PAIRS. Someday you will retire. What year will that be?
What money will you live on when you retire?

WRITE. Write about your life when you are retired. See page 273.

Lesson 8 Request a schedule change

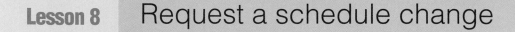

Listening and Speaking

1 BEFORE YOU LISTEN

CLASS. Look at some reasons that people change their work schedules. What are some other reasons?

My son is starting school.

I'm taking classes now.

My wife needs the car during the day.

My husband's work schedule changed.

2 LISTEN

A CLASS. Look at the picture of Linda and Ron. Guess: What is their relationship?

a. a customer and a manager
b. an employee and a manager

CD3 T58

B 🖸 Listen to Linda and Ron's conversation. Was your guess in Exercise A correct?

CD3 T58

C 🖸 Listen again. Answer the questions.

1. Why does Linda need to talk to Ron? _____

2. When does Linda work now? _____

3. When does she want to work? _____

4. Why does she ask for a schedule change? _____

CD3 T59

D 🖸 Listen to the whole conversation. What kind of class is Linda planning to take?

CONVERSATION

CD3 T60
Listen and repeat the conversation.

Linda: Excuse me, Ron. Can I speak to you for a minute?

Ron: Sure, Linda. What's up?

Linda: I need to talk to you about my schedule.

Ron: OK. Right now you work in the mornings, right?

Linda: Yes. But I'm planning to take classes now. Could I change to evenings?

Ron: Well, let me look at the schedule. I'll get back to you.

Linda: OK. Thanks.

4 **PRACTICE**

A **PAIRS. Practice the conversation. Then make new conversations. Use your partner's name and the information in the boxes.**

A: Excuse me, _____. Can I speak to you for a minute?

B: Sure, _____. What's up?

A: I need to talk to you about my schedule.

B: OK. Right now you work _____, right?

A: Yes. But _____. Could I change to _____?

B: Well, let me look at the schedule. I'll get back to you.

A: OK. Thanks.

the second shift	Tuesdays and Thursdays	full-time
my daughter is starting school	my hours changed at my other job	my mom can't take care of my son anymore
the first shift	Mondays and Wednesdays	part-time

B **ROLE PLAY. PAIRS. Make your own conversations. Use different reasons for asking for a change in schedule.**

5 **LIFE SKILLS WRITING**   Complete a vacation request form. See page 267.

Grammar

Can / Could to ask permission

Can Could	I	speak change have	to you? to evenings? Friday off?	Sure. Of course. Yes, you **can**.

Grammar Watch

- *Could* is more formal than *can* to ask permission.
- Answer a *could* permission question with *can*.

PRACTICE

A Complete the conversations. Write questions with *can* or *could*.

1. **A:** Can I take a break now? _____

   B: Sure, you can take a break. But please wait till Marlena comes back.

2. **A:** _____

   B: Sure. No problem. We can trade shifts on Friday.

3. **A:** _____

   B: I'm sorry, but you can't have Friday off. We need you on Friday.

4. **A:** _____

   B: Yes, we can talk about the schedule. Come into my office.

5. **A:** _____

   B: Sorry, I can't cover your hours tomorrow. I have plans.

6. **A:** _____

   B: Go ahead. You can leave a little early tonight. We're not that busy.

7. **A:** _____

   B: OK. I think I can give you more hours next week. I'll see what I can do.

B PAIRS. Student A, ask for permission to do something. Use the ideas in the box or your own ideas. Student B, answer Student A's questions.

> use your dictionary   borrow your pen   copy your notes

1 GRAMMAR

A Complete the conversation. Use *can, can't, could,* and *have to.*

Nora: Excuse me. This is my first day. _____Can_____ I ask you something?

Olga: Sure. What do you want to know?

Nora: Well, do we have to wear these uniforms?

Olga: No, we don't. We _____ wear our own shirts and pants if we want. But we _____ wear work boots. No sneakers or sandals. It's for safety.

Nora: I see. One more thing. _____ I ask you a favor?

Olga: What is it?

Nora: I'm supposed to work Monday, but I _____ . You're not on the schedule for Monday. _____ you take my shift?

Olga: Sure. But ask Mr. Wang first. We _____ get his permission.

> **Safety Reminder**
> All employees must wear work boots. No sneakers or sandals allowed!

B Complete the conversations. Write information questions with the words in parentheses.

1. **A:** (who) _Who do I give my vacation request form to?_

   B: Give your vacation request form to your supervisor.

2. **A:** (what time) _____

   B: Kevin can take his break at 12:30.

3. **A:** (where) _____

   B: You store the floor cleaning equipment in the hall closet.

4. **A:** (which days) _____

   B: Tanya works on Thursday, Friday, and Saturday this week.

5. **A:** (when) _____

   B: I worked overtime on Thursday and Saturday.

Go to the CD-ROM for more practice.

2 ACT IT OUT — What do you say?

STEP 1. CLASS. Review the Lesson 2 conversation between Monica and Michelle (CD 3 track 52).

STEP 2. ROLE PLAY. PAIRS. Student A, you are a new employee. Student B, you are an experienced employee.

> **Student A:** Ask about what employees have to do and what they are not allowed to do.

> **Student B:** Explain company policy.

3 READ AND REACT — Problem-solving

STEP 1. Read about Ivan's problem.

Ivan started working in a warehouse eight years ago. He likes the job but he needs to work more hours. A few months ago Ivan's boss hired some new employees. His boss gave them a lot of overtime hours. Ivan almost never gets overtime. He doesn't think this is fair.

STEP 2. PAIRS. What is Ivan's problem? What can he do? Here are some ideas.

- He can talk to his boss.
- He can say nothing and get a second job.
- He can offer to cover other employees' hours.
- He can _____.

4 CONNECT

For your Goal-setting Activity, go to page 255.
For your Team Project, go to page 285.

Which goals can you check off? Go back to page 225.

Information Gap Activities

UNIT 1, PAGE 13

A Student B, look at Joseph Smith's identification card. Answer Student A's questions about Joseph Smith. Use the information on the identification card.

B Student B, ask questions. Complete the missing information on the application.

Name of Applicant			
First	Last	Middle	Suffix (Jr., Sr., III)
Ana	Martinez	Maria	–
Social Security Number (SSN)	Place of Birth		Date of Birth (mm–dd–yyyy)
451-100-282	New York, NY		

Sex	Height		Weight	
Male ☐ Female ☑	Feet	Inches	110	Pounds

Eye Color	Hair Color

Residence Address		
Street		Apt. #
		–
City	State	Zip Code
Yonkers	NY	10701

UNIT 5, PAGE 91

STEP 1. PAIRS. Student B, Look at the picture. Don't show your picture to your partner.

STEP 2. SAME PAIRS. Talk about the pictures. What are the people doing? What problems do you see? Take notes. What are the differences in your pictures?

A: *In my picture, a man is fixing a sink in a kitchen.*

B: *In my picture, a man is cooking . . .*

UNIT 5, PAGE 97

STEP 1. PAIRS. Student B, you have an apartment for rent. Look at your apartment information in the ad.

STEP 2. SAME PAIRS. Student B, answer Student A's questions about your apartment.

STEP 3. SAME PAIRS. Change roles. Student B, ask about student A's apartment. Take notes.

APARTMENT FOR RENT. 2 BR, 1 BA, LR, EIK, nr. laundromat and bus stop, parking avail. $950/mo. + 1 mo. sec. dep. No fee.

Ask about:	Notes
number of bedrooms	
number of bathrooms	
laundry room	
parking	
rent, fees, security deposit	

UNIT 7, PAGE 131

Read the notes about the Lee family's appointments. Some information is missing. Take turns. Ask questions with *When* and *What time*. Write the missing information.

A: *When is Walter's dentist appointment?*

B: *On Friday at . . .*

Walter—dentist, on Friday at 4:15 P.M.

Gloria's checkup with Dr. Rosen, _____ A.M., Jan. _____

Jack—blood test at the hospital, _____ P.M. on _____. (Get there by _____.)

Olivia! You need to make an appointment to see Dr. Jay in 2 weeks.

Sue—call the Dr. tomorrow; his office is open from 8:00 A.M. to 5:00 P.M.

UNIT 11, PAGE 211

STEP 1. PAIRS. Student B, study the picture. What are the people doing? Write six sentences.

A baby is sleeping.

STEP 2. SAME PAIRS. Talk about your pictures. What is different? Find at least six differences.

A: *In my picture, a baby is crying.*

B: *In my picture, a baby is sleeping.*

Unit 1   Name Game

A GROUPS OF 5. Play the Name Game.

Nellie: My name is Nellie.

Pablo: Her name is Nellie. My name is Pablo.

Jun: Her name is Nellie. His name is Pablo.
My name is Jun.

Jai Yong: Her name is Nellie. Excuse me. What's
your name again, please?

Pablo: Pablo.

Jai Yong: OK, thanks. Her name is Nellie.
His name is Pablo. Her name is Jun.
My name is Jai Yong.

Simone: Her name is Nellie. His name is Pablo.
Her name is Jun. His name is Jai Yong.
My name is Simone.

B How many classmates' names do you remember?

Unit 2   Things We Have in Common

A Read the sentences. Check (✓) all the statements that are true for you.

- ☐ I have a small family.
- ☐ I have a large family.

- ☐ Most of my family lives in this country.
- ☐ Most of my family lives in my country.

- ☐ I live with my family.
- ☐ I live with friends.

- ☐ I'm married.
- ☐ I'm single.

- ☐ I have children.
- ☐ I don't have children.

- ☐ I have a job.
- ☐ I don't have a job.

B Walk around the room. Ask your classmates questions. For example,
Do you have a large family? Find classmates who have things in common
with you. Take notes.

C CLASS. Report to the class.

*Monica and I are both married. We both live with our families. Blanca and I both have
two children.*

Unit 3 Goal Visualization: *Where, Who, What*

A CLASS. Look at the picture of Brigitte. She's an ESL student at The Greenville Adult School. Today, she's doing some food shopping. Answer the questions.

1. Where is Brigitte?
2. What is she doing?
3. What is she saying?

B GROUPS OF 3. Think about your goals for learning English: Where do you want to speak English? Who do you want to speak to? What do you want to talk about or say? Tell your group.

C Draw a picture of yourself speaking English. Show where you want to speak English and who you want to speak with. Write what you want to say or talk about.

D CLASS. Show your picture to the class. Explain your goal.

Unit 4   Outside of Class

A Think about ways you can practice English outside of class. Complete the questionnaire. Which things do you do now? Which things do you want to do in the future? Check (✓) the boxes.

Activity	I do this now.	I want to do this.
I listen to the radio in English.	☐	☐
I listen to music in English.	☐	☐
I watch TV in English.	☐	☐
I read the newspaper in English.	☐	☐
I read magazines in English.	☐	☐
I read the mail in English.	☐	☐
I read books in English.	☐	☐
I read websites in English.	☐	☐
I read with my children in English.	☐	☐
I write letters in English.	☐	☐
I write e-mails in English.	☐	☐
Other: _____	☐	☐

B GROUPS OF 3. Talk about your answers to the questionnaire.

C What do you want to do next week? Choose one activity.
Write one goal for next week.

Next week, I will _____ in English.

D SAME GROUPS. Talk about your goals. Check with each other next week.
Did you complete your goal?

Unit 5   Daily Planner

A When do you study or practice English? Write a daily planner.
Use the planner below as a model. Make one planner for every day of the week.

Day: Monday	
Activity	Time
English class	8:30 A.M.–11:30 A.M.
Use English at work	1:00 P.M.–5:00 P.M.
Listen to music in English	5:00 P.M.–5:30 P.M.
Do my homework	8:30 P.M.–9:00 P.M.

B GROUPS OF 3. Show your planners to your group.

Unit 6   My Vocabulary Learning Strategies

A CLASS. Look at the Learning Strategies on pages 7, 47, 67, and 87.

B Which strategies do you use to learn vocabulary? Check (✓) the strategies.

☐ Personalize   ☐ Use pictures

☐ Make connections   ☐ Make labels

☐ Other: _____

C GROUPS OF 5. Talk about the strategies you use.

A: *I personalize and I use pictures. What about you?*
B: *I . . .*

D Write your vocabulary goals for this week.

I want to learn _____ new words this week.
          (number)

I will use _____ to help me remember the new words.
          (title of Learning Strategy)

E SAME GROUPS. Talk about your goals. Check with each other next week.
Did you complete your goals?

Unit 7   Things That Make It Hard to Attend School

A CLASS. Think about things that make it hard for people to attend school. Make a chart on the board.

Things That Make It Hard to Attend School
The kids get sick.

B Copy the chart from Exercise A. Which things make it hard for you to attend school? Circle them.

C NETWORK. Find classmates who circled some of the same things as you. Form a group.

D GROUPS. What can you do to change the things you circled? Make a list of ideas.

Maybe my sister can watch my kids. I can watch her kids other times.

E SAME GROUPS. Make a plan. Tell your group.

I will talk to my sister about watching my kids.

Unit 8   Class Jobs

A CLASS. Look at the list of class jobs. These assistants help the teacher. Are there other jobs in your class? Write them in the list.

Assistant 1: Write today's date on the board.

Assistant 2: Erase the board.

Assistant 3: Give out supplies.

Assistant 4: Take attendance.

Assistant 5: Collect supplies.

Assistant 6: _____

Assistant 7: _____

B CLASS. Choose assistants to help your teacher. Write the students' names in the list. Change assistants every week.

(Note: For the Unit 9 Activity, each student should have a folder or binder, if possible.)

Unit 9 My Portfolio

A portfolio is a folder or binder of papers or drawings. For example, artists have portfolios of their work. You use your portfolio to keep things that show what you can do.

A Create a portfolio of your written work in English. You can include your Life Skills writing, your paragraph writing, unit tests, workbook exercises, etc. Choose papers that you feel proud of. Make a list of the papers you include.

B PAIRS. Show your portfolio to your partner. For each paper in your portfolio, tell your partner why you feel proud.

(*Note: For the Unit 10 Activity, you will need tea and cookies or other refreshments.*)

Unit 10 Getting to Know You Tea

A CLASS. Bring tea and cookies to class.
Take some of the tea and cookies.
Sit with a classmate you don't know.

B PAIRS. Take turns. Ask and answer the questions below.

Elena: *Hi. My name is Elena. What's your name?*
Dmitri: *My name is Dmitri. Hi. Where are you from? . . .*

- What's your name?
- Where are you from?
- Tell me about your family.
- What do you do? Tell me about your job.
- What is your favorite free-time activity?
- What do you like to do on the weekend?
- What kind of food do you like?
- What's your favorite holiday?
- What are your interests and special skills?

C Report to the class. Say one new thing you learned about your partner.

Dmitri likes Mexican food.

Unit 11   Study Skills and Habits

 A Do you have good study skills and habits? Take this questionnaire.

		Yes	No
In class	I come to class every day.		
	When I can't come to class, I make up the work.		
	I ask questions when I don't understand.		
	I participate in every exercise.		
Your study space	I have a specific place where I study outside of class.		
	I have good lighting where I study.		
	I sit on a comfortable chair at a table or a desk.		
	I don't watch TV or listen to music when I study.		
Your time	I study at the same time every day.		
	I plan my study schedule every week.		
	I set small study goals.		
Your studies	I review what we did in class every day.		
	I use the workbook for extra practice.		
	I look for ways to practice my English outside of class.		

B PAIRS. Compare answers.

C SAME PAIRS. Make a plan. Choose one thing you want to change about your study skills and habits. Tell your partner.

Unit 12　Now I Can . . .

A Look at the first page of each unit. Read the unit goals. Which goals did you check off? Choose one goal that you are proud of from each page. Write the goals in the chart.

Unit Number	Now I can . . .
1	
2	
3	
4	
5	
6	
7	
8	
9	
10	
11	
12	

B Report to the class. Tell the class one goal that you can do now.

Now I can write a personal check!

C CLASS. Stand up and clap for everyone. CONGRATULATIONS ON YOUR SUCCESS!

Life Skills Writing

Unit 1

A A driver's license is a common form of identification used in the U.S. Do you have a driver's license? If not, what type of identification card do you have?

B Read the form. Find *Learner permit*, *ID card*, and *Signature*. What do these words mean?

2 WRITE

Complete the form. Use true or made-up information.

 **DEPARTMENT OF MOTOR VEHICLES**

| Application for Driver License |

I AM APPLYING FOR A *(check one)*

☐ Learner Permit ☐ Driver License ☐ ID Card

IDENTIFICATION INFORMATION

LAST NAME   FIRST NAME   MIDDLE INITIAL

DATE OF BIRTH   SEX   HEIGHT   EYE COLOR

Month   Day   Year   Male ☐ Female ☐   Feet   Inches

PHONE NUMBER   SOCIAL SECURITY NUMBER

Area Code ( )

ADDRESS WHERE YOU LIVE

(Street)   (City)   (State)   (Zip Code)

ADDRESS WHERE YOU GET YOUR MAIL

(Street)   (City)   (State)   (Zip Code)

Has your name changed? ☐ Yes ☐ No

(Signature)   (Date)

Can you...complete a driver's license application? ☐

Unit 2

A A customs declaration form is used to mail packages from the U.S. to other countries. What information do you think you need to write on a customs declaration form?

B Read the form. Find *Gift, Documents, Commercial sample, Other*, and *Country of origin of goods*. What do these words mean?

2 WRITE

Imagine that you are sending a gift to a friend in another country. Complete the form. Use true or made-up information.

LC524307871US

Postal Service Customo Doolaration			Sender's Name and Address
☐ Gift ☐ Commercial sample ☐ Documents ☐ Other			
Quantity and description of contents	Weight	Value (US $)	
For Commercial items only Country of origin of goods	Total Weight	Total Value (US $)	Addressee's Name and Address
I, the undersigned, whose name and address are given, certify that the particulars given in this declaration are correct and that this item does not contain any dangerous article or articles.			
Date and sender's signature			Date and Sender's Signature

Can you...complete a post office customs form? ☐

Unit 3

BEFORE YOU WRITE

A Read the check. Find: *Pay to the order of, In the amount of,* and *Memo.*
What do these words mean?

```
Monica Butler                                                    1379
14 Apple Lane
San Francisco,
CA 94105                              DATE ____9/18/08_____

PAY TO THE    Pacific Gas and Electric Company     | $ | 87.65 |
ORDER OF _____|   |_____|

IN THE        Eighty-seven and 65/100 _____ DOLLARS
AMOUNT OF _____

FIRST SAVINGS BANK
CA

MEMO ____Utility bill_____              Monica Butler

122213311:  5556665656  1379
```

B Read the check again. Complete the sentences.

1. The check is from _____.

2. The check is to _____.

3. The date on the check is _____.

4. The amount of the check is _____.

5. The check is payment for _____.

WRITE

**Imagine you are
buying a jacket
from the Oakville
Department Store.
The total is $59.95.
Write the check.
Use today's date.**

```
                                                              101
                                    DATE _____
PAY TO THE
ORDER OF _____| $ | _____ |

IN THE
AMOUNT OF _____ DOLLARS
National Bank
CA

MEMO _____     _____
356621035:  8214600186  101
```

Can you...write a personal check? ☐

Unit 4

A Have you ever visited your local library? Look at the list of things you can do at a library. Which would you like to do?

☐ check out books and movies

☐ bring your children to a story hour

☐ get help finding a job

☐ take an English class

☐ use a computer

☐ other: _____

B Look at the instructions on the library card application. What do you need to do to get a library card?

2 WRITE

Complete the library card application. Use true or made-up information.

GREENVILLE PUBLIC LIBRARY

Adult Library Card Application

Date: _____

You may apply for a Greenville Public Library card if you live or work in the city of Greenville. The library card is free to all Greenville residents. You are responsible for all materials checked out on your card.

Instructions:
Complete this application. Bring the application and one piece of identification to the circulation desk. Identification must include your name and address. Acceptable identification includes: a driver's license or state identification card, a utility bill, or a bank statement.

Please print. Enter only one letter or number in each box.

Name and Mailing Address

Last Name   First Name   Middle Initial

Mailing Address   Apt. #

City   State   Zip Code

(Area Code)   Telephone Number   Date of Birth (month/day/year)   Male   Female   Adult   Senior Citizen (Age 62 or over)

E-mail Address

Can you...complete a library card application?   ☐

Unit 5

A Do you live in an apartment or a house? How long have you lived there?

B Read the form. Find *Landlord*, *Evicted*, *Salary*, and *References*. What do these words mean?

2 WRITE

Imagine you want to rent an apartment. Complete the form. Use true or made-up information.

Apartment Rental Application

Full Name _____ Phone Number _____

Date of Birth _____ E-mail Address _____

List any pets you have _____

Rental History

Current Address _____

Month and year you moved in _____ Rent $ _____

Reasons for leaving _____

Landlord's Name _____ Landlord's Phone Number _____

Previous addresses for the last two years _____

_____

_____

Credit History

Have you ever not paid your rent on time? _____

Have you ever been evicted from an apartment? _____

Employment Information

Your employment status is: Full-time ☐   Part-time ☐   Student ☐   Unemployed ☐

Employer's Name _____ Employer's Phone Number _____

Salary $ _____ Dates of Employment _____

References

Please list three references and their contact information.

Name: _____ Phone: _____

Name: _____ Phone: _____

Name: _____ Phone: _____

Can you...complete an application for an apartment? ☐

Unit 6

A Read the note that Sofia's mother wrote to her teacher. Then answer the questions.

March 25, 2010

Dear Mrs. Roe,

My daughter Sofia Ramos was absent on March 23 and March 24. She had a fever and a sore throat.

Sincerely,

Carmen Ramos

---

1. Who wrote the note? _____

2. When did she write the note? _____

3. What is Sofia's teacher's name? _____

4. When was Sofia absent from school? _____

5. Why was Sofia absent from school? _____

2 WRITE

Write a note to your teacher or your child's teacher to explain an absence.

Can you...write an absence note to a teacher? ☐

Unit 7

BEFORE YOU WRITE

A Medical history forms provide information about your medical history to doctors and other health workers. Why is this information important?

B Read the form. Find *Allergies*, *Medications*, *Medical conditions*, *Health status*, *Deceased*, and *Concerns*. What do these words mean?

2 **WRITE**

Complete the form. Use true or made-up information.

MEDICAL HISTORY

Today's Date: _____

Patient's Name: _____

Date of Birth: _____

_____

Medical Allergies: _____

Food Allergies: _____

Other Allergies: _____

_____

Current medications you are taking: _____

_____

Current medical conditions: _____

Family Medical History			
Relation	Age	Health Status	If Deceased: Cause/ Age at death
Father			
Mother			
Siblings			

Please check all conditions which apply to yourself or any members of your family:

- ☐ asthma/allergies
- ☐ arthritis
- ☐ high blood pressure
- ☐ high cholesterol
- ☐ diabetes
- ☐ heart disease

- ☐ headaches
- ☐ seizures/epilepsy
- ☐ stroke
- ☐ lung disease
- ☐ liver disease
- ☐ ulcers

Other concerns: _____

_____

_____

Can you...complete a medical history form? ☐

Unit 8

Job applications provide employers with important information. Read the form. Find *Under age 18*, *Position*, and *References*. What do these words mean?

Imagine you are applying for a job as a stock clerk at Super Foods Supermarket. Complete the form. Use true or made-up information.

Super Foods Supermarket
Job Application
Personal Information

Full Name _____

Address _____

Phone Number _____ Are you under age 18? ☐ yes ☐ no

Position you are applying for _____ What day can you start work? _____

Days and hours you can work

☐ Monday from ____ to ____   ☐ Tuesday from ____ to ____

☐ Wednesday from ____ to ____   ☐ Thursday from ____ to

☐ Friday from ____ to ____   ☐ Saturday from ____ to ____

☐ Sunday from ____ to ____

Education

Name and Address of School   Degree or Diploma   Graduation Date

_____

_____

Employment History

Present or Most Recent Position

Employer _____

Address _____

Supervisor _____ Phone Number _____

Previous Position

Employer _____

Address _____

Supervisor _____ Phone Number _____

References

1. _____

2. _____

Can you...complete a job application? ☐

Unit 9

A school enrollment form provides important personal information to a school. Read the form. Find *Gender*, *Last school attended*, and *Local emergency contact*. What do these words mean?

2 WRITE

Imagine you are enrolling your child in Franklin High School. Complete the form. Use true or made-up information.

Franklin High School
Enrollment Form

Student's Full Name: _____

Gender: M__ F__   Date of Birth: _____   Phone: _____
Street Address: _____ City: _____ State: _____ Zip: _____

Last School Attended: _____

Last School's Street Address: _____

City: _____ State: _____ Zip: _____

Dates Enrolled: _____

Parents' Full Names: _____

Father's Employer: _____ Phone: _____

Mother's Employer: _____ Phone: _____

Local Emergency Contact: _____

Country of Birth: _____ Student's First Language: _____

Main Language Spoken at Home: _____

Other Languages Spoken at Home: _____

Did student study English as a second language? _____

Parent or Guardian Signature: _____

Date: _____

Can you...complete a school enrollment form? ☐

Unit 10

A What kinds of foods do you think are healthy? Do you eat healthy foods?

B Read the form. Find *Calories, Fiber, Protein, Carbohydrates, Sugar, Fat,* and *Grams.* What do these words mean?

2 WRITE

Keep a record of the food you eat today. Complete the log. Use information from the nutrition labels on the food you eat.

Healthy Eating Log

Date: _____

Food or Beverage: _orange juice_____

Calories	Carbohydrates	Fat	Protein	Sugar	Fiber
110	26g	0g	2g	22g	0g

Food or Beverage: _____

Calories	Carbohydrates	Fat	Protein	Sugar	Fiber

Food or Beverage: _____

Calories	Carbohydrates	Fat	Protein	Sugar	Fiber

Daily Totals

Calories	Carbohydrates	Fat	Protein	Sugar	Fiber

Can you...complete a healthy eating log? ☐

Unit 11

A Have you ever been in an accident at work? What information do you think you should give to your employer if you are in an accident?

B Read the form. Find *Accident, Work location*, and *Required medical attention.* What do these words mean?

2 WRITE

Imagine you had an accident at work. Complete the form with information about the accident.

Employee Accident Report
office of Human Resources

Employee name: _____

Employee Social Security number: _____

Address: _____

_____

Home phone number: _____

Job Title: _____

Date of birth: _____

Date of accident: _____ Time of accident: _____

Place of accident: _____

Employee work location: _____

Employee required medical attention   ☐ Yes   ☐ No

Other information you would like to include: _____

_____

_____

Employee signature: _____ Today's date: _____

Can you...complete an employee accident report? ☐

Unit 12

Before you can go on vacation, your employer might ask you to complete a vacation request form. Read the form. Find *Department*, *Requested*, and *Supervisor*. What do these words mean?

2 WRITE

Imagine you want to go on vacation. Complete the form. Use true or made-up information.

VACATION REQUEST FORM

Employee _____ Date of Hire _____

Department _____

Number of Vacation Days Requested _____

Dates Requested _____

Employee Signature _____ Date _____

Supervisor Signature _____ Date _____

Can you...complete a vacation request form? ☐

Writing

Unit 1

1 BEFORE YOU WRITE

A Read Cheong-Ah's tips for learning English.

My Learning Tips   Cheong-Ah Lee
  • Make vocabulary cards with a word on one side and a picture
    of the word on the other side.
  • Organize my notes into charts.
  • Watch movies with subtitles so I can read and listen at the same time.

B What is Cheong-Ah's learning style? Circle the letter.

a. auditory   b. visual   c. kinesthetic

2 WRITE

Think about your learning style. Write two tips for
learning English. Use Cheong-Ah's tips as a model.

Writing Watch

Capitalize the first word of a
sentence.

Unit 2

1 BEFORE YOU WRITE

A Read Yahia's list of responsibilities.

B Look at Yahia's list again. Do
you have some of the same
responsibilities? Check (✓) the
ones you have, too.

My responsibilities   Yahia El-kadi
— work
— pay the bills
— watch my children when my wife is at work
— go to English class
— go food shopping for the family
— go to the doctor with my mother

2 WRITE

Write a list of your responsibilities.
Use Yahia's list as a model. Write a star (*)
next to the most important ones.

Writing Watch

Use a dictionary to check the
spelling of words you don't
know.

Unit 3

1 BEFORE YOU WRITE

A Read about Zofia's next big purchase.

B Why is Zofia going to buy the computer with cash? Circle the letter.

a. She likes to make small payments every month.

b. She likes to know the total cost.

> **My Next Big Purchase   Zofia Nowak**
>
> I want to buy a computer. I'm going to pay for it with cash. I don't like credit cards. With cash I know how much everything costs. There are no surprises!

2 WRITE

Think about an expensive purchase you want to buy. How are you going to you pay for it? Why? Write about your next big purchase. Use Zofia's paragraph as a model.

> **Writing Watch**
>
> End each sentence with a period.

Unit 4

1 BEFORE YOU WRITE

A Read about what is rude and polite in Rafael's country.

> **Rafael Rodriguez**
>
> In Venezuela it is polite to say hello when you walk into a room—even to people you don't know. It's polite to say goodbye when you leave a room, too. It's polite to stand when you meet someone new. You should stand up and shake hands.

B What is rude in Spain? What is polite? Write *R* for rude and *P* for polite.

_____ Say hello to strangers.

_____ Say goodbye when you leave a room.

_____ Sit when you are introduced to someone.

2 WRITE

Write about what is rude and polite in your home country. Use Rafael's paragraph as a model.

> **Writing Watch**
>
> Capitalize the names of countries.

Unit 5

1 BEFORE YOU WRITE

A Read about Manuel's community in the United States.

B What does Manuel like about his community? What does he dislike? Write *L* for *Like* and D for *Dislike*.

_____ the schools   _____ the cost of living

_____ the jobs   _____ the housing

_____ the pay   _____ the weather

> Living in Winston   by Manuel Vega
>
>   I live in Winston. It's a nice place to live. The schools are good. There is plenty of work and the pay is good. But there are some things I don't like about Winston. It's expensive to live here and the apartments are too small. Worst of all, the weather is very cold in winter.

2 WRITE

Write about what you like and dislike about your community. Use Manuel's paragraph as a model.

> **Writing Watch**
>
> Indent the first line of each paragraph.

Unit 6

1 BEFORE YOU WRITE

A Read Joseph's autobiography.

> My Life   Joseph Bernard
>
>   I was born in Gonaives, Haiti in 1984. In 1998, my family and I moved to the United States. In 2000, I got my first job. In 2003, I finished high school. In 2007, I got married to Josette Pierre.

B Read Joseph's autobiography again. Complete his time line.

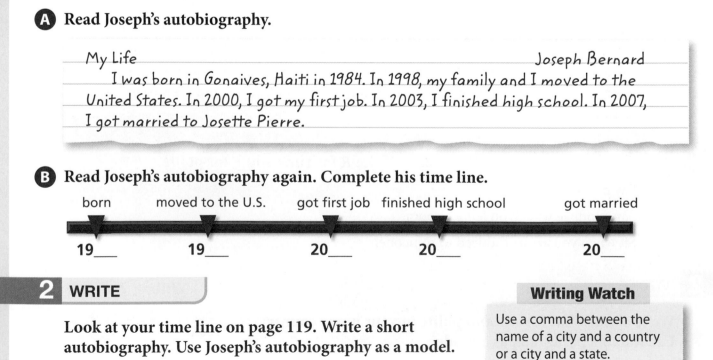

born   moved to the U.S.   got first job   finished high school   got married

19____   19____   20____   20____   20____

2 WRITE

Look at your time line on page 119. Write a short autobiography. Use Joseph's autobiography as a model.

> **Writing Watch**
>
> Use a comma between the name of a city and a country or a city and a state.

Unit 7

 BEFORE YOU WRITE

A Read about something that causes stress in Yao's life.

> Stress at work   Yao Wang
>   My job can be stressful. I work in a restaurant. Sometimes it gets very busy.
> Everyone is running around. We cannot work fast enough, and our boss gets angry.
> I don't like it when it gets so busy. Everyone is upset.

B Is Yao Wang's job stressful all the time?   ☐ Yes   ☐ No

2 **WRITE**

Write about something that causes stress in your life.
Use Yao's paragraph as a model.

Writing Watch
Check that your subjects and verbs agree. For example, *he writes*, NOT *he write*.

Unit 8

1 **BEFORE YOU WRITE**

A Read about Marie's future job.

> My Future Job   Marie Toussaint
>   I want to get a job as a nurse assistant because I like to take care of people.
> Nurse assistants work in hospitals, nursing homes, and people's homes. They help
> patients with things like eating and taking a bath. I think this is a good job for me.

B Why does Marie want to be a nurse assistant? Circle the letter.

a. to earn good money   b. to take care of people   c. to work at home

2 **WRITE**

Write about the job you want in five years.
Write about why you want that job and what the
duties are. Use Marie's paragraph as a model.

Writing Watch
Use *because* to answer *Why* and to give a reason.

Unit 9

BEFORE YOU WRITE

A Read Khalid's paragraph.

B What is Khalid's educational goal?

a. a certificate

b. a bachelor degree

c. an associate degree

> My Educational Goal   Khalid Ali
> First, I need to improve my English. After that, I want to get an associate degree at a community college. I plan to study for two years. I want to study hotel and restaurant management. Then I can get a better job and I can earn more money.

2 WRITE

Write about your educational goals. Use Khalid's paragraph as a model.

Writing Watch

Use *First*, *After that*, and *Then* to show the order that things happen.

Unit 10

1 BEFORE YOU WRITE

A Read Fabio's caffeine journal.

B Do you think Fabio consumes a lot of caffeine?

> Caffeine Journal   Fabio Barreto
> Thursday, December 2
>
> | Time | Caffeine |
> |------|----------|
> | 6:30 A.M. | cup of coffee with milk |
> | 9:30 A.M. | chocolate muffin |
> | 11:30 A.M. | iced tea |
> | 2:30 P.M. | cola |

2 WRITE

A Keep a caffeine journal for one day. Write down every time you consume something with caffeine.

Time	Caffeine

Writing Watch

Write A.M. for times before noon and P.M. for times after noon.

B Look at your caffeine journal. Did you consume a lot of caffeine?

Unit 11

1 BEFORE YOU WRITE

A Read about Aisha's ideas for making her home safer.

> How to Make My Home Safer   Aisha Said
>   There are some things I can do to make my home safer. My shower is slippery. I
> can put a mat in the shower. There are toys all over the living room. I can put the
> toys in the closet. Sometimes I leave food cooking on the stove and do other things.
> I can stay in the kitchen when I am cooking.

B Which areas of her home does Aisha plan to make safer? Check (✓) all that are true.

☐ bathroom   ☐ bedroom   ☐ living room   ☐ kitchen   ☐ stairs   ☐ yard

2 WRITE

Write about what you can do to make your home safer.
Use Aisha's paragraph as a model.

Writing Watch

Include a subject and a verb in each sentence.

Unit 12

1 BEFORE YOU WRITE

A Read about Blanca's retirement plans.

> My Retirement   Blanca Deras
>   I will retire in 2030. I will move back to my hometown in
> El Salvador. My family has a house there. I will take care of
> the garden and I will visit my family and friends.

B Read Blanca's paragraph again. Answer the questions.

1. What year will Blanca retire? _____

2. Where will she live? _____

3. What will she do? _____

2 WRITE

Write about your retirement plans. What year will you
retire? Where will you live? What will you do?
Use Blanca's paragraph as a model.

Writing Watch

Proofread your writing for grammar, punctuation, capitalization, and spelling.

Team Projects

Unit 1   Meet Your Classmates   MAKE A BOOKLET

Materials
- paper
- pens or markers
- stapler and staples
- camera (optional)

TEAMS OF 4 Captain, Co-captain, Assistant, Spokesperson

GET READY **Captain:** Ask your teammates, "Where are you from? Where do you live now? What do you do?" Give your teammates your information, too.
Assistant: Take notes.
Co-captain: Keep time. You have five minutes.

Name: _____

Home country: _____

Where he/she lives now: _____

Occupation: _____

Name: _____

Home country: _____

Where he/she lives now: _____

Occupation: _____

Name: _____

Home country: _____

Where he/she lives now: _____

Occupation: _____

Name: _____

Home country: _____

Where he/she lives now: _____

Occupation: _____

CREATE **Co-captain:** Get the materials. Then keep time. You have ten minutes.
Team: Create your booklet. Use one page for each person. Write the information on the page. Take a photo of each person if you want and put it on the page.

REPORT **Spokesperson:** Show your booklet to the class. Tell the class about your teammates.

COLLECT **Captains:** Collect the booklet pages from each group. Staple them together to make a booklet about your classmates.

UNIT 2 **What We Have in Common** <u>MAKE A POSTER</u>

TEAMS OF 4 Captain, Co-captain, Assistant, Spokesperson

GET READY **Captain:** Ask your teammates questions. Find out what you
and your teammates have in common. Are your personalities
the same or different?
Assistant: Complete the chart.
Co-captain: Keep time. You have five minutes.

Materials
- large paper
- markers
- camera (optional)

A: *I'm quiet. Are you?*
B: *Yes, I'm quiet, too. What about you, Than?*
C: *I'm usually quiet.*

How we are the same	How we are different

CREATE **Co-captain:** Get the materials. Then keep time. You have ten minutes.
Team: Create your poster. Write about what you have in common and how
you are different. Take a photo of your team if you want.

REPORT **Spokesperson:** Show your poster to the class. Tell the class about
your teammates.

Unit 3　Neighborhood Shopping　<u>MAKE A GUIDE</u>

Materials
- 4 pieces of white paper
- pens or markers
- stapler and staples

TEAMS OF 4　Captain, Co-captain, Assistant, Spokesperson

GET READY　**Captain:** Ask your teammates about their favorite stores in your area.
Assistant: Write the answers in the chart.
Co-captain: Keep time. You have five minutes.

Store name	Location	What you like to buy	Why you shop there
Shop Mart	Main Street	clothes for my kids	low prices

CREATE　**Co-captain:** Get the materials. Then keep time. You have ten minutes.
Team: Create your shopping guide. Choose one store that you talked about. Write a page for that store. Include the information in your chart.

REPORT　**Spokesperson:** Tell the class about the store.

COLLECT　**Captains:** Collect the shopping guides from each group. Staple them together to make a neighborhood shopping guide.

Unit 4   Neighborhood Activities   <u>MAKE A GUIDE</u>

TEAMS OF 3   Captain, Co-captain, Assistant, Spokesperson

GET READY   **Captain:** Ask your teammates, "What do you like to do on a special day? Where can you do that?" Ask for other information such as hours and cost.
Team: Plan three activities for a special day.
Assistant: Write the information in the chart.
Co-captain: Keep time. You have five minutes.

Materials
- 4 pieces of white paper
- pens or markers
- stapler and staples

Activity	Location	Other information (hours, cost)
picnic	Greenville Park	open 7:30 A.M. - 9:00 P.M. free

CREATE   **Co-captain:** Get the materials. Then keep time. You have ten minutes.
Team: Create your activity guide. Write a page about your three activities for a special day. Include the information in your chart. Add art if you want.

REPORT   **Spokesperson:** Show your activity guide to the class. Tell the class about the activities.

COLLECT   **Captains:** Collect the activity guides from each group. Staple them together to make a neighborhood activity guide.

Unit 5 The Perfect Home MAKE A HOUSING CLASSIFIED AD

TEAMS OF 3 Captain, Co-captain, Assistant, Spokesperson

GET READY You are a family of three.
Captain: Ask your teammates about the home you want or need.
Assistant: Complete the chart.
Co-captain: Keep time. You have five minutes.

Materials
- large paper
- markers

Number of bedrooms	
Number of bathrooms	
Size of rooms	
Cost	
Neighborhood	
Special features	☐ yard ☐ laundry ☐ fireplace ☐ garage ☐ other: _____

CREATE **Co-captain:** Get the materials. Then keep time. You have ten minutes. **Team:** Create your ad. Write a heading with the number of bedrooms and bathrooms. Write the other information in your notes. Check the abbreviations. Add art if you want. Use the housing ads on page 93 as a model.

REPORT **Spokesperson:** Show your ad to the class. Tell the class about your home.

COLLECT **Class:** Walk around the room. Look at the ads. Which home is best for you?

Unit 6   Time to Celebrate   MAKE A HOLIDAY CALENDAR

Materials
- large paper
- markers
- rulers

TEAMS OF 4   Captain, Co-captain, Assistant, Spokesperson

GET READY   Your instructor/teacher will give you three months.
Captain: Ask your teammates about the holidays you celebrate during these three months. Ask, "What holidays do you celebrate? When are the holidays? How do you celebrate the holidays? What do you do?"
Assistant: Complete the chart.
Co-captain: Keep time. You have ten minutes.

Holiday	Date	How you celebrate
Halloween	October 31	wear costumes, give candy to children

CREATE   **Co-captain:** Get the materials. Then keep time. You have ten minutes.
Team: Create your calendar. Make a calendar page for each month. Write the holidays on the correct dates. Write a short paragraph/description about how people celebrate one of the holidays on your calendar pages. Add art if you want.

REPORT   **Spokesperson:** Show your calendar to the class. Tell the class about your holidays.

Unit 7　Home Remedies <u>MAKE A BOOKLET</u>

Materials
- 4 pieces of white paper
- pens or markers
- stapler and staples

TEAMS OF 4 Captain, Co-captain, Assistant, Spokesperson

GET READY **Team:** Home remedies are ways of treating an illness that is not serious at home. Choose illnesses from the box or use your own ideas.

Captain: Ask your teammates what home remedies they use.

A: *What do you do for a burn?*
B: *I put toothpaste on the burn.*

Assistant: Complete the chart.
Co-captain: Keep time. You have five minutes.

| a burn | a cold | a headache |
| a sore throat | a stomachache | a stuffy nose |

Illness	Home remedies
a burn	*put toothpaste on the burn* *put milk on the burn*

CREATE **Co-captain:** Get the materials. Then keep time. You have ten minutes.
Team: Create your booklet. Write a page for each home remedy. (Each student writes one.)

REPORT **Spokesperson:** Tell the class about your home remedies.

COLLECT **Captains:** Collect the booklet pages from each group. Staple them together to make a booklet about home remedies.

Unit 8   Job Skills and Requirements <u>MAKE A BOOKLET</u>

TEAMS OF 4 Captain, Co-captain, Assistant, Spokesperson

hospital	hotel	school
restaurant	factory	other: _____

Materials
- 3 pieces of white paper
- pens or markers
- stapler and staples

GET READY **Team:** Choose a workplace. Each student chooses one job in this workplace.

Captain: Ask your teammates, "What skills do you need for this job? What education or experience do you need?"

Assistant: Write the answers in the chart.

Co-captain: Keep time. You have five minutes.

Workplace	Job	Skills	Education and/or experience

CREATE **Co-captain:** Get the materials. Then keep time. You have ten minutes.

Team: Create your booklet. Make a page for each job. Write about the skills, education, and/or experience you need for this job.

REPORT **Spokesperson:** Tell the class about one of the jobs.

COLLECT **Captains:** Collect the booklet pages from each group. Staple them together to make a booklet about the skills you need for different jobs.

Unit 9 Ways to Improve Your English <u>MAKE A POSTER</u>

TEAMS OF 3 Captain, Co-captain, Assistant, Supervisor

GET READY **Captain:** Ask your teammates, "What are ten ways to improve your English?"
Assistant: Take notes.
Co-captain: Keep time. You have five minutes.

> *Practice speaking outside of class. Read English books.*

> Materials
> • large paper
> • markers

CREATE **Co-captain:** Get the materials. Then keep time. You have ten minutes.
Team: Create your poster. Write the suggestions from your list.
Add pictures to the poster if you want.

REPORT **Spokesperson:** Show your poster to the class. Tell the class your suggestions.

Unit 10 Places to Shop for Food MAKE A FOOD SHOPPING GUIDE

TEAMS OF 4 Captain, Co-captain, Assistant, Spokesperson

GET READY **Captain:** Ask your teammates, "Where do you shop for food? Where is it located? Why do you shop there?"
Assistant: Complete the chart.
Co-captain: Keep time. You have five minutes.

Materials
- 3 pieces of white paper
- pens or markers
- stapler and staples

Name of store	Location	Reason for shopping there
Greenville Farmer's Market	Greenville Park	fresh fruits and vegetables, low prices

CREATE **Co-captain:** Get the materials. Then keep time. You have ten minutes.
Team: Create your shopping guide. Write where your team shops for food. Write about why your team shops at these places.

REPORT **Spokesperson:** Show your shopping guide to the class.
Tell the class about where your team shops.

COLLECT **Captains:** Collect the shopping guide from each group. Staple them together to make a class shopping guide.

Unit 11 Plan for a Fire Emergency MAKE A POSTER

TEAMS OF 3 Captain, Co-captain, Assistant, Spokesperson

GET READY Imagine there is a fire in your school.
Captain: Ask, "What will you do if there is a fire at our school? Where will you go?"
Team: Draw a map of your school building. Mark all of the exits in your classroom. Talk about what to do and where to go in case of a fire.
Assistant: Write the instructions.
Co-captain: Keep time. You have five minutes.

> *Stay calm. Leave your books. Go to the hall. Turn . . .*

Materials
- large paper
- markers

CREATE **Co-captain:** Get the materials. Then keep time. You have ten minutes.
Team: Create your poster. Draw the escape plan. Write the instructions.

REPORT **Spokesperson:** Show your escape plan to the class. Read your instructions.

Unit 12 Your Dream Company <u>MAKE AN EMPLOYEE MANUAL</u>

TEAMS OF 4 Captain, Co-captain, Assistant, Spokesperson

GET READY You are opening your dream company.
Captain: Ask your teammates, "What kind of company is it?
What's the name of the company? What are the rules for your
employees? What are the rules for taking time off?"
Assistant: Write the answers in the chart.
Co-captain: Keep time. You have five minutes.

Materials
- 1 piece of white paper
- pens or markers
- stapler and staples

Type of business	
Company name	
Employee duties	
Time-off rules	

CREATE **Co-captain:** Get the materials. Then keep time. You have ten minutes.
Team: Create your employee manual. Write the information from your charts.
Include the name of your company, the type of business, the employee duties, and
time-off rules. Each team member writes one part.

REPORT **Spokesperson:** Tell the class about your company.

COLLECT **Class:** Walk around the room. Look at the employee manuals.
Which company would you like to work for the most?

Grammar Reference

UNIT 1, Lesson 3, page 10

Contractions are short forms. Contractions join two words together. In a contraction, an apostrophe (') replaces a letter. Use contractions in speaking and informal writing.

Contractions with *be*

Affirmative			**Negative**		
I am	=	I'm	I am not	=	I'm not
you are	=	you're	you are not	=	you're not / you aren't
he is	=	he's	he is not	=	he's not / he isn't
she is	=	she's	she is not	=	she's not / she isn't
it is	=	it's	it is not	=	it's not / it isn't
we are	=	we're	we are not	=	we're not / we aren't
they are	=	they're	they are not	=	they're not / they aren't

Negative contractions with *do*

I do not	=	I don't
you do not	=	you don't
he does not	=	he doesn't
she does not	=	she doesn't
it does not	=	it doesn't
we do not	=	we don't
they do not	=	they don't

UNIT 6, Lesson 6, page 116 and UNIT 7, Lesson 6, page 136

Simple past: irregular verbs

Base form	Past tense form	Base form	Past tense form	Base form	Past tense form
be	was/were	get	got	run	ran
begin	began	give	gave	say	said
bleed	bled	go	went	see	saw
break	broke	grow	grew	send	sent
bring	brought	have	had	sing	sang
buy	bought	hurt	hurt	sit	sat
come	came	keep	keep	sleep	slept
cost	cost	know	knew	speak	spoke
cut	cut	leave	left	spend	spent
do	did	lose	lost	swim	swam
drink	drank	make	made	take	took
drive	drove	meet	met	teach	taught
eat	ate	oversleep	overslept	tell	told
fall	fell	pay	paid	think	thought
feel	felt	put	put	understand	understood
find	found	quit	quit	wake up	woke up
forget	forgot	read	read	write	wrote

UNIT 9, Lesson 6, page 176

Spelling rules for adverbs of manner

We can make many adverbs of manner from adjectives.

For most adverbs of manner, add -*ly* to an adjective. For example:

nice	$\longrightarrow$	nicely
quiet	$\longrightarrow$	quietly
normal	$\longrightarrow$	normally

If an adjective ends in *y*, change y to i and add -*ly*. For example:

happy	$\longrightarrow$	happily
noisy	$\longrightarrow$	noisily
angry	$\longrightarrow$	angrily

UNIT 9, Lesson 9, page 182

Spelling rules for possessive nouns

A possessive noun shows that a person or thing owns something.

Add 's to most singular nouns and names. For example:

student	$\longrightarrow$	student's
girl	$\longrightarrow$	girl's
Ming	$\longrightarrow$	Ming's

Add 's to singular nouns and names that end in -*s*. For example:

boss	$\longrightarrow$	boss's
Mr. Jones	$\longrightarrow$	Mr. Jones's
James	$\longrightarrow$	James's

Add ' to plural nouns that end in -*s*. For example:

parents	$\longrightarrow$	parents'
classmates	$\longrightarrow$	classmates'
boys	$\longrightarrow$	boys'

Add 's to plural nouns that do not end in -*s*. For example:

children	$\longrightarrow$	children's
people	$\longrightarrow$	people's
women	$\longrightarrow$	women's

Spelling rules for plurals and irregular nouns

Add -s to make most nouns plural. For example:

1 student	$\longrightarrow$	2 students
1 pencil	$\longrightarrow$	5 pencils
1 house	$\longrightarrow$	10 houses

Add -es to nouns that end with s, z, x, sh, or ch. For example:

1 sandwich	$\longrightarrow$	3 sandwiches
1 bus	$\longrightarrow$	4 buses
1 dish	$\longrightarrow$	5 dishes

For most nouns that end in o, just add -s. For example:

| 1 avocado | $\longrightarrow$ | 2 avocados |
| 1 radio | $\longrightarrow$ | 2 radios |

For some nouns that end in a consonant and o, add -es. For example:

1 potato	$\longrightarrow$	2 potatoes
1 tomato	$\longrightarrow$	8 tomatoes
1 hero	$\longrightarrow$	4 heroes

When a noun ends in a consonant + y, change y to i and add -es. For example:

1 baby	$\longrightarrow$	3 babies
1 country	$\longrightarrow$	15 countries
1 berry	$\longrightarrow$	20 berries

When a noun ends in f, change f to v and add -es. When a noun ends in fe, change fe to v and add -es. For example:

1 wife	$\longrightarrow$	2 wives
1 knife	$\longrightarrow$	9 knives
1 loaf	$\longrightarrow$	7 loaves

Some nouns have irregular plural forms. For example:

1 foot	$\longrightarrow$	2 feet
1 tooth	$\longrightarrow$	10 teeth
1 man	$\longrightarrow$	5 men
1 woman	$\longrightarrow$	8 women
1 child	$\longrightarrow$	7 children
1 person	$\longrightarrow$	12 people

UNIT 10, Lesson 3, page 190

Non-count nouns

Drinks	Some food		Materials	Subjects	Activities	Other
coffee	beef	meat	corduroy	art	baseball	advice
juice	bread	pasta	cotton	language arts	basketball	equipment
milk	butter	rice	denim	math	exercise	furniture
soda	cheese	salad	fleece	music	hiking	homework
tea	chicken	salt	glass	physical	jogging	information
water	chocolate	soup	leather	education	running	mail
	fish	spinach	metal	science	soccer	money
	fruit	sugar	nylon	social studies	swimming	news
	ice cream	yogurt	silk	technology	tennis	paper
	lettuce		vinyl	world languages		traffic
			wood			weather
			wool			work

UNIT 10, Lesson 6, page 196

Spelling rules for comparatives and irregular comparatives

To make comparative adjectives from one-syllable adjectives, add -er. For example:

cheap	$\longrightarrow$	cheaper
tall	$\longrightarrow$	taller
cold	$\longrightarrow$	colder

If a one-syllable adjective ends in e, add -r. For example:

nice	$\longrightarrow$	nicer
late	$\longrightarrow$	later
large	$\longrightarrow$	larger

If an adjective ends in one vowel and one consonant, double the consonant and add -er. For example:

hot	$\longrightarrow$	hotter
big	$\longrightarrow$	bigger
sad	$\longrightarrow$	sadder
thin	$\longrightarrow$	thinner

For two-syllable adjectives that end with -y, change y to i and add -er. For example:

busy	$\longrightarrow$	busier
pretty	$\longrightarrow$	prettier
easy	$\longrightarrow$	easier

UNIT 11, Lesson 3, page 210

Spelling rules for *-ing* verbs

For most verbs, add *-ing* to the base form of the verb. For example:

work	$\longrightarrow$	working
do	$\longrightarrow$	doing

For verbs that end in *e*, drop the *e* and add *-ing*. For example:

change	$\longrightarrow$	changing
leave	$\longrightarrow$	leaving
make	$\longrightarrow$	making

If the base form of a one-syllable verb ends with consonant, vowel, consonant, double the final consonant and add *-ing*. For example:

shop	$\longrightarrow$	shopping
run	$\longrightarrow$	running
cut	$\longrightarrow$	cutting
begin	$\longrightarrow$	beginning

Word List

UNIT 1

applicant, 12
application, 12
attractive, 8
auditory learner, 18
average height, 7
average weight, 7
bald, 7
beard, 7
beautiful, 8
bossy, 14
cheerful, 14
curly, 7

date of birth, 13
DOB (date of birth), 13
friendly, 15
funny, 15
goatee, 7
good-looking, 8
handsome, 8
heavy, 7
height, 7
identification card, 12
interesting, 15
kinesthetic learner, 18

laid-back, 14
learning style, 18
long hair, 7
mailing address, 12
moody, 14
mustache, 7
outgoing, 14
personality, 15
physical description, 7
pretty, 8
quiet, 15
short hair, 7

shoulder-length, 7
shy, 14
slim, 7
straight hair, 7
street address, 12
sweet, 14
talkative, 14
tall, 7
thin, 7
visual learner, 18
wavy, 7
weight, 7

UNIT 2

advice, 32
aunt, 27
brother, 27
Certificate of Mailing, 39
Certified Mail, 39
children, 27
Collect on Delivery
   (COD), 39
cousin, 27
daughter, 27
Delivery Confirmation, 39
envelope, 38
Express Mail, 38

family, 26
father, 27
father-in-law, 27
female, 26
fiancé, 27
fiancée, 27
First-Class Mail, 38
game show, 40
grandchildren, 27
granddaughter, 27
grandfather, 27
grandmother, 27
grandson, 27

have in common, 34
husband, 27
Insurance, 39
letter, 38
mailing service, 38
mailing tube, 38
male, 26
mother, 27
mother-in-law, 27
nephew, 27
niece, 27
package, 38
Parcel Post, 38

parents, 27
post office, 38
postcard, 30
pound, 38
Priority Mail, 38
Registered Mail, 39
relationship, 26
responsibility, 32
sister, 27
sister-in-law, 27
son, 27
uncle, 27
wife, 27

UNIT 3

ad, 52
ATM, 54
bakery, 55
bank, 55
big, 61
blouse, 61
boots, 47
broken, 60
button, 60
calculate change, 52
charades, 57
clearance sale, 48
clothes, 47
coat, 47
cold, 49
cool, 49
corduroy, 47

cotton, 47
credit card, 58
deli, 54
denim, 47
discount, 52
drugstore, 55
errand, 54
exchange, 50
fleece, 47
flip-flops, 52
gas station, 55
gloves, 47
grocery store, 55
hardware store, 54
hole, 60
hot, 49
jacket, 47

jeans, 47
laundromat, 54
leather, 47
library, 55
long, 61
loose, 60
material, 47
missing, 60
nylon, 47
raincoat, 47
receipt, 53
rent-to-own, 59
return (a purchase), 50
ripped, 60
sale, 52
scarf, 47
seam, 60

shorts, 49
silk, 47
sunglasses, 52
sweater, 61
sweatshirt, 47
swimsuit, 53
swimwear, 52
T-shirts, 61
tax, 52
tight, 60
too, 62
very, 62
vinyl, 47
windbreaker, 47
wool, 47
zipper, 60

UNIT 4

accept, 80
calendar, 72
clean the house, 75
club, 72
computer, 68
computer class, 68
cook, 74
decline, 80
do the dishes, 75
don't feel well, 80
errands, 81
exercise, 71
free-time, 67
get some coffee, 81
get up early, 75

go dancing, 67
go fishing, 67
go for a bike ride, 67
go for a walk, 67
go hiking, 67
go jogging, 67
go out to eat, 67
go shopping, 67
go swimming, 67
got to a meeting, 81
go to the beach, 67
go to the movies, 77
go to the park, 67
go to the zoo, 67
guitar class, 68

hate, 76
have other plans, 80
indoor, 66
invitation, 80
invite, 81
iron, 74
karate, 69
like, 76
love, 76
make some calls, 81
message board, 78
not like, 76
once, 71
outdoor, 66
painting, 69

polite, 78
read, 77
rude, 78
run some errands, 81
schedule, 73
spend time with family, 77
take a walk, 81
too busy, 80
twice, 71
use a computer, 77
vacuum, 74
watch TV, 74

UNIT 5

air-conditioning, 92
balcony, 95
basement, 92
bathroom, 92
broken, 87
building manager, 88
bulletin board, 93
bus stop, 95
ceiling, 86
clogged, 87
closet, 95
cost of living, 99
dining room, 92
dishwasher, 90
door, 86
dryer, 92
eat-in kitchen, 92

electrician, 88
elevator, 92
faucet, 86
fee, 92
fix, 88
furnished, 92
get directions, 100
go straight, 100
go through (a light), 100
heat, 87
hot water, 87
Internet posting, 93
kitchen, 95
landlady, 94
laundry room, 94
leaking, 87
living room, 92

lock, 86
locksmith, 88
mailbox, 87
microwave, 95
Midwest, 98
natural beauty, 99
newspaper ad, 93
Northeast, 98
(not) working, 87
paint, 91
pet, 92
plumber, 88
problem, 86
public transportation, 92
real estate agent, 93
region, 98
rent, 92

rental apartment, 92
security deposit, 92
sink, 86
South, 98
Southwest, 98
stove, 87
stuck, 87
toilet, 86
traffic, 99
turn left, 100
turn right, 100
utilities, 92
washer, 92
washing machine, 86
West, 98
West Coast, 98
window, 86

UNIT 6

anniversary party, 107
baby shower, 107
barbecue, 107
be born, 114
biography, 118
birthday party, 107
Christmas Day, 112
Columbus Day, 112
dance all night, 108
dress casually, 106
dress formally, 106
exhausted, 121
family reunion, 107

forget (your lunch), 120
funeral, 107
get a job, 114
get married, 114
get stuck in traffic, 120
give gifts, 106
graduate from
   school, 114
graduation party, 107
grow up, 114
have car trouble, 120
have children, 114
holiday, 107

holiday meal, 107
Independence Day, 112
Labor Day, 112
listen to family
   stories, 108
look at old photos, 108
lose (your keys), 120
Martin Luther King Jr.
   Day, 112
Memorial Day, 112
milestone, 105
New Year's Day, 112
oversleep, 120

potluck dinner, 107
Presidents' Day, 112
retirement party, 107
stay up late, 108
surprise party, 107
take the wrong train, 120
Thanksgiving Day, 112
time line, 119
to-do list, 111
unhappy, 121
upset, 121
Veterans' Day, 112
wedding, 107

UNIT 7

absence, 140
appointment, 128
appointment card, 128
break your arm, 134
break your tooth, 141
burn your hand, 134
call in sick/late, 144
chest pains, 127
cough, 127
create stress, 139
cut your finger, 134
diarrhea, 127
dizzy, 128
dosage, 133
due to, 132
earache, 127

expiration date, 132
eye drops, 133
fall, 134
feel better, 141
fever, 127
get well soon, 141
good luck, 141
have a cold, 127
have the chills, 127
have the flu, 127
headache, 127
health problem, 127
heartburn, 127
hurt your head, 134
injury, 134
itchy, 128

loss of control, 138
manage stress, 138
medical history, 133
medicine label, 132
miss work, 140
nauseous, 128
negative attitude, 138
ointment, 133
over-the-counter (OTC)
   medicine, 132
pharmacist, 133
pharmacy, 133
prescription, 132
rash, 127
reduce, 132
refill, 133

relieve, 132
sick, 141
sore throat, 127
sprain your ankle, 134
stiff neck, 127
stress, 138
supervisor, 140
swollen, 128
symptom, 128
tablespoon, 133
temporarily, 132
unhealthy habit, 138
upset stomach, 127

UNIT 8

agriculture, 158
assist customers, 147
availability, 160
benefits, 152
change jobs, 154
clean kitchen
   equipment, 147
computer system
   administrator, 146
experience, 152
field of employment, 158
flexible, 160
food service worker, 146
full-time, 152
give notice at work, 160

greet visitors, 147
handle phone calls, 147
health care, 158
help with computer
   problems, 147
help-wanted ad, 152
install computer
   hardware, 147
job application, 151
job duty, 146
job interview, 148
manager, 146
manufacturing, 158
nurse assistant, 146
operate a forklift, 148

order supplies, 148
part-time, 152
plan work schedules, 147
prefer, 152
prepare food, 147
receive shipments, 147
receptionist, 146
record patient
   information, 147
references, 152
résumé, 152
sales associate, 146
shift, 160
skill, 148
speak Spanish, 148

stock clerk, 146
stock shelves, 147
supervise employees, 147
take care of patients, 147
technology, 158
truck driver, 155
type, 148
unemployed, 154
unload materials, 147
use a cash register, 148
use a word-processing
   program, 148
warehouse worker, 146
work history, 154
work schedule, 160

UNIT 9

art, 166
Associate Degree, 178
Bachelor Degree, 178
be disrespectful, 180
behave, 180
behavior, 180
bully, 180
call someone back, 173
college, 178
college degree, 178
color, 166
community college, 178
community service, 167
Doctor of Philosophy, 178
draw, 166

elementary school, 166
financial aid, 179
fool around, 180
get along with others, 180
get extra help, 174
give someone a
  message, 173
grant, 179
high school, 166
language arts/English, 167
leave a message, 173
leave early, 169
loan, 179
Master Degree, 178
math, 167

meeting, 169
middle school, 166
misbehave, 180
music, 167
notice from school, 168
parent-teacher
  conference, 168
pay attention, 180
P.E. (physical
  education), 167
phone message, 172
preschool, 166
PTO (parent-teacher
  organization), 168
return a call, 172

science, 167
science fair, 169
scholarship, 179
school play, 169
school subject, 166
skip class, 180
social studies/history, 167
take a message, 172
technology, 167
try, 169
tuition, 179
university, 178
world languages, 167

UNIT 10

apple juice, 200
bag, 187
beans, 189
beverage, 199
bottle, 187
bottled water, 200
box, 187
bunch, 187
caffeine, 198
calories, 193
can, 187
carbohydrates, 192
cereal, 189
cheap, 196
chewing gum, 198
chocolate, 198
cholesterol, 192
coffee, 195
cola, 198
coleslaw, 200
commercial, 194
consume, 198
contain, 198

container, 187
convenience, 194
convenience store, 188
cucumber, 189
delicious, 196
dozen, 187
effect, 198
fat, 193
fattening, 196
fiber, 192
fish, 190
fish sandwich, 200
French fries, 200
fresh, 194
gallon, 187
good, 196
gram (g), 193
guest check, 200
half-gallon, 187
hamburger, 200
harmful, 199
head, 187
headache medicine, 198

healthy, 194
ice cream, 195
iced tea, 200
ingredient, 192
irritable, 199
jar, 187
lettuce, 187
lemon/lime soda, 198
low-fat, 195
macaroni and cheese, 200
mashed potatoes, 200
meatloaf, 200
menu, 200
milligram (mg), 193
mixed vegetables, 200
non-fat milk, 193
noodles, 200
nutrients, 192
nutrition label, 192
nutritious, 196
onion rings, 200
orange, 189
orange juice, 195

outdoor market, 188
picnic, 191
pint, 187
pork chop, 200
pound, 187
price, 194
protein, 192
quantity, 187
quart, 187
roast chicken, 200
salty, 196
serving, 193
shopping list, 191
soda, 200
sodium, 192
soup, 189
sugar, 192
supermarket, 188
taste, 194
tea, 198
tuna, 189
yogurt, 189

UNIT 11

911, 208
allergic reaction, 207
ambulance, 208
be hurt, 215
bleed, 207
burn yourself, 207
car accident, 214
choke, 207
cleaning supplies, 218
cloth, 212
construction accident, 214
cross street, 208
crowd of people, 217
curtain, 212

dangerous, 214
driver's license, 220
electric, 209
electrical cord, 212
electrical outlet, 212
electrical plug, 212
emergency, 206
escape plan, 212
exit, 212
explosion, 214
fall, 207
fire escape, 212
fire extinguisher, 212
fire hazard, 212

have trouble breathing, 207
heart attack, 207
heater, 212
injury, 215
location, 208
matches, 212
medical emergency, 207
police, 217
proof of insurance, 220
pull over, 220
reaction, 209
registration, 220
robbery, 214
rug, 212

run a red light, 221
safety procedure, 212
safety tip, 213
seat belt, 221
situation, 209
smoke alarm, 212
special, 221
steering wheel, 220
swallow poison, 207
tailgate, 221
taxi, 208
traffic jam, 217
traffic ticket, 220
unconscious, 207

UNIT 12

ask for a favor, 234
ask questions, 227
be on time, 226
call in late, 227
clock in/out, 227
cover someone's hours, 234
deduction, 232
disabled, 238
eat at my desk, 229
eat in the break room, 229

employee badge, 228
federal tax, 232
first shift, 241
follow directions, 227
full-time, 241
gross pay, 232
latex gloves, 227
maintain equipment, 227
manager, 228
Medicare, 232
miss work, 234
net pay, 232

orientation meeting, 228
overtime hour, 233
park, 229
part-time, 241
pay period, 232
pay stub, 232
rate of pay, 232
regular hour, 232
report a problem, 227
retired, 238
safety gear, 227
second shift, 241

Social Security, 232
Social Security benefits, 238
State Disability Insurance (SDI), 232
state tax, 232
store equipment, 227
talk to a manager, 229
trade shifts, 229
uniform, 227
wash hands, 227
work as a team, 227

Audio Script

UNIT 1

Page 8, Listen, Exercises A and B

Tania:	Hi, Eva.
Eva:	Hi, Tania. Are you coming to my party tonight?
Tania:	Of course. Are you inviting your friend?
Eva:	Which friend?
Tania:	You know—he's handsome and he has short, black hair.

Page 8, Listen, Exercise C

Tania:	Hi, Eva.
Eva:	Hi, Tania. Are you coming to my party tonight?
Tania:	Of course. Are you inviting your friend?
Eva:	Which friend?
Tania:	You know—he's handsome and he has short, black hair.
Eva:	Does he have blue eyes?
Tania:	No, he has brown eyes.
Eva:	Oh. You mean Victor. He's not my friend, he's my brother! But of course I'll introduce him to you.

Page 14, Listen, Exercises A and B

Tania:	So tell me more about Victor. What's he like?
Eva:	Well, he's outgoing and he has a lot of friends.
Tania:	Yeah? What else?
Eva:	He's sweet but he's a little quiet.

Page 14, Listen. Exercise C

Tania:	So tell me more about Victor. What's he like?
Eva:	Well, he's outgoing and he has a lot of friends.
Tania:	Yeah? What else?
Eva:	He's sweet but he's a little quiet.
Tania:	Quiet? That's not a problem.
Eva:	But you're so talkative. Don't you like talkative guys?
Tania:	No, I don't. I like guys who *listen* a lot!

Page 20, Listen, Exercises B and C

Eva:	I want to introduce you to my friend. Victor, this is Tania. Tania, this is Victor.
Victor:	Nice to meet you.
Tania:	Nice to meet you, too.
Victor:	So, are you a student?
Tania:	Yes, I am. Eva and I are in the same English class.
Victor:	Oh, that's nice. Where are you from?
Tania:	Ecuador.
Victor:	Really? What's it like?
Tania:	It's a very beautiful country.

Page 20, Listen, Exercise D

Eva:	I want to introduce you to my friend. Victor, this is Tania. Tania, this is Victor.
Victor:	Nice to meet you.
Tania:	Nice to meet you, too.
Victor:	So, are you a student?
Tania:	Yes, I am. Eva and I are in the same English class.
Victor:	Oh, that's nice. Where are you from?
Tania:	Ecuador.
Victor:	Really? What's it like?
Tania:	It's a very beautiful country. . . . So, how about you? Are you a student, too?
Victor:	No, I'm not. I work at a restaurant. I'm a cook.

UNIT 2

Page 28, Listen, Exercise B

Amy:	Tell me about your family.
Babacar:	Well, I don't have a very big family. I have a brother and two sisters.
Amy:	Do they live here?
Babacar:	My sisters live in Senegal, but my brother lives here.

Page 28, Listen, Exercise C

Amy:	Tell me about your family.
Babacar:	Well, I don't have a very big family. I have a brother and two sisters.
Amy:	Do they live here?
Babacar:	My sisters live in Senegal, but my brother lives here.
Amy:	Really? What does your brother do?
Babacar:	He works in a hospital. He's a medical assistant.
Amy:	And does he live near you?
Babacar:	Yes. In fact, we live in the same apartment.
Amy:	Wow, then he *really* lives near you!

Page 34, Listen, Exercises B and C

Ming:	Tina, is this your sister? You two look alike.
Tina:	Yeah, that's my sister, Lili.
Ming:	Do you have a lot in common?
Tina:	Actually, we do. She works in a bank, and I do, too. And we both have new babies.

Page 34, Listen, Exercise D

Ming: Tina, is this your sister? You two look alike.
Tina: Yeah, that's my sister, Lili.
Ming: Do you have a lot in common?
Tina: Actually, we do. She works in a bank, and I do, too. And we both have new babies.
Ming: That's nice.
Tina: What about you, Ming? Do you have any brothers or sisters?
Ming: I have two sisters, and we have a lot in common.
Tina: Really?
Ming: Yeah. I have two sisters, and they do, too. I don't have any brothers, and they don't, either!

Page 39, Practice

Customer: Hello. I'd like to mail this package.
Clerk: How do you want to send it?
Customer: How long does Parcel Post take?
Clerk: Two to nine days.
Customer: OK. I'll send it Parcel Post.
Clerk: Do you want Delivery Confirmation or Insurance?
Customer: Yes. Delivery Confirmation, please.

Page 40 Listen, Exercises A, B, and C

Oliver: Hello, I'm Oliver Marley, and welcome to *They're Your Family Now!*, the game show where we ask people questions about their in-laws. Please welcome our first contestant, Mr. Trevor Scanlon.
Trevor: Hello.
Oliver: Now, Trevor. Here are the rules of the game. Before the show, we asked your wife Ann ten questions about her family. Now I'm going to ask you the same questions. You get $100 for every question you answer correctly.
Trevor: OK! I'm ready.
Oliver: Great. Trevor, here's your first question. Where do your wife's grandparents live?
Trevor: Oh! That's easy. They live in San Antonio with the rest of her family.
Oliver: Right! Good start. OK. Here's your next question. How many brothers and sisters does your mother-in-law have?
Trevor: My mother-in-law?! . . . Well, there's Martha, Paula, Henry, Charles, . . . and what's his name? . . . Paul! OK. My mother-in-law has two sisters and three brothers. So that's five in total.

Oliver: That's right! Good job. Next question. What does your brother-in-law Alex do?
Trevor: Oh, wow . . . I know he works in an office . . . Um, he's an engineer?
Oliver: No, he's an accountant!
Trevor: Oh!
Oliver: Better luck on the next one. Here it is . . . When does your sister-in-law Danielle work?
Trevor: Oh, I know this one! Danielle works at night because her husband works during the day. She watches the baby all day, and he watches him at night!
Oliver: Correct! Well, so far you have three points. We have to take a break, but we'll be right back with *They're Your Family Now!*

UNIT 3

Page 48, Listen, Exercises A and B

Lindsey: Hi, this is Lindsey Campbell with WEYE's *Eye Around Town*, the program that tells you what's happening in town. So what's happening today? I'm here at the summer clearance at Big Deals, and the store is full of shoppers. Let's talk to a few of them . . . Excuse me. What's your name?
Alicia: Alicia Duran.
Lindsey: Hi, Alicia. Tell us, why are you here at Big Deals today?
Alicia: Well, I shop here a lot. They have great prices on everything you need.
Lindsey: And what do you need to buy today?
Alicia: Well, I don't *need* to buy anything, but I *want* to buy a new pair of jeans.
Lindsey: Well, I hope you find some, Alicia. Next . . . tell us your name, please.
Gladys: Gladys Flores.
Lindsey: Gladys, why are you here today?
Gladys: I'm here with my daughter. We don't need to buy anything today. We just need to return this dress. It's really easy to return things here if you have your receipt . . . Where *is* that receipt? I know it's here somewhere . . .
Lindsey: Uh . . . OK. And you, sir. Who are you, and why are you here at Big Deals today?
John: My name's John Nichols. I need to buy some shorts for my son.
Lindsey: Do you always shop here at Big Deals?

| John: | Yeah. It's so convenient. They have everything here, so I don't need to go to a lot of different stores. I really don't like to shop. |
| Lindsey: | OK, well, we need to go back to the studio now, and I want to look for a jacket while I'm here! I'm Lindsey Campbell with your *Eye Around Town*. Now back to the studio. |

Page 54, Listen, Exercises A and B

Debbie:	So, what are your plans for tomorrow?
Antonio:	Nothing. I'm going to relax. Why?
Debbie:	Well, I have a lot to do. First, I need to go to the ATM. Then I need to go to the hardware store. Then I'm going to stop at the supermarket.
Antonio:	Wow. You're going to be busy.

Page 54, Listen, Exercise C

Debbie:	So, what are your plans for tomorrow?
Antonio:	Nothing. I'm going to relax. Why?
Debbie:	Well, I have a lot to do. First, I need to go to the ATM. Then I need to go to the hardware store. Then I'm going to stop at the supermarket.
Antonio:	Wow. You're going to be busy.
Debbie:	I know. And you are, too.
Antonio:	What?
Debbie:	Yeah. You're going to help me. You're going to the laundromat, the deli, and the drug store.
Antonio:	OK. See you later.
Debbie:	Hey—where are you going?
Antonio:	To take a nap. I got tired just thinking about tomorrow.

Page 60, Listen, Exercises B and C

Shu-Chi:	Hi, Kelly. Where are you going?
Kelly:	I'm going to Kohn's. I need to return this jacket.
Shu-Chi:	How come?
Kelly:	The zipper is broken.
Shu-Chi:	That's annoying . . . Um, could you do me a favor?
Kelly:	What is it?
Shu-Chi:	Could you return a dress for me?
Kelly:	Sure. What's wrong with it?
Shu-Chi:	It's too short.

Page 60, Listen, Exercise D

Shu-Chi:	Hi, Kelly. Where are you going?
Kelly:	I'm going to Kohn's. I need to return this jacket.
Shu-Chi:	How come?
Kelly:	The zipper is broken.

Shu-Chi:	That's annoying . . . Um, could you do me a favor?
Kelly:	What is it?
Shu-Chi:	Could you return a dress for me?
Kelly:	Sure. What's wrong with it?
Shu-Chi:	It's too short.
Kelly:	Too short? Let me see it.
Shu-Chi:	Sure. It's in that bag.
Kelly:	Oh, no! Of course this is too short. It's a shirt, not a dress!

UNIT 4

Page 68, Listen, Exercises A and B

Mario:	What are you doing this weekend?
Bi-Yun:	I'm going to go to the beach with my family.
Mario:	Really? Sounds like fun.
Bi-Yun:	Yeah. We usually go to the beach on Sunday. What about you?
Mario:	Well, I have a guitar class. I have a guitar class every Saturday morning.

Page 68, Listen, Exercise C

Mario:	What are you doing this weekend?
Bi-Yun:	I'm going to go to the beach with my family.
Mario:	Really? Sounds like fun.
Bi-Yun:	Yeah. We usually go to the beach on Sunday. What about you?
Mario:	Well, I have a guitar class. I have a guitar class every Saturday morning.
Bi-Yun:	You play the guitar? Wow. That's really neat.
Mario:	Well, I don't really play . . .
Bi-Yun:	But you're taking classes, right?
Mario:	Yeah. But I don't know how to play. That's why I'm taking classes!

Page 73, Practice, Exercise A

This is the Greenville Community Center Information Line. The following information is for the month of September.

The Lunch Club meets at Hilda's Café on the second Friday of the month at 12:00 P.M.

We now have a dance class. The dance class meets on Thursdays from 3:00 to 4:00 P.M.

The Movie Club now meets on the second and fourth Saturday of the month. Movies begin at 7:00 P.M.

The ESL class meets every Monday and Wednesday from 7:00 to 9:00 P.M.

The Jogging Club meets every Saturday at 8:00 A.M.

We now have a Concert Club. The Concert Club meets on the first and third Friday of the month. Concerts start at 7:00 P.M.

Page 74, Listen, Exercises A and B

Katie: Welcome to our show. I'm your host, Katie Martin. We all have things that we need to do. And here's the problem: A lot of times we don't like the things we need to do. So, what's the solution? Well, today we're talking to Dr. Collin Goldberg, and he has some ideas. Welcome to the show, Dr. Goldberg.

Dr. Goldberg: Thanks, Katie. It's great to be here.

Katie: So, Dr. Goldberg, tell us about some of your ideas.

Dr. Goldberg: Sure. Here's the first one: When you need to do something you hate, do something you like *at the same time.* For example, if you hate to wash dishes, then do something you love *while* you wash the dishes. Wash the dishes and watch TV. Or wash the dishes and talk to a friend on the phone.

Katie: That way you're not thinking about the activity that you don't like.

Dr. Goldberg: Exactly.

Katie: That seems pretty easy. Do you have any other tips?

Dr. Goldberg: Sure. Here's another idea: Put a time limit on the activities you hate to do.

Katie: A time limit?

Dr. Goldberg: Exactly. For example, say it's 1:00 and you need to clean the house. Decide what time you're going to finish cleaning, say 3:00. When it's 3:00, you stop.

Katie: That's it?

Dr. Goldberg: Yes. It's an extremely simple idea, but it works. When you have a time limit, you know when the activity is going to end. And that can help a lot.

Katie: That makes sense.

Dr. Goldberg: Right. And here's one more: After you do something you hate, do something you like. For example, if you hate to do laundry, but you love to read, then say to yourself, "I'm going to do the laundry. Then I'm going to read for half an hour."

Katie: Dr. Goldberg, these sound like really good ideas. We have to take a break now, but we'll be back in a moment with more . . .

Page 80, Listen, Exercises B and C

Gloria: Do you want to get some lunch?

Yi-Wen: Sorry, I can't. I have to finish some work.

Gloria: Oh. Are you sure?

Yi-Wen: Yes, I'm sorry. I really can't.

Gloria: Well, how about a little later?

Yi-Wen: Thanks, but I don't think so. Not today.

Page 80, Listen, Exercise D

Gloria: Do you want to get some lunch?

Yi-Wen: Sorry, I can't. I have to finish some work.

Gloria: Oh. Are you sure?

Yi-Wen: Yes, I'm sorry. I really can't.

Gloria: Well, how about a little later?

Yi-Wen: Thanks, but I don't think so. Not today. I have a big meeting this afternoon. Hold on a second. Hello? Oh, hi, Bob. OK. Great. Thanks for calling. Guess what? My meeting was canceled.

Gloria: That's great! So now you can go to lunch?

Yi-Wen: Yes, I guess I can. Let me get my coat.

Page 81, Conversation, Exercise B

1. I have a test tomorrow.
2. I have to study.
3. He has to stay late.
4. He has a meeting.

UNIT 5

Page 88, Listen, Exercises B and C

Harry: Hello?

Joe: Hi, Harry. It's Joe.

Harry: Oh, hi, Joe. Can I call you back?

Joe: Sure. No problem.

Harry: Thanks. My radiator is broken and I'm trying to fix it.

Joe: You should call the building manager.

Page 88, Listen, Exercise D

Harry: Hello?

Joe: Hi, Harry. It's Joe.

Harry: Oh, hi, Joe. Can I call you back?

Joe: Sure. No problem.

Harry: Thanks. My radiator is broken and I'm trying to fix it.

Joe: You should call the building manager.

Harry: That's a good idea. There's just one problem.

Joe: What's that?

Harry: Well, I just got a new job. Now *I'm* the building manager!

Page 94, Listen, Exercises A and B

Landlady: Hello?
Paula: Hi, I'm calling about the apartment for rent. Can you tell me about it?
Landlady: Sure. There are two bedrooms and a large living room.
Paula: Is there a laundry room?
Landlady: No, there isn't. But there's a laundromat down the street.
Paula: I see. Is there a park nearby?
Landlady: Yes, there is—just around the corner.

Page 94, Listen, Exercise C

Landlady: Hello?
Paula: Hi, I'm calling about the apartment for rent. Can you tell me about it?
Landlady: Sure. There are two bedrooms and a large living room.
Paula: Is there a laundry room?
Landlady: No, there isn't. But there's a laundromat down the street.
Paula: I see. Is there a park nearby?
Landlady: Yes, there is—just around the corner.
Paula: Wow! And the ad says it's only $200 a month!
Landlady: Yes, sorry. That was a mistake. The rent is $2,000 a month, not $200.
Paula: Oh, well, thanks. I guess I don't need any more information. I'm looking for something under five hundred a month.

Page 100, Listen, Exercises A and B

Thank you for calling the Greenville Public Library. For directions, press 1.
Directions to the library: From the west, take Warton Avenue east. Turn left onto Brice Road. Go straight. Turn right onto Clarkson Street. Go through one traffic light. The library is on the left.
To repeat this message, press 2. To disconnect, press 0. Thank you. Good-bye.

UNIT 6

Page 108, Listen, Exercises B and C

Michelle: How was your weekend? How was the family reunion?
Sam: It was really nice, thanks. My whole family showed up.
Michelle: Sounds great.
Sam: Yeah, it was fun. We looked at old pictures and listened to family stories.

Page 108, Listen, Exercise D

Michelle: How was your weekend? How was the family reunion?
Sam: It was really nice, thanks. My whole family showed up.
Michelle: Sounds great.
Sam: Yeah, it was fun. We looked at old pictures and listened to family stories. How about you?
Michelle: My weekend was pretty good. I had a surprise party on Saturday night.
Sam: Really? Was it someone's birthday?
Michelle: No, it wasn't a birthday. I just invited some friends over. Then some other friends came over, and—surprise! It was a party!

Page 112, Recognize U.S. Holidays, Exercise C

Conversation 1
A: What time do the fireworks begin?
B: At 9:00. But let's go a little early so we can get a good spot.

Conversation 2
A: Oh, my! What a big turkey!
B: I'm so glad everyone in the family is coming to help eat it!

Conversation 3
A: Mmm. I love the smell of the tree in the house. Don't you?
B: Yes, and I love decorating the tree, too. Here are the lights!

Conversation 4
A: Well, this is it! Our last barbecue of the summer!
B: Yeah. I can't believe summer is over.
A: That's right! Tomorrow, it's back to work, and back to school!
B: Oohhh!

Conversation 5
A: How was the party last night?
B: We had a terrific time, but we didn't get home until really late. I'm glad it's a holiday today.
A: Yeah, it's a great way to start the new year!

Page 114, Listen, Exercises A and B

Amber:	Welcome to *Star Talk*, the program where we talk to today's biggest stars. I'm your host Amber Jenkins, and today I'm very excited to welcome actor Daniel Lopez!
Daniel:	Thanks. It's great to be here.
Amber:	So, Daniel, tell us about yourself and your celebrity life.
Daniel:	Uh—sure. But my life really isn't that interesting.
Amber:	Your life? Not interesting? I don't believe it. I mean, you're a huge star. Now, let's start with your childhood. You were born in California?
Daniel:	Yes, I was born in California, and that's where I grew up. I had a pretty normal childhood.
Amber:	What about school?
Daniel:	Uh, yeah. I went to school. I graduated from high school and went to college.
Amber:	And you always wanted to be an actor?
Daniel:	No, I didn't. Actually, I wanted to be a plumber when I was a kid. My dad was a plumber, and I wanted to be just like him. I started acting in college.
Amber:	OK, so you had a normal childhood. You went to school. But now your life is very different, right? You probably do lots of interesting things.
Daniel:	Uh, not really.
Amber:	Oh, come on, tell us. What did you do last night? I'll bet you went to a big, fancy party.
Daniel:	No, actually I stayed home. I watched some TV and went to bed early.
Amber:	Went to bed early? That's not glamorous at all!
Daniel:	I know, I'm telling you, I don't have a very glamorous life. I'm really just a regular guy.
Amber:	Well, there you go, listeners—Daniel Lopez is just a regular guy. We need to take a break, but we'll be back . . .

Page 115, Conversation, Exercise B

1. Maria grew up in Houston.
2. You came to the U.S. in 1995?
3. Ali graduated from college two years ago.
4. She got married last year?

Page 120, Listen, Exercises A and B

Maria:	Is everything OK? You look stressed out.
André:	Well, I had a rough morning.
Maria:	Why? What happened?
André:	First I lost my car keys.
Maria:	Oh, no!
André:	Then I got stuck in traffic.
Maria:	When did you get to work?
André:	At 10:00. I was really late.

Page 121, Listen, Exercise C

Maria:	Is everything OK? You look stressed out.
André:	Well, I had a rough morning.
Maria:	Why? What happened?
André:	First I lost my car keys.
Maria:	Oh, no!
André:	Then I got stuck in traffic.
Maria:	When did you get to work?
André:	At 10:00. I was really late.
Maria:	That's too bad.
André:	Wait—It gets worse.
Maria:	Really? What happened?
André:	When I finally got to work, I realized it was Tuesday.
Maria:	So?
André:	So, I don't work on Tuesdays! Tuesday is my day off!

UNIT 7

Page 128, Listen, Exercises B, C, and D

Receptionist:	Hello. Westview Clinic.
Roberto:	Hi. This is Roberto Cruz. I need to make an appointment, please.
Receptionist:	All right. What's the matter?
Roberto:	I have a fever and I'm nauseous.
Receptionist:	OK. Can you come on Tuesday morning? How about at 9:00?
Roberto:	Yes, that's fine.
Receptionist:	All right. What's your name again?
Roberto:	Roberto Cruz.
Receptionist:	Roberto Cruz. OK, Mr. Cruz, we'll see you on Tuesday at 9:00.
Roberto:	OK. Thank you.

Page 134, Listen, Exercise B

Manolo:	Hi, Ellie. What are you doing here?
Ellie:	Oh, hi, Manolo. I had an accident. I broke my arm.
Manolo:	Oh, no! I'm sorry to hear that.
Ellie:	Thanks. What about you?
Manolo:	I hurt my ankle at a soccer game. I think I sprained it.
Ellie:	That's too bad.

Page 134, Listen, Exercise C

Manolo: Hi, Ellie. What are you doing here?

Ellie: Oh, hi, Manolo. I had an accident. I broke my arm.

Manolo: Oh, no! I'm sorry to hear that.

Ellie: Thanks. What about you?

Manolo: I hurt my ankle at a soccer game. I think I sprained it.

Ellie: That's too bad. I guess you can't play soccer for a while.

Manolo: Oh, I don't play soccer. I just watch.

Ellie: What? So how did you hurt your ankle?

Manolo: Well, I was at a soccer game. I was hungry, so I got some food. I had a drink and a sandwich in my hands, and I fell down the stairs on the way to my seat.

Page 140, Listen, Exercise A

Paula: Hello. Paula Charles speaking.

Soo-Jin: Hi, Paula. This is Soo-Jin. I can't come in today because I have to go to the doctor. I don't feel well.

Paula: Sorry to hear that. Thanks for calling, and take care of yourself.

Soo-Jin: Thanks.

Page 140, Listen, Exercise B

Paula: Hello. Paula Charles speaking.

Soo-Jin: Hi, Paula. This is Soo-Jin. I can't come in today because I have to go to the doctor. I don't feel well.

Paula: Sorry to hear that. Thanks for calling, and take care of yourself.

Soo-Jin: Thanks.

Paula: Do you think you'll be in tomorrow?

Soo-Jin: I'm not sure. I can call you later after I go to the doctor.

Paula: All right. That sounds good.

UNIT 8

Page 148, Listen, Exercises B and C

Albert: Manny? Hi, I'm Albert Taylor, the store manager. Please have a seat.

Manny: Thank you. It's nice to meet you.

Albert: I have your application here. I see that you are working now. What are your job duties?

Manny: Well, I assist customers and stock shelves.

Albert: OK. Tell me about your skills. Can you use a cash register?

Manny: No, I can't, but I can learn.

Page 154, Listen, Exercises A and B

Albert: So, tell me more about your work experience.

Manny: Well, I came to the U.S. three years ago. First, I got a job as a gardener. Then last year I got a job as a stock clerk.

Albert: OK. So now you're a stock clerk. Why are you looking for another job?

Manny: Things in my life have changed, and now I'd like to do something different.

Page 154, Listen, Exercises C and D

Albert: So, tell me more about your work experience.

Manny: Well, I came to the U.S. three years ago. First, I got a job as a gardener. Then last year I got a job as a stock clerk.

Albert: OK. So now you're a stock clerk. Why are you looking for another job?

Manny: Things in my life have changed, and now I'd like to do something different.

Albert: I see. By the way, you wrote on your application that you were unemployed two years ago. Can you explain that?

Manny: Sure. I left my job because my mother was sick, and I had to take care of her for two months. When she got better, I got a new job.

Page 160, Listen, Exercises A and B

Albert: Let me ask you a few questions about your availability. Do you prefer mornings or afternoons?

Manny: Well, I prefer mornings, but I'm flexible.

Albert: All right. Can you work on weekends?

Manny: Yes, I can.

Albert: Great. And when could you start?

Manny: In two weeks. I need to give two weeks' notice at my job.

Page 160, Listen, Exercise C

Albert: Let me ask you a few questions about your availability. Do you prefer mornings or afternoons?

Manny: Well, I prefer mornings, but I'm flexible.

Albert: All right. Can you work on weekends?

Manny: Yes, I can.

Albert: Great. And when could you start?

Manny: In two weeks. I need to give two weeks' notice at my job.

Albert:	OK. Well, everything looks good. Do you have any questions for me?
Manny:	Yes. When can I expect to hear from you?
Albert:	Well, I have some other interviews this week. I can let you know next week.
Manny:	OK. Thank you for the opportunity to talk with you. It was nice to meet you.
Albert:	You, too.

UNIT 9

Page 168, Listen, Exercises B and C

Mrs. Duval:	Carlo brought a notice home from school today. There's a parent-teacher conference in two weeks.
Mr. Duval:	Oh yeah? What day?
Mrs. Duval:	Thursday the 19th at 6:00. My mother will watch the kids. That way we can both go.
Mr. Duval:	Oh, I have to work that day until 9:00, but I'll try to change my shift.

Page 168, Listen, Exercise D

Mrs. Duval:	Carlo brought a notice home from school today. There's a parent-teacher conference in two weeks.
Mr. Duval:	Oh yeah? What day?
Mrs. Duval:	Thursday the 19th at 6:00. My mother will watch the kids. That way we can both go.
Mr. Duval:	Oh, I have to work that day until 9:00, but I'll try to change my shift.
Mrs. Duval:	I hope you can.
Mr. Duval:	Me, too. When is Carlo's band concert? I know it's coming up.
Mrs. Duval:	That's Monday the 23rd.
Mr. Duval:	OK. I'll definitely go to that.

Page 172, Take a phone message, Exercises B and C

Receptionist:	Winter Hill Elementary School.
Elsa:	Hello. This is Elsa Vega. May I speak to Mr. Taylor please?
Receptionist:	I'm sorry. He's not available right now. May I take a message?
Elsa:	Yes, please. I have a question about my daughter Maria's math homework. Please ask him to call me back.
Receptionist:	Sure. What's your number?
Elsa:	It's 718-555-4343.
Receptionist:	OK. I'll give him the message.
Elsa:	Thank you.

Page 172, Take a phone message, Exercise D

Beto:	Hello.
Mr. Taylor:	Hi. May I please speak with Ms. Vega?
Beto:	I'm sorry. She isn't here right now. May I take a message?
Mr. Taylor:	Yes, please. This is Mr. Taylor from Winter Hill Elementary School. Please ask her to call me back.
Beto:	OK. What's your number?
Mr. Taylor:	My number is 718-555-8185.
Beto:	718-555-8185. All right. I'll give her the message.
Mr. Taylor:	Thank you.

Page 174, Listen, Exercises B and C

Mr. Thompson:	Hi, I'm Harold Thompson, Carlo's teacher. Nice to meet you.
Mrs. Duval:	I'm Carlo's mother, Annette Duval. Nice to meet you, too. So, how's Carlo doing?
Mr. Thompson:	Carlo's a good student. I enjoy having him in class.
Mrs. Duval:	That's good to hear.
Mr. Thompson:	He does very well in math. He works carefully.
Mrs. Duval:	He likes math a lot. What about social studies?
Mr. Thompson:	Well, he's having a little trouble in that class. He needs to do his homework.
Mrs. Duval:	OK. I'll talk to him.

Page 174, Listen, Exercise D

Mr. Thompson:	Hi, I'm Harold Thompson, Carlo's teacher. Nice to meet you.
Mrs. Duval:	I'm Carlo's mother, Annette Duval. Nice to meet you, too. So, how's Carlo doing?
Mr. Thompson:	Carlo's a good student. I enjoy having him in class.
Mrs. Duval:	That's good to hear.
Mr. Thompson:	He does very well in math. He works carefully.
Mrs. Duval:	He likes math a lot. What about social studies?
Mr. Thompson:	Well, he's having a little trouble in that class. He needs to do his homework.
Mrs. Duval:	OK. I'll talk to him.
Mr. Thompson:	Have you thought about signing up Carlo for homework help after school?
Mrs. Duval:	Homework help? What's that?
Mr. Thompson:	It's an after-school program. Older kids from the high school come and help students with their homework. The program is free, and students can get the extra help they need.

Page 180, Listen, Exercises A and B

Mrs. Herrera: Where's Luis?
Mr. Herrera: He's at a friend's house. Why? What's up?
Mrs. Herrera: Well, his teacher called. He's having some trouble at school.
Mr. Herrera: Uh-oh. What kind of trouble?
Mrs. Herrera: She said he's not paying attention and skipping class.
Mr. Herrera: What? Well, we need to talk to him right away.
Mrs. Herrera: Definitely. Let's all talk tonight after dinner.

Page 180, Listen, Exercise C

Mrs. Herrera: Where's Luis?
Mr. Herrera: He's at a friend's house. Why? What's up?
Mrs. Herrera: Well, his teacher called. He's having some trouble at school.
Mr. Herrera: Uh-oh. What kind of trouble?
Mrs. Herrera: She said he's not paying attention and skipping class.
Mr. Herrera: What? Well, we need to talk to him right away.
Mrs. Herrera: Definitely. Let's all talk tonight after dinner.
Mr. Herrera: This is so strange. Luis never has problems at school.
Mrs. Herrera: I know. He's usually a great student.

UNIT 10

Page 186, Practice, Exercise A

1. a bag of potato chips
2. a bunch of grapes
3. a head of cauliflower
4. a box of cereal
5. a can of tuna fish
6. a dozen eggs
7. a jar of pickles
8. a bottle of soda
9. a container of yogurt
10. a pint of milk
11. a quart of orange juice
12. a half-gallon of ice cream
13. a gallon of water
14. a pound of cheese

Page 188, Listen, Exercises B and C

Agnes: Hi, Yuka. I'm going to the grocery store for some milk. Do you need anything?
Yuka: Uh, let me see. Could you get a can of tomatoes?
Agnes: A can of tomatoes? Sure, no problem.
Yuka: Oh, and I need some onions.
Agnes: How many onions?
Yuka: Two.
Agnes: All right. A can of tomatoes and two onions. I'll be back in a little while.

Page 188, Listen, Exercise D

Agnes: Hi, Yuka. I'm going to the grocery store for some milk. Do you need anything?
Yuka: Uh, let me see. Could you get a can of tomatoes?
Agnes: A can of tomatoes? Sure, no problem.
Yuka: Oh, and I need some onions.
Agnes: How many onions?
Yuka: Two.
Agnes: All right. A can of tomatoes and two onions. I'll be back in a little while.
Yuka: Wait a second, since you're going, we could use a jar of mayonnaise, a loaf of bread, and a box of cereal. Hey, what are you doing?
Agnes: I'm looking for a pen and paper. I need to write all this down!

Page 194, Listen, Exercises A and B

Your family is important to you. You want to take care of them. You want to give them food that tastes good and that's good for them. Better taste, healthier meals. That's what you get from French's Chicken. With no added chemicals, French's Chicken is better for you than any other brand of chicken. Never frozen, French's Chicken is fresher than other chicken. Try it. You'll taste the difference.

Page 198, Before you Read, Exercise C

The following products have caffeine: cola, coffee, tea, chocolate, and some headache medicines. Coffee has the most caffeine but some headache medicines have almost as much caffeine as coffee.

Page 200, Listen, Exercise A

Waitress: Here are your iced teas. Are you ready to order?
Ernesto: Yes. I'd like the meatloaf.
Waitress: And what would you like with that?
Ernesto: A side of mixed vegetables.
Waitress: OK. Meatloaf with mixed vegetables.
Ernesto: And a hamburger with a side of onion rings.
Waitress: A hamburger with onion rings.
Ernesto: Oh, and could we have some sugar?
Waitress: Sure. Here you go. I'll be right back with your salads.

Page 200, Listen, Exercise B

Waitress: Here are your iced teas. Are you ready to order?
Ernesto: Yes. I'd like the meatloaf.
Waitress: And what would you like with that?
Ernesto: A side of mixed vegetables.
Waitress: OK. Meatloaf with mixed vegetables.
Ernesto: And a hamburger with a side of onion rings.
Waitress: A hamburger with onion rings.
Ernesto: Oh, and could we have some sugar?
Waitress: Sure. Here you go. I'll be right back with your salads.
Angela: Excuse me. I want to order something, too.
Waitress: Oh! Aren't you having the hamburger?
Angela: Actually, no. The meatloaf and the hamburger are both for him.
Ernesto: Yeah. I'm pretty hungry!

UNIT 11

Page 208, Listen, Exercises B, C, and D

Operator: 9-1-1. What's your emergency?
Olivia: I think a man is having a heart attack.
Operator: OK. What's the location of the emergency?
Olivia: Dave's Sports Shop at 103 Elm Street.
Operator: What are the cross streets?
Olivia: 17th and 18th Avenues.
Operator: All right. What's your name?
Olivia: Olivia Ramos.

Page 208, Listen, Exercise E

Operator: 9-1-1. What's your emergency?
Olivia: I think a man is having a heart attack.
Operator: OK. What's the location of the emergency?
Olivia: Dave's Sports Shop at 103 Elm Street.
Operator: What are the cross streets?
Olivia: 17th and 18th Avenues.
Operator: All right. What's your name?

Olivia: Olivia Ramos.
Operator: All right, Ms. Ramos. An ambulance is on its way. But don't hang up. Stay on the line with me until the ambulance gets there.
Olivia: OK. I'll just tell the man that the ambulance is coming.

Page 214, Listen, Exercises B and C

Mr. Novak: Did you hear what happened yesterday?
Mrs. Novak: No. What happened?
Mr. Novak: There was a gas explosion downtown.
Mrs. Novak: Oh my gosh. That's terrible. Was anybody hurt?
Mr. Novak: Yes. Two people went to the hospital.

Page 215, Conversation, Exercise B

1. here, here 2. art, heart 3. high, I 4. Ow!, Ow!
5. ear, hear 6. high, high

Page 214, Listen, Exercise D

Mr. Novak: Did you hear what happened yesterday?
Mrs. Novak: No. What happened?
Mr. Novak: There was a gas explosion downtown.
Mrs. Novak: Oh my gosh. That's terrible. Was anybody hurt?
Mr. Novak: Yes. Two people went to the hospital.
Mrs. Novak: How did it happen? Do they know?
Mr. Novak: No, not yet. They're looking into the cause.
Mrs. Novak: I'll bet traffic is terrible around there.
Mr. Novak: Oh, yeah. It says here a lot of the streets are closed downtown.

Page 220, Listen, Exercise A

Hi, I'm Officer Ramirez, and I'm here today to talk to you about what to do if you're pulled over by a police officer.

So imagine: You're driving along, and everything's great. But suddenly you hear a siren, and behind you there's a police car with flashing lights. That can be really scary. But stay calm and follow this simple advice.

Anytime you see a police car with flashing lights or hear a siren, look for a place to pull over quickly. Always pull over to the right, even if you're in the left lane. Use your turn signal, and pull over to a safe spot.

After you stop your car, roll down your window. Wait for the police officer and stay in your car. Don't get out. If it's dark, turn on the light inside your car. Put your hands on the steering wheel where the officer can see them.

The officer will probably ask for your license, registration, and proof of insurance. Wait for the officer to ask for your documents. Then tell him what you're going to do. For example, say, "I'm going to get my wallet. It's in my purse."

Cooperate and be polite. Follow the officer's instructions. Do not argue with the officer. The officer will give you a warning or a ticket. If you get a ticket, there are instructions on the ticket about how to pay it. You don't pay the officer at that time. Never offer any money or other gifts to an officer.

Finally, don't start your car or leave until the officer gives you permission to go.

Remember, stay calm and listen to the police officer. Police officers want to help and protect you.

UNIT 12

Page 228, Listen, Exercises A and B

Hello, everybody. I'm Michelle Rivera from human resources. Welcome to the Greenville Hotel. I think that you will find this a great place to work. We're going to start our orientation meeting by talking about company policies, and then we'll take a tour of the building.

Let's start with employee responsibilities. We'll give you an employee ID badge at the end of this meeting. You must wear your employee ID badge during your work shift. This is very important.

Also, all employees must follow the dress code. Your manager will explain the dress code for your department. Employees in housekeeping and food service must wear a uniform. Please get your uniforms at the end of this orientation.

Here's another very important responsibility: You must clock in at the start of your shift and clock out at the end of the shift. Please be on time! And you must also clock in and out when you take your break. During your six-hour shift you must take a thirty-minute break. You must not clock in or clock out for another employee.

Are there any questions? No? OK. Now, some information about our sick day policy. Please open your company policy booklet to page 5 . . .

Page 234, Listen, Exercises B and C

Luis:	Hi, Rachel. Can I ask you a favor?
Rachel:	Sure. What is it?
Luis:	I'm on the schedule for Monday, but I can't come in.
Rachel:	Oh, what's up?
Luis:	I have to study for a test. Can you take my shift for me?
Rachel:	What time do you start?
Luis:	9:30.
Rachel:	No problem.

Page 234, Listen, Exercise D

Luis:	Hi, Rachel. Can I ask you a favor?
Rachel:	Sure. What is it?
Luis:	I'm on the schedule for Monday, but I can't come in.
Rachel:	Oh, what's up?
Luis:	I have to study for a test. Can you take my shift for me?
Rachel:	What time do you start?
Luis:	9:30.
Rachel:	No problem. I can use the extra hours. By the way, who's working that day?
Luis:	I don't know. Let's check the schedule . . . . Oh, Tim's working that day.
Rachel:	Tim? Oh, definitely! I like working with him!

Page 240, Listen, Exercises B and C

Linda:	Excuse me, Ron. Can I speak to you for a minute?
Ron:	Sure, Linda. What's up?
Linda:	I need to talk to you about my schedule.
Ron:	OK. Right now you work in the mornings, right?
Linda:	Yes. But I'm planning to take classes now. Could I change to evenings?
Ron:	Well, let me look at the schedule. I'll get back to you.
Linda:	OK. Thanks.

Page 240, Listen, Exercise D

Linda:	Excuse me, Ron. Can I speak to you for a minute?
Ron:	Sure, Linda. What's up?
Linda:	I need to talk to you about my schedule.
Ron:	OK. Right now you work in the mornings, right?
Linda:	Yes. But I'm planning to take classes now. Could I change to evenings?
Ron:	Well, let me look at the schedule. I'll get back to you.
Linda:	OK. Thanks.
Ron:	By the way, what classes are you planning to take?
Linda:	Business classes. Someday I want to be a manager.
Ron:	Oh, that's great. Let me know if I can help.

Index

Map of the United States and Canada

Map of the World

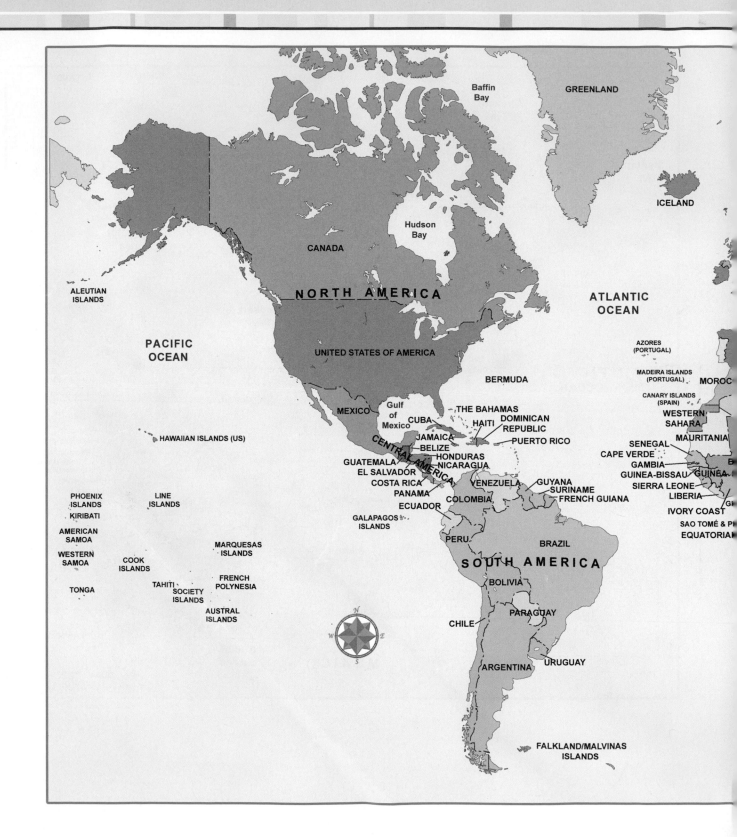

Baffin Bay

GREENLAND

ICELAND

Hudson Bay

CANADA

ALEUTIAN ISLANDS

NORTH AMERICA

ATLANTIC OCEAN

PACIFIC OCEAN

UNITED STATES OF AMERICA

AZORES (PORTUGAL)

MADEIRA ISLANDS (PORTUGAL)

MOROC

BERMUDA

CANARY ISLANDS (SPAIN)

WESTERN SAHARA

MEXICO

Gulf of Mexico

THE BAHAMAS

CUBA

HAITI

DOMINICAN REPUBLIC

HAWAIIAN ISLANDS (US)

JAMAICA

PUERTO RICO

MAURITANIA

CENTRAL AMERICA

BELIZE

HONDURAS

SENEGAL

CAPE VERDE

GUATEMALA

NICARAGUA

GAMBIA

EL SALVADOR

GUINEA-BISSAU

GUINEA

COSTA RICA

VENEZUELA

GUYANA

SIERRA LEONE

PHOENIX ISLANDS

LINE ISLANDS

PANAMA

SURINAME

LIBERIA

KIRIBATI

COLOMBIA

FRENCH GUIANA

IVORY COAST

ECUADOR

AMERICAN SAMOA

GALAPAGOS ISLANDS

SAO TOMÉ & P

WESTERN SAMOA

COOK ISLANDS

MARQUESAS ISLANDS

PERU

BRAZIL

EQUATORIAL

SOUTH AMERICA

TONGA

TAHITI

SOCIETY ISLANDS

FRENCH POLYNESIA

BOLIVIA

AUSTRAL ISLANDS

PARAGUAY

CHILE

URUGUAY

ARGENTINA

FALKLAND/MALVINAS ISLANDS